American Insider's Guide to

Toys & Games

Hello boys!
Tell 'em you built it with
GILBERT "Big-Boy" Tools
"Constructed for Service"

Boys, here's your chance to give Mother and Dad the surprise of their lives! Build with your own hands furniture, airplanes, toys, bird houses, and hundreds of other practical things—just like skillful builders do. Tell Dad you want to join the group of real fellows who build things with Gilbert "Big Boy" tools. Tell him today you'll start right in as soon as you get your Big Boy Set. Lift the lid of one of my big red brass-bound tool chests and you open up a whole new world of exciting thrills. Put on the sporty carpenter's apron, call in your pals and show them how a real builder goes to work. Oh, Boy! how their eyes will pop! My Boy Builder's Plan Book tells exactly how each job is done. And there's a tool for every purpose. I know what you need and I've built these tools for real service.

Find out right away how smart you are with your hands. Look over my Big Boy Tool Chests and machine shop outfits at any good store. Take Dad along. Tell him you want to be a full-fledged member of this happy group of builders. Pick out your set, get it home quickly, and start right in building wonderful things.

When You Buy Your Tool Chest
See that you get these Feature Tools

A.C.Gilbert

NO. 780 $10.00

Let's Go

If you want to make things hum, the thing for you is my brand new Motor-Driven Machine Shop, the greatest thing I've made for boys since I invented Erector. Yes sir, it's a complete scientific work shop—a combination portable lathe, demountable drill, emery wheel for grinding knives and sharpening tools. There's a real scratch brush for removing rough surfaces from metal, and a buffing wheel for finishing and polishing metal. And—Boy, here's big news—this workshop's equipped with a 1/8 H. P. Universal Motor for A. C. or D. C., with toggle switch, cord and plug. It would take a whole page to tell you everything about this marvelous outfit. Send that coupon in to me and get the booklet that tells you all in words and pictures.

BOYS

This big chest of tools (Number 780) is the treasured possession of thousands of red-blooded boys. They wouldn't swap it for a million dollars. But you can get yours at any good store. There are 26 pieces in all—18 pounds of scientific fun—the kind of fun you'll never get tired of. A saw that bites its way right through wood, a plane that shaves like a master, a sturdy brace and bit, chisels, and dozens of other he-man tools for the boy builder. And two complete books that show clearly and exactly how to build hundreds of wonderful useful things. Now boys, be sure you get my big red brass-bound BIG BOY Tool Chest, because I know what you need and have spent ten years planning this fun for you.

A. C. Gilbert's Olympic Sports Book

You will want to know all about this greater 1928 Erector and Big Boy Tool Chests. It is easy to get the whole story, together with a series of exciting sports talks by America's most famous athletes. All between the covers of A. C. Gilbert's brand new book that comes free to your door for the asking. The little coupon below brings this free book to you. Just write in your name and address and mail the coupon today.

GILBERT "Big-Boy" Tool Chests
Consist of
BOY'S SIZE
No. 701—For the little fellow—Contains 11 pieces with Plan Book...........Price $1.00
No. 701E—Dandy set for the beginner—Contains 13 pieces with Plan Book. Price $1.50
No. 702—Practical young carpenter's set. 16 pieces with Plan Book..........Price $2.50
No. 707—Handy, practical set for boys. 19 pieces including Plan Book.......Price $3.50
No. 765—Feature set in Boy's size group. Dandy set. 23 pieces. Real tools for practical service. Packed in big red chest with Plan Book.................Price $5.00

DAD'S SIZE
No. 780—Household Treasure Chest. 26 pieces of real he-man tools including big 16 in. Cross-Cut Saw, 15 in. Steel Level and 7¾ in. Plane. A regular outfit. Two Plan Books. Packed in brass-bound chest..Price $10.00
No. 785—Handy carpenters set. Practical, selected, high grade tools. 33 pieces, two Plan Books, 15 in. Steel Level, 16 in. Cross-Cut and Dandy Keyhole Saw, also 9 in. Plane. Packed in brass-bound chest................Price $15.00
No. 790—Feature set of "Big Boy" Line. 36 pieces including 14 in. Plane, Ratchet Brace, 15 in. Level, 20 in. Cross, 18 in. Rip, and Dandy Keyhole Saws. Two Plan Books. Every needed tool for master builders. Packed in big red chest, brass corners and lock.........................Price $25.00

THE NEW 1928 LINE INCLUDES THESE IMPORTANT DESIRABLE FEATURES
When you are looking for a genuine Chest of Tools, be sure to get these big exclusive features, contained in the Dad size Chests:
1. BIG BOY TOOL CHESTS have more and better tools than any other chest of equal value.
2. All-metal spirit level. In No. 765 and up.
3. High quality, ground face Block Plane. In No. 765 and up.
4. Bench Plane. The kind that real carpenters use. In No. 785 and up.
5. LePage's Glue with Home Workshop Booklet. In all Dad Size Chests.
6. New 1928 Plan Book. In all sets.
7. Carpenter's apron. In all Dad Size Chests.
8. Drop forged hammers. In Dad Size Chests.
9. Big-boy Saws.
10. Metal Tray.
11. Big Red Brass-bound Chest.

A. C. GILBERT'S RADIO SPORTS TALKS—Every Monday Night, 6:30 Eastern Time, 5:30 Central Time. See full announcement pages 50-51

A. C. Gilbert's OLYMPIC SPORTS BOOK

FREE:- Send for it!

When answering advertisements please mention BOYS' LIFE

December

Advertisement for Gilbert Tools from Boys' Life *magazine, December 1928.*

MILLER'S

American Insider's Guide to

Toys & Games

Tim Luke

General Editor: Lita Solis-Cohen

American Insider's Guide to Toys and Games

A Miller's-Mitchell Beazley book
Published by Octopus Publishing Group Ltd.
2–4 Heron Quays
London E14 4JP
U.K.

Commissioning Editor: Anna Sanderson
Executive Art Editor: Rhonda Fisher
U.S. Project Manager: Joseph Gonzalez

Produced by:
designsection
Caxton Road
Frome
Somerset BA11 1DY
U.K.

General Editor: Lita Solis-Cohen
Editor: Julian Flanders
Graphic Design: Carole McDonald
Proofreader: Matt Levine
Indexer: Indexing Specialists

ISBN 1 84000 380 4

Set in Perpetua.
Printed and bound in Hong Kong.

Front cover picture: a highly lithographed tinplate wind-up toy featuring Topper and Hopalong Cassidy with lasso on seesaw, Marx, 1940s, $700–$900
Back cover picture: a rare, clockwork, lithographed, tinplate Popeye and Olive Oyl jigging toy with original box (not shown), Marx, 1930s, $600–$800
Back flap picture: a clockwork Amos and Andy toy car, Marx, 1930s, $700–$900

CONTENTS

INTRODUCTION	6
THE HISTORY OF TOYS	8
WHY WE COLLECT THINGS	14
TAKING CARE OF YOUR COLLECTION	16
BUYING AND SELLING	18
THE ESSENTIALS	27
FACT FILE—WOODEN TOYS	32
FACT FILE—TINPLATE TOYS	41
COLOR REVIEW ◆ ANTIQUE TOYS: 1880s–1900s	49
FACT FILE—CAST-IRON TOYS	71
FACT FILE—BOARD GAMES	86
FACT FILE—WIND-UP TOYS	91
COLOR REVIEW ◆ INDUSTRIAL-AGE TOYS: 1910s–1930s	97
FACT FILE—TOY TRAINS	118
FACT FILE—PRESSED-STEEL TOYS	123
FACT FILE—PLUSH TOYS	135
COLOR REVIEW ◆ POST-WAR TOYS: 1940s–1960s	145
FACT FILE—TOY SOLDIERS	161
FACT FILE—DIE-CAST TOYS	167
FACT FILE—CHARACTER TOYS	176
FACT FILE—NOVELTY TOYS	179
FACT FILE—BATTERY-OPERATED TOYS	183
FACT FILE—PLASTIC TOYS	189
COLOR REVIEW ◆ POPULAR-CULTURE TOYS: 1970s–1990s	193
TOY COMPANIES: A QUICK REFERENCE GUIDE	209
USEFUL ADDRESSES	212
GLOSSARY	214
BIBLIOGRAPHY	217
INDEX	218
ACKNOWLEDGMENTS	224

INTRODUCTION

The concept of toys is as old as civilization itself. Fragile, handcrafted toys have been found in ancient Egyptian tombs. These early playthings included carved wooden animals and dolls made of wood and linens. Even simple mechanical toys and board games have been found during archeological digs. Based on the Egyptian practice of building tombs and filling them with items the dead may have needed in the next life, it is hard to determine if the artifacts were only ceremonial or were also made for the children of the time period.

At the time of the Roman Empire, children played with marbles made of fired clay, stone, or glass and had rag dolls similar to the ones we see today. Since playthings have been with us for so long, it is not suprising that toy collecting is so popular. We all relate to toys—trains and cars, games and dolls. Every culture throughout history has shared a love of toys.

THE SECONDARY MARKET

During the Victorian era, toy manufacturers had no idea that they would be affecting the future collectibles market with the choices of designs and colors of paint which they used to decorate their toys. At the time, their main focus was to produce quality items that would be popular sellers, producing enough revenue to cover the expense of production and, hopefully, make a small profit. As time passed, automation resulted in increased production and profits.

What we now call the "secondary," or collectibles market for toys didn't really begin until the 1930s, and the term "secondary market" didn't come into common use until much later. The 1980s brought with them a vogue for "limited edition" toys and reproductions of nostalgic toys. Today, entire companies have been created to manufacture reproduction cast-iron, battery-operated, and wind-up toys.

THE INTERNET EFFECT

The old aphorism "History repeats itself" applies to toys, as well as everything else. Just as the Industrial

A trade catalogue from 1880 for the toys and novelties manufactured by the E.I. Horsman Co. Representatives used these catalogues to showcase the items offered by the company to buyers across the country.

Revolution of the 19th century drastically changed society, the technological advances of the last part of the 20th century have dramatically changed our world, as well. Today, everything seems to happen at the speed of your modem or the click of your computer mouse. The networking of the collecting community has transformed the collectibles market by providing equal access to material offered for sale by people the world over. The trade show and antiques mall are no longer the only arenas. To be a collector today, you have to be computer literate, because it is on the Internet that you will discover those fantastic finds. The hunt has moved into cyberspace, where all are welcome and knowledge is power. Get connected, and you will discover how much fun it can be.

Examples of collector edition items made for Star Wars *collectors.*

HOW THIS BOOK WORKS

The goal of this book is to introduce the most innovative toy companies from the late 19th and 20th centuries—those that helped shape the state of the market today. By focusing on these companies, the materials they used, and the items they produced, this guide will help increase the knowledge of those of you who already have a collection and, I hope, motivate others to start a collection for themselves.

With the population in America expanding at the beginning of the 19th century and economic prosperity growing, toy companies increased production to meet the demand. This demand helped to establish home-grown companies like Marx, Buddy "L," and Lionel, as well as overseas outfits like Lehmann, Schuco, Steiff, and Märklin.

The Fact Files feature company profiles that will give you an understanding of the history of each firm and the type of toys that they produced, and explain what you should look for as a collector of their products. The book also features four Color Reviews, each of which concentrates on a particular era of toy production and explains the concerns of the toy industry at the time. These reviews are designed to provide a colorful overview of the history of collectible toys in the 20th century.

With the vast number of manufacturers and the huge range of toys produced, this book only provides highlights of the most popular companies. Many of the toys are illustrated together with information about the materials of which they are made and the date of manufacture. Whenever possible, identification clues and descriptions of what to look for, along with collectors' stories and insiders' tips, are also included in each entry. Enjoy the stories, but more importantly, look beyond the toys to see the rich history and unique qualities possessed by each piece that you come across.

Modern examples of clay and pottery marbles are similar in appearance to the ones made in ancient Rome.

Since only artifacts remain from ancient civilizations, with no documentation relating to the playthings of the time periods, it is difficult to pinpoint the exact beginning of toy making. We do know that after the fall of the Roman Empire, the "Dark Ages" ensued, during which time there were very few advances in technology, science, or culture. Since toys are a direct reflection of the society for which they are made, it stands to reason that this period saw few advances or variations on the clay items with which Roman children had played. It was not until the late 16th century that the seeds of the toy industry we know today began to take root.

EARLY TOY PRODUCTION

During the 15th century, Nuremberg in Germany established itself as a major stop on the trade routes in Europe. The city's many craftsmen made household utensils, religious articles, and toys. As time went by,

the peasants in neighboring regions also made toys, and agents from Nuremberg collected them for sale in the city. As the market for these toys grew, the network of families involved in their production expanded. Some carvers spent their entire lifetimes carving the same two or three items that had become popular in the rest of the world. For the next 200 years, this cottage industry flourished. Noah's Arks and the wooden Christmas villages that were made in this region are widely collected today. Other materials, such as foil papers, cardboard, leather, and—by the late 1700s—silver and tin plate, were used. By this time, across the ocean, a new nation was beginning to take shape.

THE INFLUENCE OF PRINTING

The great age of European discoveries—from the late 15th century through the 18th century—would alter humankind's view of the world and how it was portrayed in maps. The English colonies in America were settled in the first quarter of the 17th century, and throughout the colonial era, manufactured goods were sent to the colonies from England. One of the first industries to take root in the New World was printing. Newspapers, broadsides, lottery tickets, and psalm books were soon followed by printed board games, cards, and puzzles for both adults and children. One early American game, "Lottery of the Pious (or The Spiritual Treasure Casket)," was printed in 1744. Most of these early games reflected the strict moral and religious code of the times.

The American Revolution, which began in 1775, was fought and won by idealists and forward thinkers who laid the foundations for the United States of America. The colonies had to prove to the British that they could be free and self-sufficient. Craftsmen relied more on materials found in the New World and less on imports from abroad. Workshops to make household items and furniture were set up, and before long, the United States was recognized as an economic force in the international community.

THE ROOTS OF MASS PRODUCTION

In the mid-19th century, the cottage industry of woodcarving was waning, in part due to advances in machine-operated mass production in factories. As early as the 1840s, mechanical methods of stamping tinplate, molding papier-mâché, and casting iron revolutionized the toy industry. No longer did an entire toy have to be made by hand. In America, a few manufacturers began to produce toys commercially, on a small scale compared with their European counterparts.

Once again, history affected the overall production of toys in America in the middle of the 19th century. The Northern and Southern states declared a Civil War, and foundries up and down the Atlantic, and particularly in New England, were built to provide the military supplies and ammunition needed for the conflict. After the war, demand for military supplies diminished, and foundries and factories built to make weapons began to turn out household items and toys.

During this period, some of the most sought-after early American tinplate and cast-iron toys were produced. Wind-up clockwork mechanisms, used in watches at the time, were placed in tin toys to add movement to them. The method of sand casting in the production of cast-iron toys was perfected in America. The early

toy manufacturers were also artisans, refining their craft and adding hand-painted details to the mass-produced playthings. Bell toys, still banks, horse-drawn fire engines, and mechanical banks were just a few examples of the cast-iron craftsmanship and artistry of the day. Manufacturers in Europe had been using iron for parts, wheels, and other structural supports for some years, but had never quite appreciated the versatility of the substance like the American craftsmen did. The British produced a few cast-iron mechanical banks, but could not duplicate the sand-casting techniques used in America. This resulted in the American craftsmen cornering the cast-iron toy market in the late 19th and early 20th centuries.

A line illustration of a velocipide and rider stick toy that would have been a popular item with children in the Victorian era.

Per dozen, $4.00

An 1890s catalogue illustration for Crandall's Lively Horseman. The toys cost $4.00 per dozen.

THE LITHOGRAPHIC PROCESS

While the Americans were sand casting iron, the Germans and French were mass producing tinplate toys and perfecting the lithographic process to add a variety of colors and designs to them. Popular during this period were wind-up toys that used stamped tinplate gears rather than the heavy brass clockwork mechanisms used by American toy makers. This made the European toys move faster.

There were whirling toys and fast-moving trains and trolleys, all built with their own methods of locomotion and colorful lithography on the tin. The German companies, Lehmann, Bing, and Märklin, established themselves as leaders in the industry. They exported toys around the world, most notably

to America. By 1900, it is estimated that almost one-third of all tinplate toys manufactured in Germany were sold in the United States.

DEMAND INCREASES

The 19th century was a time of economic expansion. Entire families worked 12-hour days to meet the demand for many manufactured products. Children as young as five or six were put to work. With little supervision, there were injuries and deaths until labor reform declared that children were no longer allowed to work in factories.

Victorian children with more leisure time were given games and toys to amuse and educate them. Mechanical banks were entertaining and taught thrift. Toys were manufactured in the likenesses of fairy-tale characters, like Mother Goose; were used to illustrate Bible characters, like Jonah and the whale; and depicted newspaper cartoon characters of the time, like Little Nemo.

THE MOTHER OF INVENTION

The end of the 19th century saw the horse and carriage replaced by the train and the automobile. Steamships replaced sailing ships, and by the early 20th century, airplanes were taking off. Every advance in transportation and technology was reflected in the toys of the 20th century. The material used for family cars was used for toy cars, too. Large trucks and pedal cars and trains were made of pressed steel. In time, steel and tinplate gave way to composition, a material made of wood chips, pulp, and sawdust mixed with glue that looked like wood but was cheaper and easier to mold. Rubber, and finally, celluloid and plastic replaced composition. Every new material brought with it the promise of greater durability and cost savings in production. Steam and

A family portrait of children from the 1890s with an American tinplate locomotive.
Notice the play wear and paint loss on the engine. This was a well-loved toy.

A December 1949 magazine advertisement showcasing the variety of items offered by the Tootsietoy company.

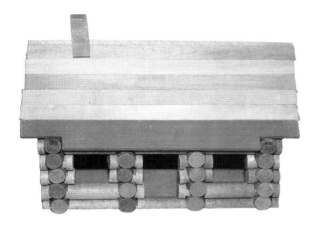

As the century closed, digital and virtual-reality games were the innovative toys of the day. Nintendo's Gameboy and Playstation captured the attention of the public. Are these the collectibles of the future? Only time will tell.

Interlocking logs, like those used in this log cabin from c. 1920, became all the rage with the success of John Lloyd Wright's Lincoln Logs.

electricity were harnessed to run toy trains, and by the middle of the century, battery-operated toys dominated toy production.

VIRTUAL TOYS

In the 1960s, the public's interest in space exploration resulted in the production of thousands of battery-operated and wind-up robots, spaceships, and futuristic vehicles of all kinds made of plastic, tin, rubber, and steel.

In the 1980s, the words "limited edition" and "collector's item" first appeared on toys. Children bombarded by TV commercials and peer pressure demanded more toys. There were ugly scenes at various top stores one Christmas when the new line of Cabbage Patch dolls ran out and the stores were unable to obtain more stock.

The last decade of the century saw the peak of the licensing phenomenon which began in the 1930s with Walt Disney. Licensed products from films, TV shows, comic strips, and digital games all provided the toy industry with characters that had world-wide appeal.

A Nintendo Gameboy color model CGB-001 electronic game with "The Legend of Zelda" game cartridge.

WHY WE COLLECT THINGS

Having been in the collectibles business and playing with toys my entire life, I am often asked what the next trend will be or to predict the collectability of new toys. Remember that the collectibles market is like the stock market. When a manufacturer or an individual pitches a 20 to 50 percent return on the initial investment, run the other way. I have discovered that there are seven basic reasons or "keys" that drive

A young boy hangs his Gund animals out to dry after a minor cleaning. This is not a recommended cleaning technique.

collectors to collect. This applies primarily to toys but is also applicable to just about any area of collecting. These keys provide a brief explanation of the psychology of collecting. They provide insight into what drives collectors to pay outrageous amounts of money for what can be conceived by an outsider to be a frivolous waste of time and resources. All seven of these factors must be in harmonic convergence for an item to reach collectible status.

THE 7 KEYS

Nostalgia: This is the number one reason people collect. There is something about objects from our past that have the power to transport us back to our youth, trigger a memory of a loved one, or in some way make us feel better about ourselves today.

Collecting in general is an emotionally based hobby, and when you mix emotions with desire, it is very difficult to predict the outcome. This is why there is no accurate formula for creating or manipulating the collectors' market.

Attraction: This is where I stress to collectors that if you are attracted to an item and want to collect it, invest all of your energy in researching and educating yourself on the item. DO NOT COLLECT TO INVEST. If you desire to invest, then play the stock market. If your toy or collectible happens to increase in value, it should be as a result of your pursuit of quality items that you found attractive and you fully researched. I say this because if the item does not increase in value, you will still have an item that you like and will not mind having around. Remember, collectible markets are similar to the stock market; the values go up and then down. If you have done your homework, you will get a good feeling for the cyclical motion of your own area of collecting.

Durability: Collectors in every area will agree that you take on a certain amount of responsibility when you start to collect. You must properly research your area of interest. You will discover if you collect vintage authentic automobiles that you need to have a large facility to warehouse, maintain, and protect your collection. When you add an item to it, you will need to consider whether the new piece is fragile and in need of extra care. When you acquire it, the responsibility for its continued existence in the world is in your hands.

Value: Look in the marketplace for comparable buys before you make that big purchase. Remember that value can be tracked through auction results or confirmed private sales. Price, on the other hand, is only the dollar amount being asked and may not reflect the true "value" of the piece. If you have done your research, you will not be taken advantage of by overpaying for or underselling an item.

Provenance: Collectors will pay a premium if there is undisputable and accurate proof of the previous ownership of the collectible. This history or lineage of a collectible, as seen at the Jacqueline Kennedy auction at Sotheby's or the Marilyn Monroe sale at Christie's, gives collectors the opportunity to get "up close and personal" with their idols. This is also true with toys, as seen in Bill Bertoia's auction of the Stan Sax collection of mechanical banks. Collectors knew that this was one of the best collections and were prepared to pay a premium for the banks in that sale.

Condition: The materials used to create a collectible item in any area of collecting must be considered when starting a collection. The deteriorating effects that time and the elements have on those materials should be taken into account when looking for an item to collect. We are constantly being assaulted by environmental factors, and everything is in a continual state of deterioration. The UV rays of the sun cause fading. Pollution and smog, cold and humidity not only affect our climate but also our collectibles. Over time, these forces can be destructive. Collectors take the condition of an item, how it has been maintained, and the overall appearance into consideration when purchasing and selling a new collectible. A simple rule: Always buy the best original condition that you can afford.

Rarity and desirability: These go hand in hand. Just because an item is rare or old does not make it desirable if no other collector likes it or is collecting it. There is a simple formula. The value of an item increases with its desirability. If the desirability is maintained in a market, adding rarity to the equation exponentially increases the value of the object. But I have a caution for collectors who overvalue the word "rare." Today, dealers and Internet auction sites may come across an item with which they are not familiar, and instead of doing research on it, they simply call it rare. Do your homework, and ask people in your area of collecting what the "rare" or hard-to-find examples look like.

If you remember these seven keys, you will be better equipped when you hit the local flea market or garage sale on your quest for the nostalgic, durable item to which you are attracted that has a fantastic provenance, is in great condition, and has desirability in the marketplace.

TAKING CARE OF YOUR COLLECTION

The type of care your collection requires depends on the type of toys you collect. However, there are several golden rules for every collection. It is important to remember to keep your items out of direct sunlight and to ensure that they are kept in a stable environment that is not too dry or too humid. Above all, it is essential to make an inventory of your collection—a list of everything you have. This is one thing that collectors often neglect to do. One easy way of doing this is to be sure to take photographs of every item you acquire. This is important for insurance purposes and will aid in recognizing any items that might be missing.

DISPLAY

Often, when I am participating in an appraisal fair, collectors will bring items that have been in their families for generations, and they often ask if they should display the items. My response is, "Most definitely." A collection should be enjoyed and shared with others. You should also document the items as much as possible, so look for old family photographs that may have the items in the background or showcase the individual who first bought them together with their purchases. This helps in establishing when the item was first bought. The next step is to get current family photographs of the children with the items to document ownership, time period, and provide the collector with a visual history to pass down to future generations.

Displaying your toys can be fun and entertaining, not to mention a creative challenge. Make sure they are secure on a stable surface without any chance of falling or accidentally being bumped or pushed off the surface. Toys are like magnets. Children and adults want to pick them up, turn them over, and try

A much-loved collection of toys on display amongst reference books in the author's office.

to wind the mechanisms. If you do not want people to handle your collectible toys, make sure they are difficult to reach or behind glass. This will ensure the longevity of your collection. Also, never be afraid to tell visitors that they must ask you if they can handle any items.

REPAIR AND RESTORATION

Often, the subject of repair and restoration arises when a toy is not complete or is in need of a little attention. Each case is different. However, the general rule is that if the restoration or repair is going to damage the original integrity of the toy, then you probably should not be in favor of it. On the other hand, if the work would help preserve the integrity of the toy, without compromising its essence, then I would say go for it.

Certain areas of collecting are more accepting of these procedures. For example, the repainting of an old cast-iron mechanical bank turns the collectors off, while the repainting of an old pedal car is generally accepted. The reason for this is scale—most pedal cars were large and so were often left outside to face the elements rather than being put away with the rest of the toys. Few have survived in their original condition. If the restoration has been done properly, then it makes the toy more desirable because it will be closer to its original condition. It also means that the restoration has helped to preserve the toy and give it a longer life by not letting it rust out and disintegrate.

If you do decide to use a restorer, take care to find a reputable one, and discuss the options and level of repair required for each job. Be sure to get a quote for the job and a description of what will be done to the toy in writing before you leave the toy with the restorer. Keep this record with your inventory for future reference, and always remember to look the

When cleaning a mohair bear, use a brush, and gently comb through the fibers to lift any surface dust.

piece over when it is returned to be sure that the job has been done satisfactorily.

CLEANING

Cleaning can ruin a perfectly good toy and destroy its value, so be sure to know the materials your toys are made of to avoid a vital mistake. Cast-iron toys should not be soaked in soapy water, nor should wind-up toys be placed in water, or the mechanisms will rust. Toys were made to be durable, and for the most part, a simple, careful dry-cloth dusting will suffice. If a more intense job or a deep clean is required, consult a restorer or professional who deals with the medium. If you are in any doubt about what to do, ask for assistance; it will save you money and agitation in the long run. Check the helpful resource section in the back of this book for the names of restorers around the country.

The author as auctioneer: Tim Luke with gavel in hand.

During my tenure as a licensed auctioneer, I have worked for Christie's auction house in New York, and later, as auctioneer for Bertoia auctions in New Jersey. I have been exposed to some of the best collections from around the world. In December 1991, I presided over the high-profile Christie's sale of "Mint and Boxed Collection of Antique Toys," which realized more that $1 million, including a record for a toy at auction, the George Brown tinplate hose reel, at $231,000 (see opposite). In May 1998, I wielded my gavel at the Bertoia auction of the Stan Sax collection of mechanical banks where the "Old Woman in the Shoe" bank realized a record-breaking $426,000 (see below right).

LIVE AUCTIONS

I usually refer to auctioneering as "the second-oldest profession in the world." The auction process dates as far back as the Roman Empire, and the basic principle of traditional auctions has not changed over the course of history—the highest bidder is the successful buyer. Do not be off put or intimidated by the high-profile auctions. The prices at the majority of auctions I have done run the gamut from $25 to $2,500, and if the auctioneer is good, you will understand what is being said, where the bid increment is, and who is the successful bidder.

Helpful tips at auction

There are some important things to remember when attending an auction that will keep you from overextending yourself. Most auction houses will have a printed catalogue of the items being offered. It is very important to review the catalogue and inspect the toys for which you may want to place a bid. If you are not able to attend the sale yourself, then call the gallery, and have someone provide you with a condition report on each item of interest. The reason for this is that all auction houses are selling things "as is," which means the house does not make any warranties or guarantees about the items being sold. Also, photographs in the catalogue may distort an item, making it look better or worse that it actually is. All of

Preparing for the auction itself

The next step is to register to receive an auction paddle. This consists of filling out a form with your name, address, and billing information. Once it is completed, you should receive a numbered paddle to use during the auction. This helps the auctioneer recognize interested bidders and allows the auction to move along, because the auctioneer only has to record the final bid and successful bidder number. A good auctioneer will usually sell between 80 and 100 lots per hour.

Once you have previewed the auction and looked over the items in which you are interested, you need to establish your limit—the highest price you are willing to go on each item. With all of this established, enjoy the excitement of the auction and wait patiently for your lot to be called. Once the bidding begins, be sure to establish eye contact with the auctioneer so that he or she knows you are a serious bidder. Then, at the appropriate moment, lift your paddle. Remember, always hold to your limits!

The advantage of selling at auction

Selling at auction should be easy and exciting, but don't forget that you will have to pay a commission to the auction house handling your items, in addition to photography charges, insurance, and, sometimes, marketing fees. Make sure you sign and receive a copy of a consignment contract that clearly spells out the terms and arrangements for the sale of your items.

The main advantage of selling at auction is that you will have a variety of bidders in competition over your items, with the highest bidder winning. This will ensure that you get the best price at that time.

The "Charles" tinplate hose reel fire toy that sold for $231,000.00.

these factors play a role in the sale of the item. The catalogue will also provide the terms of the sale. Most every live auction house has a buyer's premium. This is a percentage fee that will be added to the final bid, and will be listed in the terms and conditions section of a catalogue. It should also be announced by the auctioneer at the beginning of the sale. Typically, the percentage is between 10 and 15 percent, with Christie's and Sotheby's higher, at 17.5 to 20 percent, respectively. Note that in addition to the buyer's premium, there may also be sales tax. Finally, if the item is too cumbersome to carry out of the gallery, there will be shipping charges. All these charges are added to the final gavel price. An invoice should be presented at the time of payment with all the charges clearly indicated. Also included in the terms and conditions of the sale will be information on the forms of payment, such as whether credit cards are accepted or not.

DEALERS

Buying toys from dealers should be educational and enable you to add nice new pieces to your collection. Before approaching a dealer, make sure you talk with other collectors about that dealer. Ask around, and find out what people think. Be sure to ask for as much information as possible from the dealer about the background or provenance of any toy in which you might be interested. Also ask questions about the market and the type of toys you are interested in collecting. Establishing a good relationship with a dealer is important. You will learn quickly who the players are and what their reputations are within your collecting area. One easy way to test the standards of dealers is to ask them if they will refund your money should an item you buy from them turn out to be a fake. If dealers are reputable, they will stand behind everything they sell and comply with your request for a refund.

Buying

When you are buying from a dealer, you are paying for the convenience of not having to attend an auction, a garage sale, or a flea market. But this will probably mean paying higher prices. Also, keep in mind that if the dealer maintains a shop, then the rent, the cost of electricity, and so on will also factor into the final selling price. It is acceptable to ask for the "best price," but if the dealer's best price is not close to what you are willing to spend... then move on. If the price is right, be sure to get a receipt that includes full details about the toy, including the manufacturer, date of sale, and price paid. Keep a file of documents on all the items you add to your collection, and be sure to update it every time you buy. This will come in handy for insurance purposes and will help in the unlikely event of any authenticity dispute that might arise should you go on to sell the piece in the future.

It is important to get to know dealers before doing business with them. A good look at the items they are offering will provide you with useful information about them.

Selling

Selling to a dealer can be tricky, so it is important for the collector to understand the process. Dealers buy wholesale; this means that they usually only offer half of the perceived value to buy an item in order for them to mark the item up, sell it to their stable of clients, and make a certain percentage profit. It can be advantageous if you need cash quickly, because a dealer will pay you directly. When you sell at auction, it can take 30 days before your check is sent. Of course, every situation is different, but if you are selling a collection, be sure to do your homework. Research all of your alternatives and get several opinions of value before parting with your items. Don't undersell your pieces. After all, the more money you get, the more you will have to spend on other pieces.

TRADE SHOWS AND FLEA MARKETS

Trade shows and flea markets are like conventions for collectors. Take advantage of the wealth of knowledge possessed by the exhibitors and attendees at these functions by discussing your collecting habits or quandaries with as many people as you can. Company histories or background information on pieces in your collection that may have you stumped

could be readily available from the dealers and collectors who attend these shows. Make connections and network with people who have similar collecting tastes. There are several regional shows that features toys, with hundreds of dealers and collectors selling their wares, so check your local papers and trade magazines for details.

When you buy at a flea market or a show, it is difficult to get your money back should you discover that you have bought a fake, unless you get a receipt with a guarantee. Be sure to shop around and check out many examples and booths before putting your money down on an item. You should be prepared to make mistakes, because that is how we all learn. One bad purchase, and believe me, you will not make that mistake again. This is all part of the journey of amassing a collection.

Make the best of any trade show you attend. Talk to other collectors and dealers, make connections, and network with others who share your areas of interest.

The home page of Sothebys.com, the great international auction house's Internet "branch."

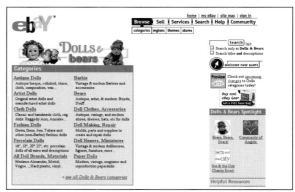

An Internet phonomenon eBay, has become a powerhouse as an on-line auction venue.

INTERNET AUCTIONS

The Internet has provided a fantastic opportunity to bring collectors around the globe together through the on-line auction format. Personally, I have been buying and selling on-line since 1997, and I find it time saving and a great way to close the gap of distance and the expense of travel in search of collectibles. To better understand the on-line format for auctions, it is a good idea to attend and familiarize yourself with the process of live auctions. The same basic principle applies—the highest bidder is the successful bidder. The same basic rules should be followed in the process of on-line auctions that were previously mentioned regarding the live auction format (*see pages 18–19*). These rules will help promote a positive experience. The most important rule is to figure out how high you want to bid on an item. Once you have established your limit, stick to it, or you may end up overpaying for your collectible.

Don't forget the fine print

Another important rule of thumb is to read the fine print. Make sure you read all the conditions of sale for each on-line auction house you use—in particular, whether there is a buyer's premium. If there is one, it will probably range from 10 to 15 percent in addition to your bid. Remember also to check out the sales tax information.

Like their live counterparts, Internet auctions typically sell items "as is," which means that it is the responsibility of the potential buyer to make all necessary inspections of any items they are interested in prior to the auction. In a live auction, you usually have a day or so before the auction to look over the items. But since there are no physical catalogues for on-line auctions, you will have to inspect the items by looking at photographs on the web sites. Make sure that the photographs match the descriptions of the items, are clear, and show as much of each item as possible. If something is missing or the description is not complete, e-mail or call the seller and ask for the missing details. If you have additional questions about an item for which you want to place a bid, always contact the seller or auction house *before* you place your bid. This will alleviate any embarrassing or difficult situations when the sale is over, leaving you, the successful bidder, with an item that you don't really want.

Honor your bid

If you are the successful bidder in an on-line auction, you have entered into a legally binding contract and must honor your bid just as you would at a live auction. Please don't be put off by the Internet. The on-line auction process can be confusing at first, but with time and patience, you will find the entire experience thrilling and fun. Plus, you will find some fantastic toys for which you might search for years, and all from the comfort of your own home.

Careful, it can be addictive! On-line auctions are fun, but you must use constraint if you have an addictive personality. Collectors all around the world agree that if you are not careful, all of your time and money will be spent surfing the auction boards. Just like in a live auction, try not to get caught up in the excitement and hype that these on-line auctions can generate. Here are a few tips. Establish a limit on the most money you are willing to pay for an item, and be prepared to walk away if you are outbid. This will help you keep your feet on the ground and not blow the budget on the one must-have collectible. Also, do your homework—know what it is you are bidding on and roughly what it's worth. Always ask the seller questions if you require any additional information before bidding.

Where do you start?

The best way to find your way around the Internet is to try it. That way, you will learn quickly. However, there are several sites that I would recommend. The best site, as you would expect, is that of one of the major auction houses. Sotheby's on-line auction site is easy to navigate and very clear, and while it does not specialize in toys and games, it has some very good quality items to sell. The address is:
www.sothebys.com

Another good site, and one that always has a great selection of dolls and bears, is eBay. Its prices are reasonable, and the site is presented in an interesting way. The address is:
www.ebay.com

The final site that I think you should start with is mine, of course. It's called TreasureQuest Auction Galleries Inc., and we've been going since 1997. We run a full selection of auctions, have a clear set of terms and conditions, and offer an appraisal service for any items that a collector might want valued. Why not pay the site a visit? After all, it's free to do so, and you never know—you might find just what you're looking for. The address is:
www.tqag.com

It is also important to know or have an idea of who you are doing business with and buying from. There is a feedback forum set up at eBay where successful buyers can rate their experience with the seller and the seller can also rate the buyer. This is helpful in "getting to know" the other parties involved with your on-line transactions. TreasureQuest provides clients with a toll-free telephone number to ask questions and make payments for their items.

A TreasureQuest employee processing a bidder's payment at their galleries in Jupiter, Florida.

DISTINGUISHING THE REAL FROM THE FAKE

Toys have increased in desirability over the years, and the fascination of collectors has driven prices to extremes, particularly when a rare and desirable toy hits the market. Whenever there are increased visibility and reports of high prices paid by collectors, the proportion of reproductions and fakes in the marketplace goes up. The promise of money brings out the sharks. There are several areas of toy collecting, especially in early cast-iron toys, in which reproductions and repainted items are presented as originals, when in fact, they are simply very good copies.

The following is a guide that I hope collectors will find useful in properly identifying real toys and reproductions. The best weapon to use against

AMOS AND ANDY CAR, 1930s
Tinplate

ORIGINAL

Look for:

- richer colors in lithography
- wear to mechanism
- dents or signs of playwear

REPRODUCTION

Look for:

- washed out colors in lithography
- blurry or out of focus look to the lithography
- shiny tinplate mechanism and undercarriage
- no signs of wear

AMOS AND ANDY CAR, 1980s
Tinplate

Undercarriage of reproduction.

buying fakes is knowledge. You should become familiar with time periods, learn when certain materials were popular and frequently used, and know how to recognize the color and tint of paints used during those periods. Remember, not all fakes are deliberately sold as such; even the sellers may be ignorant of an item's provenance.

The two areas of toy collecting in which you are most likely to get reproductions are tinplate wind-up toys and cast-iron toys. It is important for collectors of such items to know what they should look like in order to avoid falling for fakes. Reproductions made from these materials are often "distressed"—artificially aged to appear older than they are—so as to fool the unsuspecting collector. Arm yourself with the knowledge of how things should look, and you won't be fooled.

**PADDY AND PIG
BANK, 1885**
Cast-iron

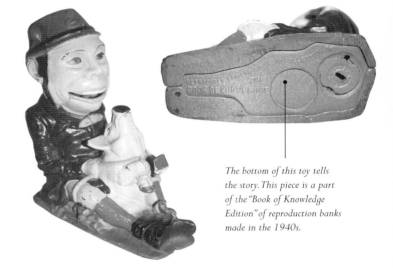

The bottom of this toy tells the story. This piece is a part of the "Book of Knowledge Edition" of reproduction banks made in the 1940s.

**PADDY AND PIG
BANK, 1940s**
Cast-iron

ORIGINAL

Look for:

- ◆ muted or aged colors of paint
- ◆ smooth casting
- ◆ seams that match up closely
- ◆ lack of file marks
- ◆ use of older screws or bolts

REPRODUCTION

Look for:

- ◆ bright and excessive use of color
- ◆ bumpy or grainy casting
- ◆ uneven seams
- ◆ file marks, usually on the bottom of the toy
- ◆ brush strokes or uneven use of paint
- ◆ use of modern screws or new springs

It is amazing the lengths that people will go to in order to take advantage of the unsuspecting collector. I have heard stories of toys being buried in the backyard for a week and left out in a rainstorm to "distress" them and make them look old. Despite the wide variety of techniques used to alter the appearance of toys, there are a few foolproof ways to detect the age and authenticity of tinplate and cast-iron toys.

Tinplate

The lithographic process employed to decorate toys between the turn of the 19th century and the 1930s was artistic, done in rich colors with great attention to the design details and finishing techniques. Toys made after World War II—and this will include most reproductions and fakes—could not duplicate the artistic or visual quality of the original toys. The earlier lithographic process was outdated and too costly to duplicate, so new techniques and color palettes were created, resulting in washed colors or color variations in the toys being reproduced. These defects can be detected with a magnifying glass. The reproduction will feature a dot matrix of lithography—an assortment of dots organized in uniform rows, similar to what is seen when photographs in a newspaper are viewed under magnification. Original tinplate lithography used a different technique. Under magnification, the item will lack the dot-matrix pattern. Another feature that might be seen on an original piece is hand-painted detail, which was often used to embellish the lithography.

Cast-Iron

Understanding the history of the various techniques used to produce cast-iron toys will assist collectors in detecting reproductions and fakes even if only armed with the naked eye. The process of manufacturing cast-iron toys dates back to the foundries of the mid-1800s and utilized a process called sand casting. This meant that a mold was impressed into wet sand in a frame, and molten iron was poured in and cooled to create the master cast for the production line. The process was repeated with the cast and the final product was hand-painted and sold on to the public.

The pigments and colors of paints used during the 1880s and 1900s were made with chemicals or ingredients that are no longer available. This means that it is impossible to replicate the shades of paint used. Also, casting techniques have advanced over the years, and original molds of antique toys simply do not exist any longer. Today's replicas are made using the original toy as the pattern. Making replicas as detailed as the original is therefore almost impossible. It is also true that since cast-iron shrinks when it cools, a replica made from an original toy will be smaller than the original. This can be a key factor in detecting a fake, especially in the area of cast-iron banks. In the following chapter, there is a chart of original base sizes for cast-iron mechanical banks (*see pages 30–31*). If you happen to find a toy that is smaller than its equivalent listed in the chart, this will indicate that you have found a reproduction.

Reproduction cast-iron toys often have a grainy or bumpy appearance. You may also find file marks where stray iron has been filed off and smoothed out. The pieces of the toy will not necessarily fit together perfectly and there may be large gaps between pieces. Original cast-iron toys will be smooth to the touch and the pieces that comprise the toy will fit together perfectly.

While it is possible to be fooled into thinking you have found an original and valuable antique toy, be suspicious and be wary. If you remember these key elements, you'll greatly lower your chances of making costly mistakes.

THE ESSENTIALS

When you decide to become a toy collector, you need to establish when your toys were made. The materials used in the production of the toys, the size of the toys, and the marks on them all help in the identification process. It is important for collectors to develop their own sets of skills in determining age and authenticity. The stories of a collectible and where it came from do not always paint the correct picture of a toy's background.

For example, when I was doing an appraisal fair a few years back, a young woman came up to me and told me that her grandfather, who was born in the 1890s, played with a particular plastic, battery-operated toy when he was a child. I gently reminded her that plastic and batteries were not used in toy production until later in the 20th century, and suggested that her grandfather had picked up the toy later in his life, because he found the toy amusing. She was, naturally, rather disappointed. Another time, a woman brought me an item for valuation. She told me that the person who sold it to her had informed her that the item came from a house where a 90-year-old woman lived, and this was one of her prized possessions. But just because a toy is part of a 90-year-old woman's possessions, you cannot assume, as this woman mistakenly did, that the 90-year-old had played with it as a child. The item was not that old, and in fact, was a reproduction.

In all cases, it is the responsibility of the collectors to arm themselves with enough information to fend off unwanted items by identifying the fakes and reproductions in the marketplace. Overall, the toy market has posted gains in several areas, especially in cast-iron mechanical banks and pressed steel toys. While American tin toys continue to interest collectors, their prices have fluctuated recently.

Just like the stock market, there are ups and downs in the marketplace for toys, and the values given in this book are based on conservative estimations. There are many factors that affect the value of items, such as the economy or other uncontrollable circumstances, but at the end of the day, it is quality material in good condition that is desirable to collectors and will consistently fetch a good market value regardless of outside influences.

MATERIALS

All of the toys in this book fall within one or a combination of classifications by medium or material used to produce the toy. All of these media provide clues to the observant collector as to the date and time period the toy was produced. The dates for the use of each medium are approximations based on the period in which the medium was most popular and manufacturers were making the greatest use of it.

This toy, made by George Borgfeld, is typical of 1920s tinplate playthings.

27

PRIMARY TOY MATERIALS

CAST-IRON: 1840s–1940s

- Cast-iron was predominantly used by American toy makers.
- Some cast-iron toys were made in Germany or the U.K.
- Toys made of cast-iron include mechanical banks, still banks, horse-drawn vehicles, automobiles, planes, trains, doll-house furniture, stoves, bell toys, boats, and miscellaneous figural items.
- Beware of fakes, reproductions, and misrepresentations in the marketplace (*see pages 24–26*).
- Taiwanese fakes have flooded the market, so be aware of the poor quality and grainy or bumpy casting that indicate a fake.

CELLULOID: 1890–1950s

- Originally, celluloid was made from a mixture of nitro cellulose apyroxlin, and powdered camphor.
- The material was patented in the United States in 1869 by the Hyatt brothers, who stumbled on the substance in their search for a material suitable for making billiard balls.
- Celluloid accessories were common in the U.S., but celluloid toys were made in quantity in Asia in the 1940s.
- Today, celluloid toys are desirable but fragile and easily damaged.
- Celluloid toys include primarily figural toys, but the material was often used as an accent with other materials.

COMPOSITION: 1890s–1940s

- Composition was made from a mixture of kaolin (white china clay), sawdust, and glue.
- It was extensively used by both American and German toy manufacturers.
- Toys made of composition include figures, dolls, soldiers, and parts for some vehicle toys.

DIE-CAST METAL: 1906–Present

- Lead was originally used in the production of these toys; however, in the 1930s, due to fears over safety, the material was often replaced by mazac. Despite these fears, some manufacturers continued to use lead until the 1950s.
- The new material, mazac, was a magnesium-zinc alloy first used by Tootsietoy and still used today.
- Die-cast toys are made from metal cast under pressure in a mold.
- There are two types of die-cast toys: hollow-cast and solid-cast. As the names imply, hollow-cast toys have hollow centers, while solid-cast toys are completely filled with metal.
- Barclay's and Britain's soldiers are hollow-cast, while Heyde's are solid cast. Manoil used a combination of both techniques.
- Die-cast toys include soldiers, vehicles, and figures.

PAPER: 1830s–1950s

- Paper was often used in conjunction with other materials to produce toys.
- Prior to 1860, paper was made of a high fiber content that was more alkaline and more likely to survive.
- After 1860, paper was made from wood pulp that was highly acidic, causing paper to yellow and crumble over time.
- Paper items were often used as accents on toys and were usually lithographed or painted and then applied to toys.

PLASTIC: 1950s–Present

- Toys made of plastic originated in Asia in the early 1950s, and by the end of the decade, toy manufacturers in Europe and America were making them, too.
- They include dolls, action figures, vehicles, and toy guns.

RUBBER: 1930s

- Early rubber toys were made of natural material.
- Synthetic rubber was developed in the mid-1950s.
- Rubber was used for accessory items on toys. The early white rubber tires on vehicle toys from the 1930s often deteriorated.
- The Sun Rubber Company is most noted for the quality of its rubber toy production.
- Most rubber toys are cracked and faded from wear and neglect.
- Rubber toys include some Disney toys, dolls, and vehicles.

TINPLATE: 1850s–1940s

- Toys were made from tinplated iron or steel.
- Cloth, paper, wood, glass, celluloid, and vinyl were often used in conjunction with tinplate to create toys.
- Tinplate factories opened in America during the 1830s, but few examples from the factories were exported abroad.
- *See pages 24–26* for examples of how to tell originals from fakes.
- Tinplate toys include wind-up, character, and battery-operated toys, which were lithographed or hand-painted.

WOOD: 1830s–1930s

- Wood is one of the oldest materials used to make toys.
- It was a readily available commodity and inexpensive material to use. Records indicate that Middle Eastern people from 3100 to 2686 BC hand carved wooden carts and figures.
- Wood is still used today, but not as much as in its heyday.
- Its fragility and susceptibility to rot make finding early wooden toys difficult.
- Wooden toys include rocking horses, riding toys, vehicles, dolls, doll houses, and a variety of blocks, puzzles, and games.

TOY MARKS

Maker's marks on toys can often provide collectors with valuable information about a toy and document the time period of its production. However, deciphering marks is not as easy as it sounds.

Toys and products made after 1891 and imported into the United States needed to be marked with the countries of origin before the items were allowed into the country. We have President William McKinley and his Tariff Act of 1891 to thank for this.

Japanese marks

After World War II, the United States occupied Japan between 1945 and 1952 and assisted with the rebuilding of the country's economy. This included the production of novelties, ceramic pieces, and toys. Any of these items made for export were required to be marked "Occupied Japan" to satisfy the export requirements. This regulation lasted through April 28, 1952, when the sanction was lifted and the occupation by the United States ended. Due to the relatively short length of the occupation and the types of items produced, "Occupied Japan" items have become a favorite with collectors around the world.

Prior to the World War II, items from Japan were usually marked "Japan"; those made after the occupation are marked "Made in Japan." However, it is important that collectors remember that certain items that were made during the occupation period may only be marked "Japan," even if their boxes are marked "Occupied Japan." This is because the manufacturers already had these particular items in production when the new regulations were announced. In order to ensure that they were able to ship the items, they made sure that the legend "Occupied Japan" appeared on the boxes.

German marks

Prior to World War II, German toys that were exported into the U.S. did list the country of origin as mandated, but in some cases also included the abbreviation "D.R.G.M." or "Deutsches Reichs Gebrauchsmuster," which indicated that the toy had a registered German patent on it. After World War II, the U.S. occupied Germany, and between 1947 and 1953, exported items had to be marked: "U.S. Zone, Germany."

In 1949, toys began to be marked with the words, "Made in Western Germany." This marking continued through the 1960s. Since then, toys have simply been marked "Germany."

TOY MECHANISMS

Live steam: Steam power was usually found in boats and early locomotives. A simple brass boiler was heated externally by a spirit lamp, generating steam power for a single- or twin-cylinder engine. Toys with this feature remain very popular, but some people find them dirty and a little dangerous.

Clockwork: Powered by wound springs of various sizes, a clockwork mechanism would power a toy for a couple of minutes or more. Some early American clockwork toys ran for up to 30 minutes. They also had the advantage of not being dirty.

Electric motor: Early motors used alternating currents. These were poorly insulated, prone to shorting, and often dangerous. They were used until low-voltage systems became popular in the 1930s.

Lightweight electric mechanism: Such mechanisms were popular in toys made in Japan after 1945. Batteries were stored in the base of the toy or in a control panel.

Friction motor: These consist of a free-spinning, laminated iron disc that powers the toy when the disc is spinning.

KEY TO MECHANICAL BANK BASE DIMENSIONS

When cast-iron mechanical banks were being reproduced in the mid-1900s, the originals were used to create molds for casting. The use of originals as molds, coupled with the fact that cast-iron shrinks when it cools, means that all reproduction banks will have smaller dimensions than the originals listed here.

The numbers represented in the key were obtained by taking each measurement at the center of the bank's length or width. Banks with round bases are marked with a "D" to indicate diameter. Oftentimes, it is difficult to spot a reproduction or fake; this key will prove useful in determining the authenticity of your cast-iron mechanical banks.

Artillery Bank, c. 1900s

Boy Robbing Bird's Nest, c. 1906

Boy on Trapeze, 1888

BANK NAME	LENGTH	WIDTH
Acrobats	7¼ in (18.4 cm)	2⅞ in (7.4 cm)
Always Did Spise a Mule (Boy Over)	10¼ in (26 cm)	2⅞ in (7.4 cm)
Artillery Bank	7 15/16 in (20.2 cm)	
Bad Accident	10¼ in (26 cm)	3⅜ in (8.6 cm)
Bill-E-Grin	2½ in (5.7 cm)	3⅜ in (8.6 cm)
Bird on Roof	3¼ in (8.3 cm)	4 3/16 in (10.6 cm)
Boy and Bull Dog	4⅞ in (12.4 cm)	2¾ in (7 cm)
Boy on Trapeze	4⅞ in (11.3 cm)	4⅞ in (11.3 cm)
Boy Robbing Bird's Nest	6 in (15.2 cm)	3¼ in (8.3 cm)
Boy Stealing Watermelon	–	1¼ in (3.2 cm)
Buffalo Bucking	7¾ in (18.4 cm)	2 13/16 in (7.1 cm)
Bull Dog Bank	5⅝ in (14.3 cm)	3⅛ in (7.9 cm)
Cabin	4¼ in (10.8 cm)	2⅞ in (7.4 cm)
Cannon U.S. & Spain	8⅜ in (21.3 cm)	–
Chimpanzee	5⅞ in (14.9 cm)	–
Clown on Globe	4 15/16 in (12.5 cm)	–
Cow, Kicking Milking	10 in (25.4 cm)	–
Creedmore	10¼ in (26 cm)	–
Darktown Battery	9⅞ in (25.1 cm)	–
Dentist	9¼ in (23.5cm)	–
Dinah	4 in (10.2 cm)	–
Eagle, Eaglets	6¾ in (17.1 cm)	–
Football Player	10 3/16 in (25.9 cm)	–
Frogs, Two	8½ in (21 cm)	–
Girl in Victorian Chair	2¼ in (5.7 cm)	2¼ in (5.7 cm)
Girl Skipping Rope	8 3/16 in (20.8 cm)	–
Goat, Billy	5½ in (13.3 cm)	–
Goat, Butting	4 13/16 in (12.2 cm)	–
Goat, Frog, and Old Man	7 11/16 in (19.5 cm)	–
Harlequin	6¼ in (15.9 cm)	4¼ in (10.8 cm)
Horse Race—Large Base	–	4 7/16 in (11.3 cm) D
Horse Race—Small Base	–	4 1/16 (10.3 cm) D

Dinah, c. 1910s

Harlequin, c. 1880s

Monkey Bank, c. 1900s

BANK NAME	LENGTH	WIDTH
Humpty Dumpty	3⅝ in (9.2 cm)	—
Indian Shooting Bear	10⅜ in (26.4 cm)	—
Jolly N.	—	3⁵⁄₁₆ in (8.4 cm)
Jonah and the Whale	10⁵⁄₁₆ in (26.2 cm)	—
Leap Frog	7⁹⁄₁₆ in (19.2 cm)	—
Lion and Monkeys	9⅛ in (23.2 cm)	—
Little Moe	3⁵⁄₁₆ in (8.4 cm)	2 in (5.1 cm)
Magic	—	4 in (10.2 cm)
Magician	—	3¾ in (9.5 cm)
Monkey—Coconut	—	3¼ in (8.3cm)
Monkey—Modern	8⅞ in (9.8 cm)	—
Mule, Barn	8⅝ in (22 cm)	—
Mule, Bucking	—	2½ in (6.4 cm)
North Pole	3¹⁵⁄₁₆ in (10 cm)	—
Organ Bank	—	4¹⁄₁₆ in (10.3 cm)
Owl Moves Head	3⅞ in (9.8 cm)	3¹⁄₁₆ in (7.8 cm)
Paddy and Pig	7¹⁄₁₆ in (17.9 cm)	—
Perfection		2¹¹⁄₁₆ in (6.8 cm)
Professor Pug Frog	10⅛ in (25.7 cm)	—
Punch and Judy	5¼ in (13.3 cm)	3¾ in (9.5 cm)
Santa Claus	4⅛ in (10.5 cm)	—
Shoot the Chutes	9⅞ in (25.1 cm)	—
Squirrel, Stump	6¾ in (17.2 cm)	—
Tammany	—	2⅞ in (7.3 cm)
Teddy and Bear	—	10³⁄₁₆ in (25.9 cm)
Trick Pony Bank	7¹⁄₁₆ in (17.9 cm)	—
Uncle Remus	5⅞ in (14.9 cm)	3¹³⁄₁₆ in (9.7 cm)
Uncle Sam	¹⁵⁄₁₆ in (0.9 cm)	4 in (10.2 cm)
Uncle Tom with Lapels	4⅛ in (10.5 cm)	—
Uncle Tom without Lapels	4⅛ in (10.5 cm)	—
William Tell	10⅝ in (27 cm)	—
World's Fair	8¼ in (21 cm)	—

Organ Bank, c. 1880s

Owl Moves Head, c. 1880s

Punch and Judy, c. 1930s

31

WOODEN TOYS

Wooden toys and playthings make up the oldest mass-produced category of toy production. Records indicate that hand-carved playthings can be traced back to 3100 BC, several examples of which have been unearthed in ancient Egyptian tombs. This ancient lineage is also reflected in toys manufactured in the 20th and 21st centuries, and wooden toys are still the most primitive in appearance, often retaining the folk-art flavor of their predecessors.

In America, wooden toys were first manufactured around 1830. Over the years, various techniques were used to decorate these toys, including painting, stenciling, printing, and applying lithographed paper to the surfaces of the toys. Early American toys made from the late 1800s to the early 1900s were hand-painted with great attention to detail and artistry, giving them a homemade appearance. Between 1880 and 1910, a brass template of a design was often placed on the wooden surface of a toy, and paint was applied to create the stencilled design. Some toys from this period had a printed design impressed directly into the wood, leaving an indentation.

Another technique of toy decoration, developed in the 1860s, was color lithography. The earliest examples of these toys were lithographed game boards. After 1875, toys were made with color lithography printed directly on the wood or on paper then glued to the wood.

Overall, wood is a durable and flexible material from which to make toys, but it is easily affected by climate changes and very vulnerable to damp conditions. This means that wooden toys are prone to rot and other damage associated with damp conditions. Ironically, this makes the discovery of a fine, 19th-century wooden toy—such as a rocking horse, a velocipede, or a baby buggy—a premium find.

Antique wooden toys found these days are usually representations of modes of transportation or buildings. Most are decorated with colorful lithographed paper. While many examples are very simple, some feature ornate carving.

Perhaps the most popular antique wooden toys were doll houses, and many of them open up to reveal several interior rooms furnished with miniature wooden furniture pieces. The furniture was, of course, sold separately.

R. Bliss Manufacturing Company

The house opens to reveal the interior, which would have been filled with miniature furnishings.

A pioneer and leader in the field of lithographed paper-on-wood toys, the Bliss Manufacturing Company was founded by Rufus Bliss in 1832 in Pawtucket, Rhode Island. The company's range of products included architectural blocks, carriages, trains, trolley cars, paddle-wheel boats, battleships, fire toys, and doll houses—all distinguished by their accurate details and high-quality craftsmanship. Bliss pull-toys, and especially their ornate and very popular doll houses, entertained and educated Victorian-era children and continue to captivate collectors today.

Ads for Bliss pull-toys, doll houses, and other playthings began appearing as early as 1871. Always an innovator, Bliss was the first company to produce a toy telephone set. It continued to improve on the lithographic processes that made its toys so colorful and appealing to children and adults alike.

The toy division was sold to Manson & Parker of Winchendon, Massachusetts, in 1914 and continued to produce toys through 1935. Only a few toys by Bliss come on the market each year. Early pieces are scarce.

VICTORIAN STYLE DOLL HOUSE, c. 1905

This ornate doll house, featuring painted and stained wood with lithographed paper, has a peaked roof, two chimneys, and front and side porches.

$2,000–$3,000

INSIDER'S TIPS

Bliss toys border on folk art and are highly collectible. Make sure to check the paper carefully for restorations and repainting. Be wary of colors that seem too bright; they've probably been touched up.

WHAT TO LOOK FOR:

- ornately designed, lithographed paper-on-wood toys
- simple and accurate representations of boats, trains, and carriages of the period
- high-quality lithography with a variety of rich colors
- colors possibly faded and pieces missing, e.g., sailboats may lack masts

Crandall

Asa Crandall ran a family woodworking business from a factory in Covington, Pennsylvania. When he died in 1849, the business passed into the hands of his 16-year-old son, Charles M. Crandall. Over the next decade, with the post-Civil War economy of the United States booming, the young Crandall persevered with the business. The company began producing a variety of furniture pieces and wood objects, including particularly popular wooden croquet sets packaged in wooden boxes. The boxes had tongue-and-groove corners, a feature that helped change and shape the direction of the company forever.

The business continued to grow and prosper with Charles at the helm, and in order to meet expanding demand, he moved the operation to Montrose, Pennsylvania, in the 1860s. The croquet sets continued to be popular, and occasionally, Charles would take home the grooved scraps from the boxes for his children. They never seemed to exhaust the infinite possibilities of the grooved corners and found constant delight in the wooden scraps. Watching his children's playing inspired Charles to create his first children's play set of Crandall Building Blocks

in 1867. Shortly afterward, he patented his interlocking tongue-and-groove wooden toys and almost sold the entire first year's production. The tremendous success of the interlocking blocks helped facilitate the creation of Crandall's most popular product, The Acrobats. The interlocking concept was also applied to Crandall's District School 1875, Crandall's Heavy Artillery soldier blocks, and the Crandall Menagerie.

Crandall set up a new business outside of New York City in 1885, establishing the Waverly Toy Works in Waverly, New York. The business in Montrose was handed over to his son Fredrick, but one year later, in 1886, a fire devastated the factory, and the remainder of the operation was moved to Elkland, Pennsylvania. Production resumed through the turn of the century before the factory finally closed its doors in 1907. Charles Crandall died in 1905.

Crandall toys continue to amaze and delight collectors today. The simple, folk-art quality captures the time period brilliantly. All of the Crandall toys were packaged in wooden boxes, as opposed to paper ones. This is why many Crandall toys survive in good condition today.

THE ACROBATS,
c. 1875
This set features interlocking wooden figures that provided hours of entertainment for Victorian children.
$1,000–$2,000

It is important to keep these toys in their sets, complete with the slide-top lid.

Fisher-Price

Exploring the historical aspects of a toy company often provides collectors with insight into the minds of its creators and the reasons behind the designs of some of the world's favorite toys. The enduring popularity of Fisher-Price toys was apparent at Christie's 1993 auction of "collectible toys from the collection of Lawrence Scripps Wilkinson." Lot 54 that day was a Fisher-Price paper-on-wood Mickey Mouse and Pluto Band, *c.* 1935, modestly estimated at between $400 and $600. That particular lot received much attention, and collectors around the country were calling in for condition reports on its lithography and asking to places bids over the phone during the auction. The gavel eventually came down on this colorful toy at $2,300—a clear indication that vintage Fisher-Price toys in good condition are most desirable.

The company began operations October 1, 1930, in East Aurora, New York. Its founders, Herman Fisher and Irving Price, had met through mutual friends. Herman Fisher had worked for All-Fair Toys, a producer of board games. Irving Price had a background with the F.W. Woolworth Company, with whom he had acquired sound management experience. They combined forces with Helen M. Schelle, who at the time ran the Walker Toy Shop in Binghamton, New York. Helen Schelle possessed an incredible eye for children's toys, and her experience in the toy trade had earned her extensive contacts with buyers in New York City. She became the first secretary and treasurer for the Fisher-Price toy company. They were joined by artist and designer Margaret Price, whose background was as a writer and illustrator for Rand McNally, Harper & Brothers, and Strecher Lithography.

The new team worked hard to bring their inaugural toy line to market. The "Sixteen Hopefuls," as they were known, included Granny Doodle, Barky Puppy, and the whimsical Woodsy-Wee Zoo. As well as insisting on attention to detail and the use of vibrant colors, the company established five criteria for the production of their toys:

1. *Intrinsic play value*
2. *Ingenuity*
3. *Strong construction*
4. *Good value for money*
5. *Action*

MALLARD DUCK #141 SNAP-QUACK, 1940s
Designed by nationally known wildlife artist Lynn Bogue, this pull-toy was manufactured in the late 1940s.
$300–$500

Toys are numbered and feature the company's logo.

JUMBO #780 XYLOPHONE PLAYER, 1937
This toy is complete with the wooden balls on the xylophone hammers that are often missing. This greatly enhances the toy's value.
$600–$800

Fisher-Price took the manufacturing world by storm. The colors and sturdiness of the toys amazed and delighted children and adults everywhere. The first shipment was delivered to Macy's in New York City in 1931. By the end of the year, over 700 stores carried Fisher-Price toys. The line continued to build, adding comic characters like Popeye, Mickey Mouse, and Donald Duck to the production line.

As the years passed, the company incorporated pull-toys, push-toys, and educational toys. The action of the toys or the noise they produced always seemed to attract children to them. Today, collectors still look for the vibrant colors within the paper lithography and will take special note to see if the action aspect of the toy is still functional. Most toys have experienced significant play wear, because they were durable and were often passed from sibling to sibling.

IDENTIFICATION

- if the piece is all wood, it was produced between 1931 and 1949
- the 1950s saw the introduction of plastic into Fisher-Price toys
- by 1964, plastic had totally replaced wood in Fisher-Price toy production

KATY KACKLER #4, c. 1950s
This toy illustrates in the feather work the attention to detail that set the company apart from others.
$50–$150

MOO-OO COW #155, c. 1950s
This is an early example of a wooden toy that incorporated plastic—in this case, in the ears. By the early 1960s, plastic began to overtake wood in toy production.
$50–$100

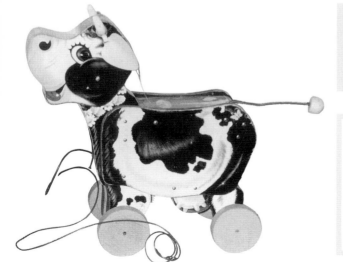

WHAT TO LOOK FOR:

- all Fisher-Price toys are marked somewhere with the company logo and a product number

INSIDER'S TIPS

The most desirable pieces and the hardest to find are pre-World War II, all-wood character pieces. The more plastic used in the production of a Fisher-Price toy, the more recent and, therefore, less valuable it is.

Gibbs Manufacturing Company

While Connecticut was the cradle of early toy manufacturers, a number of enduring toy companies were also founded in Ohio in the latter half of the 19th and well into the 20th century. The Gibbs Manufacturing Company was founded in Canton, Ohio, in 1830 by Lewis E. Gibbs, producing wooden barrels and tubs, and later adding rakes and other hardware to its lines. Lewis was no stranger to business, having worked as a child for his father, Joshua Gibbs, an inventor and plow manufacturer. Farm equipment, particularly plows, was essential in the Ohio farmlands, as well as across the Great Plains, and Lewis introduced advancements in the production of metal plows that farmers across the Midwest warmly welcomed. His innovations ensured that the company's sales increased.

Gibbs was unexpectedly thrust into the toy business and the national political arena when William McKinley's presidential campaign manager contacted him, requesting that he create a political giveaway. McKinley was from Canton, Ohio, and the idea of a hometown businessman creating a novelty for a hometown presidential candidate virtually assured a successful campaign. Lewis was flattered and rose to the occasion by manufacturing a spring-driven top that featured pictures of McKinley and his running mate along with the slogans "McKinley on Top" and "I Spin For McKinley." Lewis Gibbs's ingenuity can be credited with helping McKinley be elected president.

Due to the success of the toy top, the company continued to manufacture toys with motion and action. Tops remained in the line that also included push- and pull-toys, animals with moving legs that pulled a variety of wagons and carts, an Irishman dancing a jig, and a cat with a bobbing head. The company developed the slogan, "You have only to put Gibbs toys on your counters and they sell themselves." The toys were attractive, and children enjoyed the motion of the tops and the movable features of the horse-drawn toys and floor toys.

Lewis continued to run the company until his death in 1914. His sons and other family members ran the company smoothly and efficiently after that, and they expanded the line to include advertizing toys to order and lithographed paper-on-wood toys. The extensive toy line, coupled with competitive pricing (anywhere from 1¢ to 35¢) helped sustain the company through the lean Depression years.

Although the Gibbs Manufacturing Company never dominated the marketplace, the company managed to continue toy production until 1969.

WHAT TO LOOK FOR:

- simple platform pull-toys, usually featuring a circus animal
- early toys were numbered and named, e.g. "No. 27 U.S. Mail"

SEESAW TOY, c. 1920s
Gibbs was known for toys with motion. This one is gravity activated and moves up and down as the boy and girl make their way to the base of the toy.
$100–$300

A. Schoenhut Company

Based in Philadelphia, Pennsylvania, the Schoenhut Company has a long and distinctive history as an American toy manufacturer. The company was founded by Albert Schoenhut, a German immigrant who arrived in Philadelphia shortly after the Civil War. He worked for John Deiser & Sons, an importer, and learned to repair the toy pianos the firm imported from Germany. Soon, Schoenhut was making his own American pianos. In 1873, he set up his own company, which began producing quality toy pianos that, unlike the competition, produced a pleasant, on-pitch tone. In fact, the pianos were so popular that the company did not produce anything else until 1903.

In 1903, the Schoenhut Company expanded its line to include a variety of wooden toys. This led to the debut of the Humpty-Dumpty Circus. This circus set was simple and came with only a few pieces.

HUMPTY-DUMPTY BOXED CIRCUS SET, c. 1920s
Performing horses, props, and circus performers were all part of the many accessories included with the Schoenhut circus.
$100–$300 each

HUMPTY-DUMPTY BOXED CIRCUS SET, c. 1920s
This set has a paper-lithographed lid depicting a colorful arrangement of the circus figures and props inside. The box measures 18 x 30 inches (46 x 76 cm).
$2,000–$3,000

WHAT TO LOOK FOR:

- dolls have carved limbs with steel joints
- early circus set figures and animals are all-wood; later versions include figures with porcelain heads and wooden bodies and limbs
- wooden figures with glass eyes are rare and more desirable to collectors
- dolls are usually marked on the body with a paper label: "Schoenhut Toys Made In USA"

Its popularity resulted in Schoenhut increasing production, as well as introducing a variety of accessories for the set, including wooden figures of a ringmaster, acrobats, a lion tamer, animals, clowns, and ladders. All the pieces for the early sets were made of wood and hand-carved.

In addition to the popular circus set, Schoenhut also produced dolls, boats, toy guns, blocks, shooting galleries, horse-drawn carriages, and other playthings to entertain children. The company ceased production in 1935.

KEYSTONE COP AND CLOWN ROLY-POLY TOYS, c. 1910
These were made of papier-mâché, hand-painted, and weighted to remain upright.
$300–$500 each

MILK DELIVERY WAGON, c. 1910
This toy features a carved figure and horse on a wheeled base with milk advertising on the side panels of the wagon.
$1,000–$2,000

ALSO WORTH COLLECTING:
Lincoln Logs

John Lloyd Wright, son of architect Frank Lloyd Wright, started the Lincoln Logs toy company in Chicago in 1916. John had traveled with his father to Tokyo, where the elder Lloyd Wright had been commissioned to provide a design for the Imperial Hotel that would withstand earthquakes. The overlapping construction in the building's foundations inspired John to create a toy that has entertained children for more than 80 years. Lincoln Logs continue to be manufactured to this day by Playskool, a division of Hasbro, Inc. Today, Lincoln Logs sets vary in price from **$25–$300,** depending on condition and completeness.

Tinkertoys

Inspiration has a multitude of sources, but in toy production, the key to success is to design something that will capture a limited attention span for as long as possible, and then sell it to as many people as you can. For Charles Pajeau, an Evanston, Illinois, tombstone cutter, inspiration arrived while watching his children play with their mother's wooden thread spools and knitting needles. He combined the knitting needles' design and the concept of the circular shape with holes from the spool, and added more holes to create a new toy with multiple design possibilities.

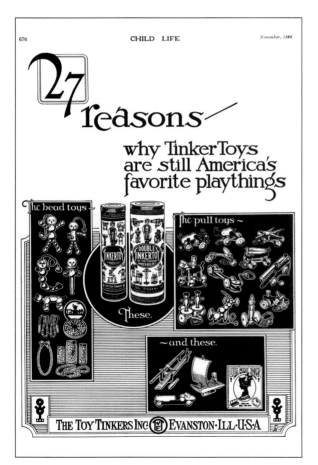

Pajeau tinkered with his invention for a couple of years before presenting its prototype at the New York Toy Fair around 1915. Being a novice in the toy industry and having no reputation, Pajeau was assigned a table placed in the far corner of the hall. He made no sales. Returning to Grand Central Terminal for the journey home, he was hit once again by inspiration. In one last desperate attempt to make a sale, he convinced two drugstores in the terminal to carry his creation in exchange for 40¢ on every dollar sold. Pajeau created elaborate window displays for both stores which featured various creations made with his Tinkertoys. For one store, he assembled an elaborate windmill and positioned an electric fan so that it blew on the windmill and made its sails turn. He also hired people to sit in the windows, demonstrating the multiple construction possibilities of his invention and just how easy it was to use. The crowds gathered, and the sales skyrocketed. A similar window display was arranged at a Philadelphia department store, resulting in over 900,000 sets sold.

Since Pajeau took the initiative and walked into that drugstore at New York's Grand Central Terminal, close to 200 million sets have been sold.

WHAT TO LOOK FOR:

◆ the Tinkertoy logo with the trademark circular canister (as shown in the advertisement on the left)

An advertisement for Tinkertoys from the November 1928 issue of *Child Life* Magazine.

Tinplate cars and other playthings are some of the earliest metal toys ever made, which is one of the reasons why they continue be so popular among collectors today. These early toys are similar to wooden toys in that they often have a folk-art appearance and can be very simple in design.

In the latter part of the 19th century, tinned sheet steel, or tinplate, helped to revolutionize the food industry, as well as providing a wonderful resource for toy manufacturers. Tinplate was often combined with other materials, such as glass, paper, wood, or cloth, in the manufacture of play items. The designs were often intricate, and the artisans who created the early tinplate toys took great pride in their creations, many featuring delicate, hand-painted decorations that used stenciling, lithography, or enameling.

One of the first tin ore mines in America opened in Galena, Illinois, during the 1840s, sparking the domestic production of tin products and decreasing American reliance on imported tin. Early tin toys were produced in larger quantities from around 1880 through the early part of the 1900s.

The mass production of tinplate wind-up toys did not begin until the early 20th century. Due to rationing and shortages during World War II, the production of tinplate toys ceased in America and moved to Japan, Korea, and China. In the 1970s, these Asian manufacturers began to use plastic, which was cheaper, more malleable, and durable.

Tinplate toys are subject to rust if improperly stored in a damp environment. It is essential that tinplate toy collectors look after items in their collection with great care, and store them in a dry environment.

The auction market for tinplate toys fluctuates, and I always encourage collectors to seek out information on the trends in the marketplace before buying or selling. Despite the fact that many of these toys are of a similar type, they have widely differing values. For example, American tinplate items can fetch good prices because of their aesthetic qualities. Certain manufacturers produced similar toys, yet the toys that were produced by Lehmann are harder to find than those produced by Marx, and therefore, far more valuable.

Gebrüder Bing

Brothers Ignaz and Adolf Bing started out as tinware dealers in Nuremberg, Germany, around 1864. At first, their business was limited to the distribution of household items and toys. By 1882, the company had developed a number of successful toy lines that included spring-driven boats, cars, and double-decker buses. They also produced construction sets and a phonograph that played records at three different speeds. Their most innovative and popular items were toy trains.

At the turn of the century, the Bing brothers took the first steps toward the mass production of toys. Their major contribution to the toy world, and their eventual trademark, was the use of superior clockwork mechanisms in their mechanical toys. They were also known for their techniques of cutting and shaping metal. Gerbrüder Bing excelled in the use of highly detailed and colorful lithography on metal, as well.

As the company continued to prosper, it expanded production in 1906 to include teddy bears and elaborate tin ocean liners. These items all featured superior craftsmanship and an attention to detail that created an enormous demand from the children of the day—a demand that still exists among collectors.

Production levels increased and warehouses were filled with stock to keep up with the level of international demand for Bing toys. Management troubles plagued the company, and in 1919, a business partner named Werke purchased the company. The stock market crash of 1929 affected demand and halted the creation of new items for distribution. The company began to falter, and in 1932, with increased inventory and lack of buyers, Gerbrüder Bing was forced to cease toy production. In 1933, Karl Bub took over the Bing train production, while the Fleischmann firm grabbed the toy boat inventory.

WHAT TO LOOK FOR:

♦ all Bing toys feature the company logo; see *Identification* box opposite for details of how it has changed over the years

♦ high quality of lithography on toys

LONDON BUS, 1910
This beautifully designed vehicle features extensive graphics and a clockwork mechanism.
$10,000–$20,000

TRAIN SET, c. 1930
This hand-painted train set features a classic 0-4-0 wheel configuration on the locomotive. The set is I gauge and includes the passenger cars.
$2,500–$3,500

Authentic replication, attention to detail, and quality of paint all add up to a higher value on the toy.

TWO-STALL GARAGE WITH A PAIR OF AUTOMOBILES,
c. 1930s

The sedan and open touring car are both clockwork activated.
$400–$600

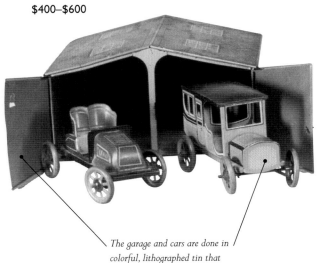

The garage and cars are done in colorful, lithographed tin that features great graphics, and as a result, the unrestored toy will command a higher price when sold.

IDENTIFICATION

- ◆ between 1900 and 1906, the letters "GBN" (for Gebrüder Bing, Nuremberg) were enclosed in a diamond outline crest (below left)
- ◆ from 1906 to 1919, the company's teddy bears had a metal chip placed in the bears' ears, while trains featured the "GBN" logo enclosed in a circle (below middle)
- ◆ from 1919 to 1923, the circle was replaced with a square
- ◆ from 1923 on, a small "W" was added to incorporate the name of Werke into the company logo (below right)

INSIDER'S TIPS

Some trains, boats, and automobiles may have chipped or missing paint. This will not affect their value unless the piece is a fake that has been artificially aged to deceive the buyer.

Boats were popular playthings in this time period; wear to this ship's hull is a sign that it has not been restored.

BATTLESHIP, 1930s

This tinplate boat, measuring 19½ inches (49.5 cm) in length, features a clockwork mechanism, lifeboats, and searchlights.
$2,000–$3,000

George W. Brown Company

George W. Brown, a clockmaker's apprentice, and his associate, Chauncey Goodrich, established their toy company in 1856, in Forestville, Connecticut. They were the first American toy makers to use clockwork mechanisms in tinplate toys, including boats, animal-drawn vehicles, tops, rattles, wagons, buckets, fire engines, and a train. Due to lack of labeling, their products can be difficult to positively identify, but George Brown's sketchbook survives.

The artistry and craftsmanship of Brown and Goodrich was reflected in the delicate designs they executed on tinplate and metal. All their toys were produced with intricate detail and precision. The company continued producing toys through 1862. After that, Brown began to alter its focus from toys to a more practical commodity, brass burners.

In 1868, Brown sold out to the Bristol Brass & Clock Company. A year later, Brown teamed up with Elisha Stevens of J. & E. Stevens (*see pages 82–83*) to create the Stevens & Brown Manufacturing Company. In 1880, however, the partnership was dissolved.

GRAND CENTRAL DEPOT TROLLEY,
c. 1880s
This tinplate horse-drawn trolley set features stencilled decorations and cut-out windows. The horses are standard Brown design.
$1,000–$2,000

WHAT TO LOOK FOR:

◆ toys made of tinplate with elaborate hand-painted stenciling or decorations

◆ simple designs

◆ toys with a folk-art, early Americana feel

COLLECTOR'S STORY

Brown may be gone, but he is certainly not forgotten. In December 1991, Christie's in New York hosted an auction of "Mint and Boxed" toys on behalf of the trustees of a bankrupt company. The toys included items made by some of the best manufacturers in the world. One toy in particular, Lot 15, was called "The Charles" (*see page 19*). This tinplate hose reel fire toy is an "only known" example and represents American toy craftsmanship at its finest. The auction room was filled with collectors. The sale was part of a bankruptcy, so the lots had no reserves—that is, minimum prices below which they would not be sold. This encouraged bidding, and record prices were set.

The auctioneer called out, "Lot 15, The Charles by George Brown, who would like to start the bidding on this lot at one dollar?" Before long, the bidding sailed over $100,000, quickly ending at $231,000—at the time a record for a toy at auction. The atmosphere in the auction gallery was electric. Overall, the entire auction of 361 lots realized over $1 million.

Georges Carette & Cie.

A German company with a reputation for quality and innovative toy designs, Carette & Cie. was started up in 1886 in Nuremberg, Germany, by a Parisian, Georges Carette. A family friend invested in the company as a silent partner, and financial backing also came from a competitor, the German toy maker Gebrüder Bing (*see pages 42–43*).

At the Columbian Exposition in Chicago in 1893, the company introduced one of the earliest toy electric streetcars. It continued to dominate the field with its production of both live-steam and spring-driven trains. Carette continued perfecting the process of lithography-on-metal and expanded production to include boats, cars, and even magic lanterns.

World War II almost brought the company's production to a halt. Once the realities of the conflict became apparent, the French-born Carette, married to a German wife, was forced to leave Germany and his company behind. The company closed its doors for good in 1917.

TONNEAY No. 50, c. 1910
This lithographed tinplate auto features a high roof, a rear entrance, and a clockwork mechanism. It showcases original features such as the figures, headlamps, and white rubber tires.
$2,000–$3,000

If these vehicles are displayed, be sure to rotate the wheels every couple of months to reduce the risk of wear to the rubber.

LIMOUSINE, c. 1910
This limousine features nickel-plated headlamps, side-mounted lanterns, and a driver. The toy has a clockwork mechanism.
$3,000–$5,000

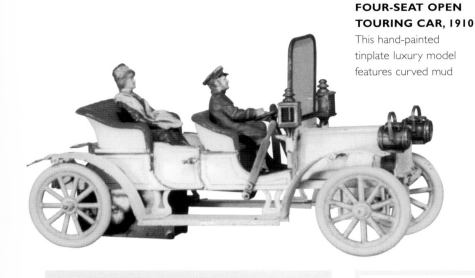

FOUR-SEAT OPEN TOURING CAR, 1910

This hand-painted tinplate luxury model features curved mud guards, nickel headlights, and side lanterns. The auto is activated by a clockwork mechanism. $8,000–$15,000

WHAT TO LOOK FOR:

- toys with high-quality craftsmanship
- attention to detail, with working lights on automobiles
- sturdy mechanisms and overall realism in the designs of the toys
- company logos (chronological, left to right)

G.C.& Cᵒ N.

INSIDER'S TIPS

Look out for reproduction trains, boats, and automobiles that have been artificially distressed to appear old.

Chips or missing paint are okay on old pieces. Repainting or touched-up paint should be noted on the receipt.

Figures that are repainted, restored, or replaced should be noted.

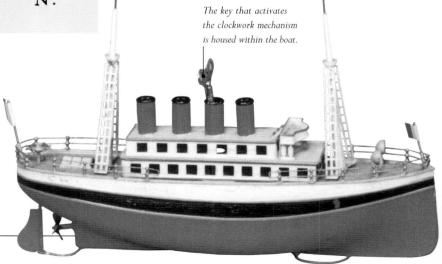

The key that activates the clockwork mechanism is housed within the boat.

HAND-PAINTED TINPLATE OCEAN LINER, 1930s

This boat is activated by a clockwork mechanism. $800–$1,200

James Fallows & Sons

James Fallows was a pioneer in American toy production. As a young English immigrant, he began his career working as a manufacturer's foreman for Francis, Field, and Francis in Philadelphia, Pennsylvania. In 1874, he formed his own company. He worked mainly in tin, adding cast-iron wheels to his bell toys, and he made some toys of papier-mâché. He propelled his toys with clockwork mechanisms.

By 1877, Fallows had perfected and patented his own process for embossing designs on tinplate—an art form in itself. These highly decorative designs and Fallows's personal trademark, "IXL,"

which stands for "I excel," make identification of a Fallows-designed toy quite straightforward. With his newly patented embossing process, Fallows went on to create his own toy design and manufacturing business. There is clearly an artistry and decorative simplicity to the toys he designed during this period.

For nearly the next two decades, Fallows created and manufactured his own designs of tinplate toys. His business began to fade around 1890, about the time that lithographed toys were beginning to gain popularity.

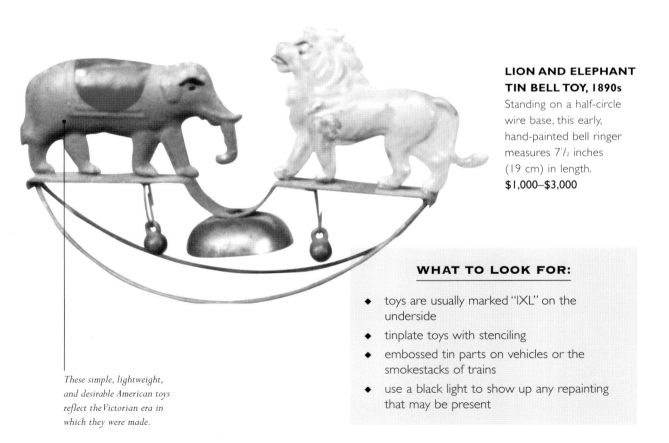

LION AND ELEPHANT TIN BELL TOY, 1890s
Standing on a half-circle wire base, this early, hand-painted bell ringer measures 7 1/2 inches (19 cm) in length.
$1,000–$3,000

These simple, lightweight, and desirable American toys reflect the Victorian era in which they were made.

WHAT TO LOOK FOR:

- toys are usually marked "IXL" on the underside
- tinplate toys with stenciling
- embossed tin parts on vehicles or the smokestacks of trains
- use a black light to show up any repainting that may be present

Hull & Stafford

Hull & Stafford, of Clinton, Connecticut, is known for producing mechanical tin toys manufactured as two halves fastened together by tabs. The historical background of this popular company is, however, a bit of a mystery, as records were destroyed, lost, or never properly kept. There are several theories. One theory is that Hull & Stafford evolved from Hull & Wright, a rival toy company also located in Clinton,

which started business in 1866. Another notion is that Hull & Stafford was an offshoot of the Union Manufacturing Company, again located in Clinton, which registered customers from 1854 to 1899.

Regardless of the company history, the fact remains that the toys made by Hull & Stafford were popular with Victorian children and have remained desirable with toy collectors today.

The toy was first stencil-decorated, and then the windows were stamped out prior to final assembly.

PROSPECT PARK TWIN HORSE-DRAWN OMNIBUS, c. 1880
This exquisite horse-drawn carriage is made of tinplate and features typical American stenciled accents.
$10,000–$15,000

WHAT TO LOOK FOR:

- tinplate toys made in equal halves and fastened by tabs
- stenciled decorations hand-painted in primary colors
- simple designs with a folk-art appearance

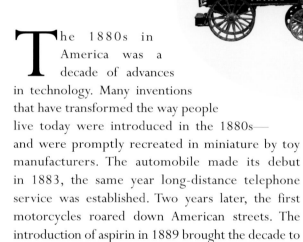

The 1880s in America was a decade of advances in technology. Many inventions that have transformed the way people live today were introduced in the 1880s— and were promptly recreated in miniature by toy manufacturers. The automobile made its debut in 1883, the same year long-distance telephone service was established. Two years later, the first motorcycles roared down American streets. The introduction of aspirin in 1889 brought the decade to a close with an extremely hopeful development for the health of all humankind.

The dawn of the 20th century brought with it even greater advances in technology. Automobiles and electricity made the horse-drawn buggy and kerosene lamp obsolete, while in 1903, the Wright brothers completed their first successful airplane flight, opening a new era in transportation that would make the world a much smaller place.

In the toy world, leading companies like Dent, Carette, and Märklin were all competing for the public's attention with innovative new toy lines. The early years of the century also witnessed the birth of everyone's favorite toy: President Theodore Roosevelt's refusal to shoot a bear cub during a

hunting trip led to the creation of the cuddly bear named Teddy in the president's honor.

Toy manufacturers of this era used wood, tinplate, and cast-iron to produce thousands of clever new playthings for children. Companies like Arcade, George Brown, and Fallows were early pioneers in the production of popular transportation toys. The companies represented in this and subsequent Color Reviews exemplify the design skills and innovative ideas of toymakers from the late 19th through the late 20th century. Featured in the Color Reviews are some rare toys, as well as more common and easy-to-find items, all reproduced in full color to assist collectors in identification.

It is interesting to note that in 1891, President William McKinley enacted a Tariff Act that required all products made after that date for import into the United States to be marked with the country of origin before being allowed into the country. Rather than permanently marking the toys themselves, some companies only marked the packaging. This is why some toys produced after the enactment of the Tariff Act are unmarked. Even so, we still have President McKinkley to thank for providing collectors with an important clue to the origins of toys.

Steiff

FULLY JOINTED, WOOL PLUSH BEAR, 1930s

In an effort to experiment with cheaper materials, Steiff created bears using alternatives like cotton, velvet, and wool. The wool material was not well received and lacked the versatility of mohair. As a result, few of these bears were manufactured, making them a rare commodity today on the secondary market. **$4,000–$6,000**

FULLY JOINTED, MOHAIR BEAR, c. 1907

This bear, in excellent condition, features a blank button in the ear, excelsior stuffing, shoe-button eyes, stitched nose, mouth, and claws, and felt pads. Bears from this time period can be distinguished by the eyes, which are anchored into the diagonal seam on the face of the bear. **$4,000–$6,000**

CENTER SEAM, FULLY JOINTED, WHITE MOHAIR BEAR, c. 1907

At this early stage of the company's history, most bears were made of shades of brown mohair, and other colors were rarely used. Often, the white bears from this time period found today are dirty or discolored. The center seam refers to the seam that goes from the tip of the nose to the back of the head. This was an economical use of mohair, and every seventh bear was made with leftover fabric, making this type of bear an especially rare find on the secondary market. **$4,000–$6,000**

Strauss Manufacturing Corporation and Fernand Martin

STRAUSS HAM AND SAM MINSTREL TEAM, 1921

This lithographed, clockwork-activated toy features a seated piano player and a standing banjo player.
$300–$500

FERNAND MARTIN "L'ENTRAVÉE," 1910

A fine example of the diverse nature of toys produced by the company. Here, we see a lady all dressed in red with an ermine muff. The clothes are well tailored on a tin body and there is a wind-up mechanism.
$1,500–$3,000

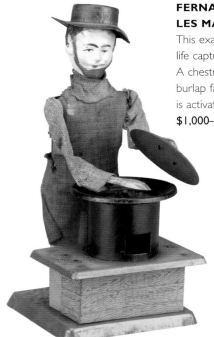

FERNAND MARTIN "CHAUDS LES MARRONS," 1910

This example is another slice of life captured by the toy company. A chestnut vendor dressed in a burlap fabric over a tin body frame is activated by a wind-up mechanism.
$1,000–$2,000

R. Bliss Manufacturing Company
and George W. Brown Company

BLISS HORSE-DRAWN CHARIOT, *c.* 1890

This is an elaborate, lithographed, paper-on-wood toy with ornate details.
$1,000–$3,000

BLISS DOLL HOUSE, 1900

This lithographed, paper-on-wood toy has ornate details.
$1,000–$2,000

BROWN TINPLATE "CHARLES" HOSE REEL, *c.* 1875

This early American fire toy is finished in royal blue and white with beautiful, hand-painted, decorative scrollwork, twin brass bells, and large cast wheels. It achieved a world-record price for a tin toy at auction when it was sold in 1991, because it is the best example of a George Brown toy and the only one of its kind known in existence.
$200,000–$300,000

Parker Brothers

"BUNNY TIDDLEDY WINKS" GAME, 1900s

The company took the basic game of tiddlywinks and added the bunny to enhance the graphics of the box top.

$10–$20

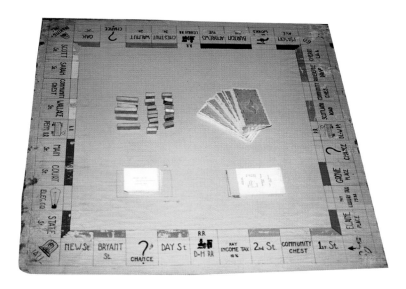

"MONOPOLY" GAME AND BOARD, 1935

This edition was issued just before Parker Brothers purchased the rights to "Monopoly" from Charles Darrow. The set features an oilcloth board, wooden buildings, $100 bills in gold, and $500 bills in pink. Players would use personal tokens as game pieces.

$3,000–$7,000

Georges Carette & Cie.
and Wilkins Toy Company

CARETTE LIMOUSINE, c. 1910
This lithographed tinplate car features running boards, nickel-plated headlamps, and side lanterns. The vehicle is activated by a clockwork mechanism.
$1,000–$3,000

CARETTE LANDAULET, c. 1911
This lithographed tinplate car features a foldable, soft-top passenger compartment with a seated woman and a roof rack. The toy is activated by a clockwork mechanism.
$5,000–$7,000

WILKINS *CITY OF NEW YORK* PADDLE-WHEEL BOAT, 1900s
This cast-iron boat features an articulated action when the toy is pulled across the floor.
$2,000–$4,000

Dent Hardware Company and James Fallows & Sons

DENT *LOS ANGELES* DIRIGIBLE, 1920s

This airship has nickel disc wheels and side observation decks. "Los Angeles" is embossed on both sides.

$600–$800

FALLOWS ELEPHANT BELL TOY, 1890s

This tinplate platform bell toy features a hand-painted elephant and an exposed bell and ringer.

$800–$1,200

FALLOWS HOOP TOY, 1890s

The elephant was a popular subject for toys in the late 19th century. This hand-painted hoop toy was used by a toddler learning to walk.

$700–$900

Gong Bell Manufacturing Company and Watrous

GONG BELL INDEPENDENCE BELL TOY, *c.* 1876

This toy, produced for the centennial of the United States, features a cast-iron platform embossed with the words "Independence 1776–1876," a large bell with an eagle finial, and cast, heart-spoke wheels.

$1,000–$3,000

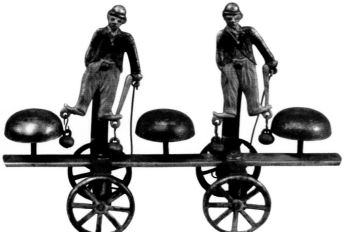

WATROUS CHARLIE CHAPLIN TRIPLE-BELL RINGER, 1910

This nickel and cast-iron toy has three bells and spoke wheels, and is all on a single-frame base.

$300–$500

WATROUS STEEPLECHASE BELL TOY, 1900

This toy features a horse and jockey made of cast metal with a nickel bell and cast, heart-spoke wheels.

$300–$500

Hubley Manufacturing Company

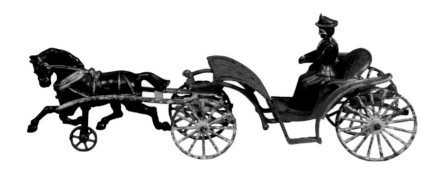

HORSE-DRAWN PHAETON, 1890s

One of the earliest cast-iron toys made by Hubley, this is a fine example of an open carriage with a hitch frame. It features curved fenders, yellow spoke wheels, and a female driver.
$800–$1,200

ROYAL CIRCUS TIGER CAGE WAGON, 1930s

This ornate, cast-iron, horse-drawn circus wagon has a pair of lions in the cage.
$300–$500

SURFER, 1940s

Hubley's broad range of subjects included this cast-iron surfer on a rolling wave on wheels.
$700–$900

E.R. Ives & Company
and Kenton Hardware Company

IVES FIRE PATROL WAGON, 1890s

This toy is made of cast-iron and features an open, bench-seat wagon with seven firemen and the words "Fire Patrol" embossed on the sides of the cart.

$400–$800

KENTON AMBULANCE, 1900s

This nickeled, cast-iron ambulance has lanterns, headlights, and a seated figure.

$500–$900

KENTON CONTRACTOR'S TRUCK, 1920s

This truck is made of cast-iron and features three open dump buckets on the bed of the truck and disc wheels.

$400–$800

Keyser & Rex
and McLoughlin Brothers

KEYSER & REX SANTA CLAUS, 1890s

This Santa Claus in a sleigh drawn by reindeer is made of cast-iron painted red with yellow runners and frame.
$2,000–$3,000

McLOUGHLIN BROTHERS "THE SUSCEPTIBLES" GAME, 1890s

The colorful box cover and game board depict a courtship scene, providing a glimpse of a turn-of-the-century dating game.
$200–$400

McLOUGHLIN BROTHERS "INDIA" GAME, 1890s

With its exotic and vibrantly colored box graphics, this "India" game reflects the Victorians' interest in faraway places.
$40–$80

Märklin

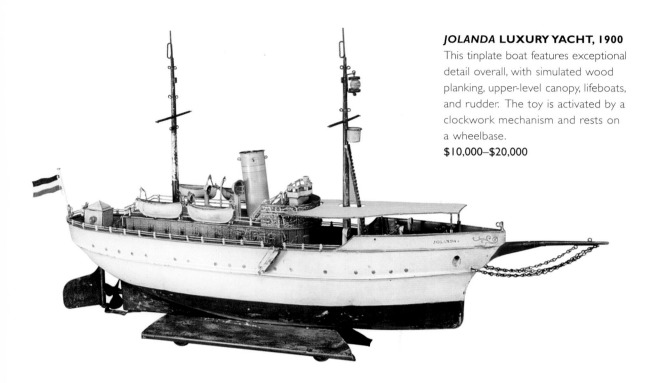

JOLANDA LUXURY YACHT, 1900
This tinplate boat features exceptional detail overall, with simulated wood planking, upper-level canopy, lifeboats, and rudder. The toy is activated by a clockwork mechanism and rests on a wheelbase.
$10,000–$20,000

"EAGLE" PASSENGER TRAIN SET, 1900
This is an early 1-gauge, hand-painted tinplate train set featuring a steam locomotive with matching tender and two coaches painted yellow and green. This highly detailed set was made for the American market, as is indicated by the American eagles stencilled on the sides of the passenger cars.
$7,000–$10,000

SNOWPLOW CAR, *c.* 1901
This 2-gauge tinplate car features a hand-painted orange body with an olive green and black plow. The track snow-remover is a replica of a common piece of train equipment of the period.
$1,000–$2,000

WOOD WAGON, *c.* 1901
This 2-gauge car features a bench seat with ladder steps.
$400–$600

TAR WAGON, *c.* 1901
This hand-painted tin tar wagon has a brake box and a faucet on the front.
$700–$900

WORKING WAGONS, *c.* 1901
This set of three cars represents the working, industrial wagons produced by Märklin. They all performed some work-related function and so differed from the simple designs of the passenger or Pullman cars.
$2,000–$4,000 for the set

Pratt & Letchworth
and W.S. Reed

**PRATT & LETCHWORTH
HORSE-DRAWN CART, 1890s**

This painted, cast-iron open cart
has a bench seat, spoke wheels,
and a driver.

$700–$900

REED CLIPPER SHIP, 1877

This clipper ship is made of wood
covered with colorful lithographed
paper. The toy is complete with
three large paper sails, cargo,
and sailors.

$1,000–$2,000

Shepard Hardware

TRICK PONY BANK, 1885
This bank was designed by Julius Mueller. The penny is placed in the horse's mouth, and when the lever is pulled, the coin is deposited in the trough and falls into the bank.
$700–$1,200

CIRCUS BANK, 1887
A coin is pushed into the slot, and when the crank is turned, the clown and pony cart go around in a circle.
$10,000–$15,000

MASON BANK, 1887
This bank was designed by Shepard and Adams. The hod carrier receives the coin and throws it forward, depositing it in the bank as the mason raises and lowers his trowel.
$2,000–$4,000

J. & E. Stevens Company

GIRL SKIPPING BANK, 1890

This popular and ornate cast-iron mechanical bank with clockwork mechanism was designed by James Bowen and patented in 1890.
A penny is placed between the paws of the squirrel, barely visible on the right of the bank. When the bank is wound, the rope turns, the girl skips and turns her head, and the penny falls into the trap.
$20,000–$30,000

RECLINING CHINA MAN BANK, c.1885

Designed by James H. Bowen, this toy is activated by placing the coin in the opening and pressing the lever, causing the figure to show his card hand of four aces while he salutes the depositor. As the coin falls into the receptacle, a rat runs out of the end of the log.
$2,000–$4,000

EAGLE AND EAGLETS BANK, 1883

A coin is placed in the eagle's beak. Press the lever, and the eaglets rise from the nest, crying for food. As the eagle bends forward to feed them, the coin falls into the nest and disappears into the receptacle below. The bank is shown here with its original wooden box.
$1,000–$3,000

E.R. Ives & Company

In 1868, Edward Riley Ives founded this company in Plymouth, Connecticut. He started out making baskets and hot-air novelty toys, which worked when fastened to a stove or a heating vent. In the early days, Ives worked at the Blakeslee Carriage Shop in Plymouth, which was owned by his brother-in-law, Cornelius Blakeslee. In 1872, they joined in a partnership of Ives & Blakeslee, and then in 1873, Ives, Blakeslee, & Co. As the company grew, the partners relocated to nearby Bridgeport.

As Bridgeport developed into a major manufacturing city in the 1880s, Ives took full advantage of the location by utilizing local designers. His toys gained popularity for their originality and fine construction. They usually combined a clockwork mechanism with wood or tinplate and had a variety of attention-grabbing actions.

Edward's son, Harry, took over the company when his father died in 1895. By this time, it had been renamed the Ives Corporation. Harry helped build Ives into one of the most prestigious and respected toy manufacturers in America. He was also very active in the creation of the Toy Manufacturers of America, the leading U.S. toy trade association.

Sadly, the company's successes were to be curtailed. Despite Harry's continuous efforts, the economic devastation of the Depression proved too much. The Ives Corporation filed for bankruptcy in 1929 and was dissolved in 1932.

WHAT TO LOOK FOR:

- toys were not marked but have clockwork mechanisms that can run for up to 30 minutes
- early toys resemble folk art
- strong mechanical toys made of wood and metal

CLOCKWORK FIREHOUSE, 1890s
This cast-iron and wood firehouse comes with a twin, horse-drawn, cast-iron pumper. If the toy is wound, bells and alarms sound when the doors open.
$2,500–$3,500

CLOCKWORK PARLOR OARSMAN, 1869
This is a hand-painted tin boat with a dressed oarsman. This early floor toy runs on wheels as the sailor goes through his rowing motions.
$3,000–$4,000

COLLECTOR'S STORY

During a toy auction at Christie's some years ago, there was an item offered that I estimated at between $10,000 and $15,000. The early clockwork toy featured a black woman washing clothes and a white woman ironing. When the toy was wound, they both went to work performing their tasks. During the auction, preview dealers and collectors were speculating on the toy's manufacturer and history. There were no apparent markings that conclusively confirmed the manufacturer. A pair of dealers from New York was quite sure the piece was European. One collector asked my opinion. Looking at the shape of the women's heads, and the positioning and construction of the arms, along with the folk-art flavor of the piece, my gut reaction was that it was made by Ives.

When the lot in question came up, I noticed that the room fell silent, and I observed dealers in the room shooting glances around to see if anyone was going to bid on the toy with the mysterious background. A common tactic at live auctions is not to bid on an item, so that after the sale, a dealer will contact the auction house and make a ridiculously low offer in hopes that the consignor needs the money and will accept the offer. Luckily for me, an anonymous telephone bidder, as well as the collector who had asked my opinion at the preview, were both interested. Between them, they pushed the bidding up to $10,000, with the collector in the room finally clinching the deal.

A few weeks later, the collector contacted me and informed me that as he had cleaned the toy and examined all of its internal parts, he had discovered a small tag hidden inside the toy which read "Pat. Pending," confirming that the toy was indeed American and most likely produced by Ives.

IVES WIDE-GAUGE CIRCUS SET, 1930s

This circus set comes complete with a backdrop featuring paper lithographed scenery, a circus tent, animals, figures, and a rare train set, #1134.

$35,000–$45,000

The paper background and accompanying circus pieces give the set its value.

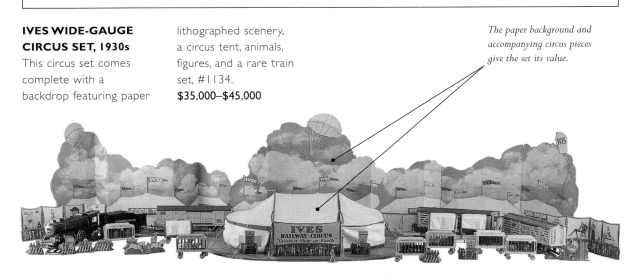

Märklin

Founded in 1859 by tinsmith Theodor Märklin and his wife Caroline in Goppingen, Germany, Märklin is rightly regarded as having set the standard for quality, design, and craftmanship in the toy world.

Initially producing doll-sized, tinplate kitchenware, the company took off when the Märklins' two sons took over the business in 1880. Like other toy companies, their products often reflected in miniature the changing world at the turn of the century. The Märklin company seemed to perceive this world with extreme clarity and sharp focus. The attention to every detail, right down

LIGHT POST AND BAGGAGE CAR, 1890s
Train accessories like these two platform items make fine additions to any train collection.
$200–$400 each

FIRE PUMPER, 1890s
This early item consists of hand-painted tin and features chain-driven gears activated by an intricate clockwork mechanism.
$20,000–$25,000

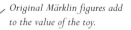

Original Märklin figures add to the value of the toy.

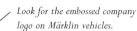

Look for the embossed company logo on Märklin vehicles.

to the spokes on the wheels of their vehicles, set them apart early on. The production line was vast, and they explored every possible design for zeppelins, cars, trains, boats, carousels, and carriages. The craftsmanship of their output earned the company a well-to-do clientele all around the world.

The designs were close to exact replicas in miniature of the full-size vehicles on which they were modeled. The mechanisms used were superior to those of their competitors. As clockwork gave way to steam and electricity, Märklin incorporated them into the design of its toys without sacrificing the integrity of the design. In 1891, the company introduced the first standardized tinplate track for trains in Europe. This became known as standard gauge.

MILITARY ARMORED CAR, 1950s
This vehicle is made of lithographed tin and painted in camouflage colors. It features a revolving rooftop gun.
$1,000–$2,000

STANDARD OIL TRUCK, 1950s
Made of pressed steel, this oil truck moves using a clockwork mechanism.
$1,000–$2,000

WHAT TO LOOK FOR:

- quality paint and fine attention to detail
- quality materials used in construction of toys
- company logo, usually easy to find

INSIDER'S TIPS

Look out for repainting or artificially distressed work on trains, boats, and automobiles. This will devalue the piece.

Some pieces will have chipped or missing paint, which is okay, provided other paint was not applied in an attempt to fix them up.

Ohio Art

While toy production in the U.S. remained primarily domestic until the 1900s, it was Germany that first began exporting toys so cheaply that many home-based manufacturers couldn't compete. Some $3 million worth of toys and games were imported in 1900, and by 1914, imports captured half of the market. With the declaration of war by the United States on Germany on April 6, 1917, drastic restrictions were placed on materials used by the toy industry. The Toy Manufacturers of America became an active lobbying group in Washington, D.C., and convinced Congress that despite the war, American children were entitled to toys and playthings made by domestic companies. It pushed for a 75 percent tariff on all imports. The legislation strengthened the domestic companies and eased the way for other fledgling companies to make a profit.

Ohio Art was one of the companies that benefited from this legislation. The company was founded in 1908 by a dentist, H.S. Winzeler, who also owned a grocery business in Bryan, Ohio. His initial idea was to create metal picture frames for works of art—hence the name of the company. In 1908, his creations were being sold in Sears, Kresge's, and other major outlets around the country.

This all changed in March of 1917, when Ohio Art purchased the Erie Toy Plant and entered the toy business. It began by creating, among other items, a galvanized tin windmill, and progressed to manufacturing items for other companies like a climbing monkey on a string for Ferdinand Strauss (*see page 116*). Eventually, Winzeler sold the Erie Toy Plant to toy giant Louis Marx (*see pages 96 and 113*).

Ohio Art continues to manufacture toys today and has introduced a variety of tin toys, sand pails, shovels, and tea sets. But it was the introduction in 1960 of Etch A Sketch that will forever leave the company's mark on American popular culture.

ROY ROGERS TOY LANTERN, c. 1950
This lithographed tin toy features horseshoe handles and colorful graphics of America's best-loved cowboy.
$100–$300

INSIDER'S TIPS

Keep items out of direct sunlight, or fading will occur. These toys will rust easily, so keep out of damp or humid environments.

WHAT TO LOOK FOR:

♦ lithographed tinplate items that are colorful and bright
♦ all items should include the company logo

Wolverine Supply & Manufacturing

Wolverine first started in 1903, manufacturing tin novelties ranging in price from 5¢ to 25¢ that took America by storm. The company continued to grow, and in 1915 erected a fireproof, three-story factory facility on Page Street in Pittsburgh, Pennsylvania.

Its early toys relied on the weight of marbles or sand to set them in motion. The motion of the toy continued unattended until the supply of weight was depleted. Their highly colorful lithography, coupled with their action, made these toys very popular. The company recognized the value of quality and the level of entertainment their toys could provide, so they expanded the line to include windmills that operated in the same way. They called them Sandy-Andy Automatic toys.

In March of 1918, Wolverine broke with tradition, and, at the Toy Fair in New York City, introduced a line of toys that focused on girls. Included were tea sets, sand pails, washtubs, glass washboards, ironing boards, and miniature grocery stores. As the toy line continued to expand in size and popularity, so did the facilities used to make it. The company built an additional five-story factory to keep up with consumer demand.

By the mid-1920s, Wolverine had established itself as a major supplier of toys for both girls and boys. Popular toys from this decade included the Sandy-Andy Dancing Doll and the Over-and-Under mechanical racecar toy. These simple toys were great favorites, and by the end of 1930s, the Wolverine Company had expanded its production facilities to 93,000 square feet (8,370 m²).

The firm foundation the company established early on and its ability to keep costs low enabled it to withstand the Depression and continue production. It added airplanes, boats, buses, and other transportation toys to its lineup, and continued production through the 1950s. Later, Wolverine became a subsidiary of Spang Industries. In 1970, the company was moved to Boonville, Arkansas, and its name was changed to Today's Kids.

ZILOTONE TOY, 1930s
This Zilotone toy is made of lithographed tinplate and is activated by a clockwork mechanism.
$100–$200

WHAT TO LOOK FOR:

- the "Wolverine" name
- pieces with brightly colored lithography
- toys with simple designs and simple actions

CAST-IRON TOYS

Cast-iron toys stand out as being a truly American creation that could not be duplicated by any other country in the world. The craftsmanship and artistry of the foundries that manufactured these toys are credited with providing Victorian children with playthings to pass the time of day, as well as to teach them valuable lessons.

These toys were made in America from the end of the Civil War through World War II, when production moved overseas. In 1865, the Civil War ended and America underwent a great deal of change. Rapid industrialization drove economic growth. Foundries that had supported the war effort by manufacturing guns, ammunition, and supplies discovered that the demand for toys became so great that they could devote themselves solely to toy production.

European toy manufacturers took notice of the popularity and low prices of cast-iron toys and tried to replicate them, with little success. They could not duplicate the quality and craftsmanship of the American manufacturers. The U. S. dominated cast-iron toy production because the multitude of factories being used resulted in low manufacturing costs.

The production process was simple. A wood-carved pattern was pressed into a sand and clay mixture and then removed, leaving a cavity that was filled with molten brass or bronze and then cooled to create the pattern. This rough casting was cleaned up to become the master pattern mold for a cast-iron toy. Molten iron was poured into such molds and allowed to cool. The toys were cleaned up, hand-painted, and boxed.

Cast-iron toys surpassed the popularity of tin toys in America and continued to be produced through the mid-1930s. This popularity meant that some entrepreneurs began to make reproduction toys of much poorer quality. Collectors should familiarize themselves with the texture and colors of these reproductions, as they are far less valuable. They are identifiable by the grainy texture of the iron, the poor fit of the components, the modern screws and springs used, and the abundance of filing marks. Reproductions are also slightly smaller than the originals. The paints are too bright, are easily distinguishable as being contemporary, and are often so horridly applied that the brush strokes are visible. Though the reproductions are durable, they can break if they are dropped.

Arcade Manufacturing Company

In 1869, a foundry in Freeport, Illinois, was organized as a two-man partnership named Novelty Iron & Brass Foundry. It was dissolved in 1885 when a newer, larger factory was incorporated, called Arcade Manufacturing Company. Arcade started producing items ranging from feed grinders and plows to coffee grinders and windmills. In 1888, toys were added to the line.

A fire in 1892 and management changes in 1893 altered the course of history for this company. Larger quantities of toys began to appear in its sales catalogue, and by 1900, the company was on its way to becoming one of America's premier cast-iron toy manufacturers. Arcade was heralded for its production of cast-iron automotive toys; its slogan, "They Look Real," was the foundation of its design concepts.

In 1919, a young member of the company, struck by the numerous yellow cabs on the streets, approached the Yellow Cab Company with a proposition. In return for the sole right to make toy replicas of the cabs, Arcade gave the cab company exclusive rights to use the toy in advertisements. A deal was struck, and the toy yellow cab was such a success that a flock of toy automobile offshoots were

**FORDSON TRACTOR,
1930s**
This tractor is made of cast-iron and features a nickel driver.
$100–$200

INSIDER'S TIPS

Arcade automotive toys from the late 1920s into the 1930s featured white rubber tires or metal tires. Check the tires for replacements; rubber tires are usually in poor condition. Check the toy for repainting and quality casting.

CAR CARRIER, 1930s
This large toy is made of cast-iron with a pressed steel flat bed.
$800–$1,200

Nickel-spoked wheels on a vehicle indicate that it was most likely manufactured by Arcade.

created to meet the demand. By the end of the 1930s, over 300 different toys were available, ranging from trains and banks to stoves and novelties.

Responding to the growing demand for quality toys, Arcade included in its line doll-house furniture, cast-iron penny toys, and toy banks. Most toys manufactured since the turn of the century have the company name cast into the toy for easy identification and dating.

WHAT TO LOOK FOR

◆ primarily transportation toys with a focus on automotive vehicles
◆ company name cast into the toy
◆ character items include the Andy Gump Roadster 348 and Chester Gump in his pony cart
◆ Yellow Cab Co. cars made by Arcade

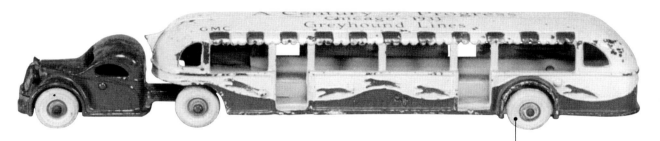

GREYHOUND BUS, 1933
This bus features the words "A Century of Progress" on its roof.

It was specially made for the 1933 World's Fair in Chicago in cast-iron with white rubber tires.
$600–$800

White rubber tires are often in poor condition.

ALSO WORTH COLLECTING:
Keyser & Rex

Louis Keyser and Alfred Rex founded this short-lived, cast-iron, mechanical bank manufacturing company in Philadelphia, Pennsylvania, in 1880. During the four years it was in business, it managed to produce some of the banks most desired by collectors today, including Stump Speaker, Lion and Monkeys, Organ bank, Uncle Tom bank, Chimpanzee bank, and Hindu with Turban. This Merry-Go-Round bank designed by R.N. Hunter, *c.* 1885, spins around when the handle is turned. The figures revolve to a chime of bells as the attendant gathers any coins on the stand. **$15,000–$30,000**

Dent Hardware Company

This toy manufacturing company was founded in 1895 in Fullerton, Pennsylvania, by English immigrant Henry H. Dent, who joined forces with four partners to produce cast-iron hardware for refrigerators and cold storage units, in addition to cast-iron toys. The company focused on quality casting methods and soon gained a reputation for exceptional work.

Attention to detail and high-quality casting techniques made Dent's automotive toys the finest produced during the 1920s. American toy manufacturers had perfected the skill of using cast-iron in a way that no foreign toy manufacturer could duplicate. Dent also experimented with other materials, like cast aluminum, but found them difficult to manipulate. Cast-iron became the material of choice for the company, and was used to produce a variety of toys. All forms of transportation were subjects of their toy design. Boats, trains, airplanes, fire wagons, horse-drawn carriages, and mechanical banks were all mass produced and became classics in their toy line.

This popular company ceased trading in 1937, but collectors still search out toys that it manufactured.

TOONERVILLE TROLLEY, 1920s
This trolley is made of cast-iron and features a cast engineer on a platform. It is shown with its original box.
$600–$800

WHAT TO LOOK FOR:

- highly detailed and quality toys
- smaller vehicles in the 4-to-12 inch (10.2 to 30.5 cm) category

HOSE-REEL WAGON, 1900

This firefighters' wagon is made of cast-iron and features an open-frame wagon, cast lanterns, a hose reel, and two firefighters. It is drawn by a team of three horses.
$700–$900

Gong Bell Manufacturing Company

The Gong Bell Manufacturing Company, based in East Hampton, Connecticut, operated from 1866 to the 1960s. The company achieved great popularity with the production of cast-iron bell toys. First patented in 1874, bell toys combined a two-wheeled base with a two-toned bell that rang when the toy was pushed or pulled. They were almost wholly an American phenomenon.

In the early years of the century, New Yorker William Barton developed a technique for casting bells in one piece, as opposed to the European alternative that soldered two pieces together. The Barton bell proved to be stronger and less expensive to produce. Barton moved from New York to establish a permanent location for the production of his bells and settled in East Hampton around 1808. His company became known as the Hampton Bell Company in 1837, and was renamed the Gong Bell Manufacturing Company in 1886. The company perfected its unique manufacturing technique and established itself as the market leader, also producing hand bells, sleigh bells, and doorbells.

Bell toys proved to be the company's most enduring products. The toys were skillfully designed, with the bells cleverly incorporated in them. A variety of bell sizes provided different sounds for each toy.

During the 1870s, the J. & E. Stevens Company (*see pages 82–83*), located in nearby Cromwell, produced the wheels for the Gong Bell toys. Stevens's very elaborate and ornate wheels complemented the toys designed by Gong Bell.

Today, these cast-iron pull toys from the turn of the century are quite desirable and collectible.

SEESAW BELL-RINGER TOY, 1890s
This bell toy features tin figures on a cast-iron base with a nickel bell.

Note the flower design cast into the wheel that adds to the decorative appeal of the toy.
$1,000–$2,000

WHAT TO LOOK FOR:

- toys are often unmarked
- early toys featured Gong Bell's bells and J. & E. Stevens's fancy wheels
- simple pull toys with a device to ring the bell; bell is usually visible and an integral part of the overall design of the toy
- bells made from one piece with no seam

INSIDER'S TIPS

The cast-iron bell toys have been reproduced with a lesser-quality cast-iron. Look for the paint quality and active bell device on originals, along with smooth casting of cast-iron.

Hubley Manufacturing Company

Around 1894, Lancaster, Pennsylvania, became the home of John E. Hubley's new company. With finances from a group of investors, a factory was built, to produce toy trains and parts. The harnessing of electricity had revolutionized society, and its effects were now felt in the realm of toy manufacturing. Hubley recognized that if his toys ran on electricity, they would stand out from the cast-iron and clockwork trains already on the market. He coined the company motto, "They're different."

Hubley's trains found quick success that continued well into the new century, only to be interrupted by a tragic factory fire in 1909. The company relocated to the abandoned Safety Buggy Company factory nearby. The traumatic effects of the fire took their toll, but two businessmen, John H. Hartman and Joseph T. Breneman, put together a group of investors who purchased the company.

The company received its biggest break from Butler Brothers, the nation's largest toy wholesaler, which placed huge orders. These orders helped changed the focus of the company from the original line of electric trains to cast-iron toys, hardware, and novelties. The first toys were horse-drawn wagons, fire engines, miniature coal stoves, circus trains, and toy guns. The company also filled orders from other toy manufacturers. Reflecting the growth and popularity of the automobile during the early 1930s,

Hubley's best lines became toy autos, accurate replicas of their real-life counterparts.

The company also recognized the importance of offering the buying public affordable toys. In addition to expensive toys, which retailed between $1.00 and $3.00, they also included 5¢, 10¢, and 25¢ toys in their line. Hubley then began to align toy production with popular manufacturers of the day, and soon consumers were seeing a Hubley Bell Telephone toy truck or a Hubley Packard toy car. Other brand names included Borden's, Old Dutch, General Electric, and Maytag.

WHAT TO LOOK FOR:

- sturdy cast-iron construction
- the company name is usually cast into the toy in an inconspicuous place
- automobiles, service vehicles, and some airplanes

INSIDER'S TIPS

Make sure to inspect the cast-iron pieces for flaws, repairs, and repainting. If the casting is bumpy or grainy, the piece is most likely a reproduction.

HARLEY DAVIDSON MOTORCYCLE, 1920s
This motorcycle with sidecar and riders is made of cast-iron and features rubber tires with spoke wheels.
$4,000–$5,000

Hubley toys were educational and had realistic or functioning parts. Dump trucks dumped, many toys could be taken apart and put back together, and even the toy grasshoppers had realistic legs. World War II halted production of cast-iron toys, and Hubley responded by changing to die-cast metal, and later, to plastics. This adaptability and quality of product has kept Hubley a household name, popular with children over the years. Collectors enjoy searching for the Hubley toys at auction and fairs across the country.

MILITARY FIGURES, 1930s

These figures are made of cast-iron and are hand-painted. From left to right, they are a minuteman figure, a sailor, and a cadet. **$200–$300 each**

BELL TELEPHONE TRUCK, 1930s

This truck is made of cast-iron and shown complete with all its accessories. **$300–$500**

ALSO WORTH COLLECTING:

Judd Manufacturing Company

An early pioneer in the production of cast-iron mechanical banks, the H.L. Judd Company was founded in 1830 in New Britain, Connecticut, by Morton Judd. Little is known about the company except that in 1855, it changed its name to M. Judd & Sons, and in 1870 to Judd Manufacturing Company. The banks manufactured by the company include models called Standing Giant, Boy Charging Dog, Peg-Leg-Beggar, and Circus Ticket Collector. This Boy Charging Dog bank was made *c.* 1870. When a coin is inserted and the lever is pulled, the boy advances as the dog moves backward, and the coin falls into the bank. **$3,000–$5,000**

Kenton Hardware Company

TRACTOR, 1930s
This tractor with three trailers is made of cast-iron and features nickel disc wheels.
$500–$700

Examine toys carefully for missing or broken parts. A small wheel has been broken off here.

The Kenton Lock Manufacturing Company was founded in May 1890 in Kenton, Ohio. It began by producing refrigerator hardware patented by F.M. Perkins of Cleveland, Ohio. Four years later, the first lines of cast-iron toys were manufactured.

The company's first toy was a cast-iron, single, horse-drawn road cart. This opened the door for the production of cast-iron mechanical banks, stoves, and more elaborate, horse-drawn fire wagons. Toy production grew to become one of the major contributors to the company's financial bottom line. In 1900, the company altered its name to the Kenton Hardware Manufacturing Company.

In 1903, the company's factory suffered a terrible fire. The company quickly responded by regrouping and rebuilding a new factory with increased manufacturing capabilities. The fire stimulated the vision of the toy manufacturing line. As the country was entering the era of motorized vehicles, Kenton recognized an opportunity to become a pioneer in manufacturing automotive toys. This vision proved to be successful and earned the company recognition as the largest manufacturer of automotive toys in the United States. But its cast-iron mechanical banks also became quite popular.

Between 1905 and 1915, the company experienced management and financial turbulence. In 1915, it was renamed the Kenton Hardware Company and Louis S. Bixler was named as president and general manager. Prior to joining Kenton, Bixler had worked for Hubley, a period that had provided him with firsthand experience in toy manufacturing. It was that experience that Bixler used to help toy production at Kenton soar. Production focused on cars and trucks. From 1920 to 1935, sales from the automotive line reached record highs and Kenton's products continued to be popular through the early 1950s. Due to financial troubles, the company ceased production in 1952, and the company assets, including toy molds and designs, were sold in 1953.

WHAT TO LOOK FOR:

- horse-drawn vehicles like fire trucks, carriages, drays, and the Overland Circus, mostly with removable figures
- toys made of cast-iron
- the company slogan, "The real thing in everything but size"

Kilgore Manufacturing Company

Kilgore began production of cast-iron toy cap guns and cannons the early 1920s in Westerville, Ohio. "Toys that last" became its motto and a phrase that pushed the company to develop the manufacture of toys that supported it.

In 1925, Kilgore decided to take over the George D. Wanner Company, based in Dayton, Ohio. Being the largest producer of kites in America, its E-Z FLY tail-less kite was a welcome addition to the Kilgore production line. In addition to kites and cap guns, the company followed the lead of other toy manufacturers by adding automotive toys to its line. Since the cap guns were made of cast-iron, the production of fire engines, cars, and trucks made of cast-iron were a natural addition to the manufacturing line. Having all the materials available allowed the company to mass produce the new line with very little extra overhead.

The toys were produced in boxed sets retailing for 50¢ and distributed around the country by Butler Brothers, the largest toy wholesaler in America. They became Kilgore's largest account. By 1929, the company was doing quite well with their focused area of toy production. Kilgore weathered the Depression by redirecting production to include only the cast-iron cap guns and paper caps. In 1937, Kilgore became one of the first toy companies to use plastic instead of cast-iron. This helped the company stay in business, producing its original product line in plastic through 1978.

ARCTIC ICE CREAM TRUCK, 1930s

This truck is made of cast-iron and features a closed cab with embossed sides and disc wheels.

$600–$800

LIVESTOCK TRUCK, 1930s

This open-bed livestock transporter is made of cast-iron and features freewheeling nickel disc wheels.

$400–$600

WHAT TO LOOK FOR:

- motto: "Toys that last"
- most cap guns from the late 1930s and 1940s will have been made by Kilgore
- quality manufacturing and casting

Kingsbury Manufacturing Company

A gift from his grandfather allowed Harry Thayer Kingsbury to purchase the Wilkins Toy Company in Keene, New Hampshire, around 1895. When the nearby Clipper Machine Works was partially destroyed by fire, Kingsbury quickly bought the company and combined his acquisitions.

The company continued to produce toys under the Wilkins name and began to make its presence felt within the industry. Following the lead of other toy manufacturers of the time, the company jumped on the toy automotive bandwagon. In 1910, it released its first line of automobiles, and cars continued to dominate the company's production up to World War I. For the next few years, the plant completely converted to manufacturing war supplies to support the American initiative overseas. Once the war was over, the company resumed production with moderate updates, using materials and designs from before the war. This lasted only until the company was back up and running.

During this rebuilding period, Kingsbury decided to drop the Wilkins name and became

the Kingsbury Manufacturing Company instead. Its new designs were based on actual cars and airplanes around at the time. Released in 1919, these miniature versions of real vehicles stimulated children to pretend they were being transported around the yard in a fast car or taking a ride around the living room in an airplane. These new designs were continually updated to mirror the constant changing designs in the real world.

In 1920, Harry's sons, Edward and Chester, joined the company. They set up the Kingsbury Machine Tool Division, which received a number of war contracts that began to dominate overall production. Kingsbury decided to sell off the toy division to Keystone in Boston in 1942. It never returned to toy production, but the tool division continued to produce tools for various companies.

FIRE PUMPER, 1920s
This fire pumper features a gold-colored boiler, yellow spoked side cranks, and white rubber tires.
$300–$600

WHAT TO LOOK FOR:

♦ automobiles, fire trucks, airplanes, and delivery trucks

Pratt & Letchworth

Credited with being one of America's largest manufacturers of cast-iron objects at the end of the 19th century, Pratt & Letchworth, based in Buffalo, New York, was founded by Samuel F. and Pascal P. Pratt, together with William P. Letchworth. It began by producing carriage and truck hardware under the formal company name of the Buffalo Malleable Iron Works.

Around 1890, Pratt & Letchworth bought a toy company and its patents from Francis Carpenter. In order to capitalize on Carpenter's work, the company redesigned the look of the toys, improving their attraction to children. Alongside the real parts produced for locomotive and automobiles, the company added cast-iron fire toys, artillery wagons, wheeled vehicles, and toy trains.

The toy business enhanced the company's core business of providing material for the booming expansion of American transportation. But due to rising costs and consumer demands for updated products that reflected the changing times, toy production ended in 1900.

HOOK AND LADDER WAGON, 1900

This early fire-fighting wagon features an open frame. It is painted black, with green and gold highlights.

$800–$1,200

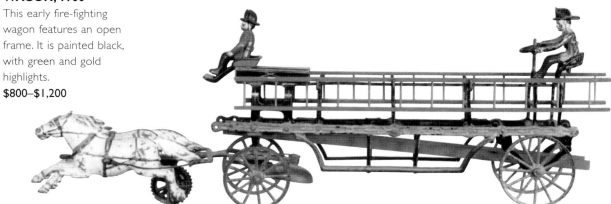

HANSOM CAB, 1900

Made of cast-iron, this hansom cab includes the driver seated above and behind the cab.

$400–$600

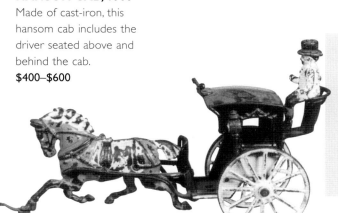

WHAT TO LOOK FOR:

- quality casting and original paint
- detail around the windows of the vehicle, detail in the horses, and the painting of any figures featured
- a direct portrait in miniature of the lifestyle at the close of the 19th century

J. & E. Stevens Company

John and Elisha Stevens, brothers from Cromwell, Connecticut, hold the distinction of being the first American mass producers of metal toys. The brothers established their company in 1843 and started out with a modest line of cast-iron hardware. Slowly, the line blossomed to include simple playthings, toy pistols, and gardening tools. Each year, the company gained greater exposure for its high-quality, cast-iron offerings.

By 1870, the company was producing over a thousand different items that included cast-iron doll furniture, stoves, toy cannons, cap guns, and tools. It even provided wheels and fittings for the Gong Bell Manufacturing Company (*see page 75*), located in a neighboring town. Making sure they hit every area, the brothers produced their version of a bell toy, the *Evening News* Baby Quieter. By the end of the 1800s, America was entering into the booming industrial era, and the Stevens company was able to capitalize on the country's prosperity by offering a wider range of products.

Despite the variety of items produced by J. & E. Stevens, only one category became popular internationally. The company's cast-iron mechanical banks were clever, captivated children for hours, and taught them a valuable lesson about saving their pennies.

It was the Stevens company's special technique for manufacturing cast-iron toys that established the standard of quality and craftsmanship that the European toy makers found impossible to duplicate. Domestically, from the end of the Civil War through the turn of the 20th century, the cast-iron mechanical banks were the most popular toys produced by the Stevens company.

BOY SCOUT CAMP BANK, c. 1915

This piece was designed by Charles A. Bailey. An extremely detailed casting, the bank works by placing a coin on the tree above the tent. When the side lever is depressed, the coin falls into the bank and the Boy Scout raises his flag in receipt.

$4,000–$8,000

The Boy Scout's arm and flag are the most vulnerable parts of this design and have often been repaired.

WHAT TO LOOK FOR:

- ◆ toys and banks that are not marked
- ◆ coin traps are often missing, but these add more to the aesthetic value of the bank than to its overall monetary value

Toys often mirror the social climate and political events of the time periods in which they were manufactured, and cast-iron mechanical banks produced at the turn of the 20th century were no exception. At the time, Native Americans were negotiating with the United States government for land rights. J. & E. Stevens produced a bank in honor of this event. It is the only bank with a Native American theme ever produced by the company.

The feet of the tackles and the areas where the players' heads connect are the most vulnerable parts of this bank.

INDIAN SHOOTING BEAR, c. 1900

This piece was designed by Charles A. Bailey. The coin is placed into position on the rifle. When the lever is pressed, the coin is shot into the bear's chest and deposited.

$3,000–$6,000

CALAMITY, 1904

Designed by James H. Bowen, this item was patented on July 30, 1904. The right and left tackles are moved back, and the coin is placed in the slot at the feet of the fullback. When the lever is pressed, the players come together, and the coin drops in. Check for repair.

$7,000–$15,000

The Native American's feathers are often replaced or repainted.

INSIDER'S TIPS

Hairline cracks often appear on the base of cast-iron toys, so examine them carefully.

Check the weakest and most delicate parts of cast-iron toys as it is at these areas that restorations or repairs may have occurred.

A black light will highlight areas of overpainting that were not part of the original bank.

ALSO WORTH COLLECTING:
Shepard Hardware

Shepard Hardware was based in Buffalo, New York, and began producing cast-iron hardware supplies in the mid-1860s. The company's founders, Walter J. and Charles G. Shepard, were granted a patent to manufacture cast-iron mechanical banks in 1882. They continued making hardware supplies but featured the banks as novelties. The company was sold in 1892.

Shepard Hardware banks were manufactured with square coin traps that had to be opened with a key. Three Shepard Hardware banks were later reissued by J. & E. Stevens.

Watrous

D.W. Watrous founded his company in 1884 in East Hampton, Connecticut. The company shared a factory with the N.N. Hill Brass Company, as Mr. Watrous was related by marriage to Mr. Hill. Bell toys became quite popular in the United States during these years, and the products made by Watrous were of comparable quality to those made by similar companies located in the region. In order to sustain the appeal of its toys,

Watrous imitated the innovation of William Barton of the Gong Bell company (*see page 75*). He cast each bell for the toys as a single piece, as opposed to soldering two pieces of the bell together, which was the practice of European bell makers.

Around 1905, Watrous was taken over by the N.N. Hill Brass Company but continued producing toys using the name Watrous.

The wheels on Watrous bell toys were made by other companies, making it difficult to identify manufacturers.

The cast-iron heart wheels were most likely made by the J. & E. Stevens Company.

JONAH AND THE WHALE BELL TOY, 1890s

The popular Bible story is illustrated in cast-iron.

As the toy is pulled across the floor, Jonah is swallowed by the whale and the bell rings.
$600–$800

WHAT TO LOOK FOR:

- toys made entirely of cast-iron
- bells cast as a single piece
- all toys feature figures on a metal base with bells

BANANA BOYS SEESAW BELL TOY, c. 1890s

This toy was pulled

across the floor, setting the boys in motion and ringing the bell.
$500–$700

Wilkins Toy Company

James S. Wilkins founded the Triumph Wringer Company in 1880. Based in Keene, New Hampshire, the company first produced toy washing machines and locomotives made from cast-iron but acted primarily as a jobber for other toy manufacturers.

Ten years later, Wilkins had acquired several patents and changed the name of the company to the Wilkins Toy Company. His first line of toys consisted of trains, horse-drawn carriages, carts, and cast-iron wagons. In 1895, Harry Thayer Kingsbury purchased the company. However, the Wilkins name was used on toys through the end of World War I.

PADDLE-WHEEL BOAT, 1900s
This boat is made of nickeled cast-iron and is modeled after the *Puritan* paddle wheeler.
$100–$300

Larger versions of the Wilkins paddle boats come with lifeboats.

The two halves of the toy fit securely together. This is one way to detect reproduction, because the recastings will not fit so nicely together.

PURITAN PADDLE WHEEL BOAT, 1900s
This carpet toy has spoke wheels for easy movement across the floor. It measures 10 inches (25.4 cm) in length.
$300–$500

WHAT TO LOOK FOR:

◆ cast-iron transportation toys
◆ carpet toys like trains, paddle boats, and horse-drawn vehicles
◆ autos with vulcanized rubber wheels

BOARD GAMES

Games consisting of a board and pieces can be traced back to the tomb of the Egyptian pharaoh, Tutankhamen, where a gaming board, playing figure, and dice were found. Board games illustrate our cultural history and reflect the social mores of the time periods in which they were produced. Games serve as a mirror for a time gone by.

Antique board games need to be displayed out of direct sunlight to decrease chances of fading, and if the game boards or box tops are framed, make sure it is in an acid-free environment, with UV Plexiglas. The collection of board games makes up a relatively small area of collecting and provides many fine example of the phrase, "Just because it is old does not make it incredibly valuable." It is desirability, coupled with condition and age, that make a toy valuable.

As antique board games have only a small following, the prices are reasonable. This is a good area for new collectors. Look for items in good condition. The game boards, box lids, and often, instructions to the games were all lithographed paper or paper that was applied to board. Paper itself contains a certain level of acidity that over time self-destructs and will not last forever. Conservation efforts are sometimes in order for antique game boards, and collectors should seek out the assistance of trained professionals in the art of paper conservation.

Games made before 1940 are most popular with game collectors, while games made between 1940 and 1960 are sought by theme collectors of baseball, space exploration, and hundreds of other categories. A "Today with Dave Garroway" game capitalized on the popularity of the morning news show, and the "Truth or Consequences" game played off the game show craze. Many games made after the mid-1960s fall into the adventure game category, one that will take some time to mature into a collectible market.

Collectors of board games should check a game over and read the instructions, which are sometimes printed on the inside of the lid of the box, to make sure that all the pieces are included. Most of the games produced after World War II will have a large number of playing pieces, such as money, cards, and game tokens, while games manufactured prior to the war will have a smaller number of pieces.

Milton Bradley

Milton Bradley's company began producing educational toys in 1861 and maintains that tradition today. The Bradley family can be traced back to 1635 in Salem, Massachusetts. Milton himself was born on November 8, 1836, in Vienna, Maine. The family stayed in Maine for 10 years before relocating to Lowell, Massachusetts.

In 1856, the young Milton Bradley was into his second year at Lawrence Scientific School. In the middle of that year, his parents decided to move to Hartford, Connecticut. Unable to support himself and attend school at the same time, he joined his family in their new home. Work was difficult to find in Hartford. However, Bradley heard word of employment opportunities in Springfield, Massachusetts, which at the time, was the fastest-growing city in New England.

Bradley arrived in Springfield late in 1856, by train—his very first exposure to locomotives and railroads. He landed the first job he applied for. The Wason Car Manufacturing Company hired him more for his enthusiasm than for his knowledge of railroad design, but he was a quick learner and worked for the company on and off for the next four years.

In 1860, Bradley was asked by the company to design a very special railroad car for the pasha of Egypt. His design was so spectacular that the company produced a color lithograph of the finished railroad car and presented it to him. That lithograph sparked the flame of what became Bradley's lifelong obsession with the lithographic process. He perfected his lithographic technique and printed an extremely popular portrait of a clean-shaven Abraham Lincoln. It remained popular until Lincoln shaved his beard. Slow sales forced Bradley to move in another direction.

"OUTLINE MAP OF THE UNITED STATES OF AMERICA" GAME, 1910
This game features colorfully lithographed pieces in the shapes of the states of the Union, which fit together like a puzzle.
$300–$400

WHAT TO LOOK FOR:

♦ board games and puzzles should have the date and name "Milton Bradley" displayed on them

♦ logo, copyright date, and patent will help establish time period of toy

INSIDER'S TIPS

It is difficult to find early board games, because the cardboard or paper used to make them has deteriorated or perished.

This area of collecting has a limited marketability and prices are still affordable.

That same year, Bradley finished developing a board game called the "Checkered Game of Life." The game was so successful that by the end of 1861, he had sold over 40,000 copies. Sticking with the educational aspect of toys his company produced a kindergarten alphabet set, building blocks featuring numbers and animals, and his most popular toy, the zoetrope. The zoetrope featured a strip of drawings showing figures in the process of an activity. The strip was placed in a drum that sat atop a pedestal and could be manually spun. As the drum spun, the figures appeared to be in motion to a viewer peering through slots in the drum.

The company has continued to grow, and during its 140 years of existence has produced thousands of puzzles, board games, card games, and educational construction toys.

"LOTTO," *c. 1930s*
This game of "Lotto" consists of cards with numbers and is played like "Bingo."
$10–$20

Look on the inside cover of the game box for instructions on playing the game.

Also Worth Collecting:
McLoughlin Brothers

McLoughlin Brothers was founded in Brooklyn, New York, in 1828 and was the first company to mass produce paper dolls and paper soldiers. The company branched out to include doll-house furniture and toy theaters with actors and scenery, as well as blocks and paper toys. The design ideas for a number of the toys manufactured for the American market showed up as revamped versions of popular European juvenile games. In 1920, the company was sold to Milton Bradley. Today, McLoughlin Brothers games, such as this "ABC of Feathers and Songs," *c.* 1880, sell for **$300–$400,** depending on their condition.

Parker Brothers

George S. Parker launched his company in 1883 in Salem, Massachusetts, with the creation of his first card game, "Banking." Three years later, he acquired the rights to games previously published by W. & S.B. Ives, providing the company with a diverse line of 125 games for their product catalogue. In 1887, George's two brothers joined the company, and the name Parker Brothers was established. The firm continued to make competitive strides in the marketplace and grew incrementally over the years. It even employed popular artist Maxfield Parrish to create colorful designs for its games and puzzles.

The United States Playing Card Company was the brothers' next target, and in 1925, Parker Brothers purchased the educational division of the card company. This allowed it to specialize in educational games for children and adults on topics ranging from finance, real estate, and banking to transportation and current events. Competition was fierce between the major players, Parker Brothers and Milton Bradley. Each company strived to introduce games that would capture the imagination of the country and that would enjoy large popular success. In 1915, Parker Brothers had a hit with "Pollyanna." Milton Bradley struck back in 1918 with "Uncle Wiggily," but neither company could conceive of the monstrous hit Parker Brothers would achieve with their version of "Monopoly" in 1935.

The origin of "Monopoly" has been traced back to 1904 and Lizzie J. Magie's "The Landlord Game," in addition to a host of similar generic games played

"SIEGE OF HAVANA" GAME, c. 1898

This was the first game to feature a real historic event on its cover.

$300–$500

Game box tops usually feature the name of its maker.

INSIDER'S TIPS

Collectors often collect games and puzzles for the artwork. As a result, games and puzzles with elaborately detailed images are more valuable and desirable to collectors.

Collectors should consider shrink-wrapping assembled puzzles with an acid-free, paper-surfaced mat board for backing to better preserve them.

Never put glue on the back of a puzzle or tape its pieces to a backing board. This will dramatically reduce its value.

Sunlight, spotlights, and floodlights have potentially damaging effects on the colors of games and puzzles. If an item is framed for display, be sure it is in an acid-free environment with UV Plexiglas.

Always check games or puzzles for signs of insect or mildew damage.

Avoid stacking game and puzzle boxes on top of each other, as those on the bottom may be crushed and irreversibly damaged.

in different regions of the country in the 1920s. Charles Darrow, credited as the inventor of "Monopoly," actually patented a version of the game which was developed by Ruth Thorp Harvey and a group of players in Atlantic City. But the game became a huge success for Parker Brothers. To further strengthen its position, Parker Brothers entered into a licensing agreement with Walt Disney, and sales soared. But game companies were not immune to corporate takeovers and acquisitions in the 1970s and 1980s, and Parker Brothers, like Milton Bradley, eventually became part of the Hasbro empire (*see page 190*).

"MONOPOLY" GAME BOX, c. 1940
The box design and two sets of patent

numbers at the top date this version of the game to the early 1940s.
$10–$30

DATING "MONOPOLY" GAMES

Game box tops and game boards contain clues that can help collectors identify and date "Monopoly" editions.

EDITION		FEATURES
Charles Darrow "Monopoly" game prior to selling rights to Parker Brothers	— 1933–1934 —	White box top featuring red strip across cover with "Monpoly" name in black inside the stripe; "© Chas B. Darrow" in corner of game board in Jail space
Parker Brothers "Monopoly" box top	— 1935 —	Features a man holding money standing above a $ sign with patent information; two patent numbers and date identify 1935 as the year of manufacture
Same as above, but only two patent numbers and no date	— 1936–1943	
Only one patent number on box	— After 1943	
"Monopoly Popular Edition" on box top	— Late 1930s	"Monopoly" printed diagonally across cover; $ sign and locomotive below name
"Monopoly Popular Edition" on box top	— 1950 —	Red border and $ sign on top of box; "Parker Brothers Trade Mark Game for its Real Estate Trading Game" at the top and "Registered U.S. Patent Office" below game name
Same as above, but green border on box	— 1954	
"Monopoly Popular Edition" with red border on lid	— After 1954 —	"Monopoly" running diagonally across cover; $ sign with locomotive below game name; manufacturing information near bottom of bow and wooden pawns as playing pieces
"Monopoly" White Box Edition No.9	— 1950s —	Lid shows game board with hotels and man running with money being chased by another man
Same as above, but with plastic houses and hotels	— 1960s	
Games feature General Mills logo	— 1960s	
Cover shows spaces from game board, including Park Place, Electric Company, Reading Railroad, and Chance	— 1960s–1970s	
Look for dates on lid and game board to determine age	— 1970s	

Wind-up toys have always been able to entertain and amuse children. They continue to make a strong showing in the marketplace and are particularly popular with baby-boomers because of the nostalgia factor. There are two major things to remember when collecting wind-ups. The first is that the mechanisms are delicate and need to be handled with care; it is especially important not to overwind them. The second is that it is essential to keep these toys away from dampness, which will rust the mechanisms and severely damage them.

Clockwork mechanisms are the oldest type of wind-up activator and the most desirable to collectors. These mechanisms were popular in toys made during the later 19th and early 20th centuries, while coil- and spring-activated mechanisms were widely used during the 20th century.

Wind-up mechanisms added whimsy and locomotion to an object. Because they were so appealing and played with so zealously, wind-up toys were often overwound and broken as a result. Broken toys were thrown away, of course, so when a surviving toy in good working condition comes to market, a collector will pay a premium for it, especially if it comes in its original box.

Today, at my own auction gallery, when we evaluate wind-ups or catalogue them for auction, we check to make sure the mechanism is functioning (and we did this when I worked at Christie's, as well). To do this, we gently wind the toy three or four rotations to ensure that the mechanism holds the wind. We make sure not to wind it again.

This tactic was proven sound at an auction I put together in 1994 while working at Christie's. One lot that day, the Girl Skipping Rope mechanical bank, featured an internal wind-up mechanism. I tested the toy prior to the auction and gave strict orders not to allow anyone to wind it again. Just before the auction, a collector asked to see it function. I said no, but assured him that the bank was in good condition and that if it did not function properly when sold, the buyer's money would be refunded. When I brought the hammer down, that same collector had paid $48,300 for it. After the sale, and before he paid, he wanted me to be present when he wound it. I can still remember his face when the toy performed flawlessly. He thanked me for taking a hard line at the viewing that accounted for its stellar performance.

J. Chein & Company

The company was founded in 1903 by Julius Chein in New York City. J. Chein & Company specialized in lithographed tin mechanical toys and developed a special production process of printing the design and color first on the sheet of tin, and then pressing it into shape. This process allowed the company to mass produce huge quantities of toys very inexpensively. To accommodate an expanding production line, the company decided to relocate their facilities to Harrison, New Jersey, in 1912.

America's response to German aggression prior to World War I was an embargo on all German products shipped to the United States. As a result, the Chein company increased its toy production and cornered the American market for lithographed tin mechanical playthings. The 1920s proved to be a decade of expansion for the company. But in 1926, while horseback riding in Central Park, Julius Chein meet his untimely death. Faced with the increasing popularity of the company's toy line, Elizabeth Chein took the helm with the assistance of her brother, Samuel Hoffman. They continued the legacy that Julius began 23 years earlier.

From this period through the 1950s, Chein mass produced mechanical toys and focused its line on Ferris wheels, roller coasters, rocket ride toys, tin banks, automobiles, and trucks. The company ceased trading in 1979.

MOTOR EXPRESS TRUCK, 1930s

This Hercules Motor Express truck is made of lithographed tin and features graphics depicting a driver in the window and stake sides on an open body.
$500–$700

POPEYE IN A BARREL, 1930s

This wind-up toy is made of lithographed tinplate and is activated by a clockwork mechanism.
$300–$400

The logo and name of the company will be present on every Chein toy.

WHAT TO LOOK FOR:

◆ colorful and lightweight wind-up toys
◆ toys in their boxes are more desirable and often priced higher

INSIDER'S TIPS

Many affordable examples of Chein toys are still available in the marketplace. Collectors should focus on those in the best condition.

Fernand Martin

Whimsical and charming are words often used to describe wind-up toys, but they are especially apt for those made by Fernand Martin beginning in 1878. In his factory in Paris, France, Martin created amusing figures inspired by scenes in the streets, the shops, or the circus. His main innovation was using fabric to costume his figures rather than colorful lithography. Drunkards, street violinists, waiters, policemen, washerwomen, and piano players all caricaturing daily life in Paris poured out of his factory. Manufactured from tinplate, wire, and lead castings, their movements were always humorous. Though the construction of the toys seems to be complex and time-consuming, the company was profitable, in part, by using the same designs year after year and only changing the fabrics or colors to suit foreign markets and changing fashions.

Martin was fascinated by the history of toys. He gave the *Conservatoire des Arts et Métiers* in Paris a large collection of his toys made over a 30-year period, making him the only 19th-century toy maker to have foreseen the historic importance of the toys he manufactured.

Fernand Martin died at the start of World War I, and his business was taken over by the Victor Bonnet Company. It continued to produce toys under the Martin name until the 1930s.

WHAT TO LOOK FOR:

- figures with a wire outline for the shape of the body
- toys with an elaborate and comical motion
- figures dressed in cloth with expressive facial features
- company logos (in chronological order, from left to right)

WASHERWOMAN, 1900

This figure, made from tin and cloth, stands on a tin base and goes through the motions of washing when the toy is wound.
$1,000–$2,000

An embossed logo will appear on bottoms of these toys.

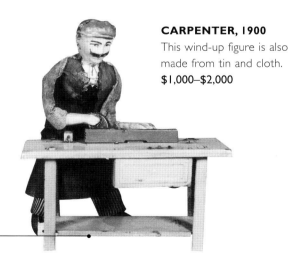

CARPENTER, 1900

This wind-up figure is also made from tin and cloth.
$1,000–$2,000

Lehmann

Based in Brandenburg, Germany, Lehmann began manufacturing tinplate containers in 1881. The company concentrated on the production of tinplate with highly colorful lithography. This provided the company with the knowledge to tap into the toy market slowly at first, and then full force. It started out with figures like dancers and boys on bicycles, and by 1914, like other toy companies around the world, moved into the production of vehicles.

MANDARIN, 1910
This hand-painted tinplate toy features two figures in blue jackets carrying a sedan chair with a seated figure. The clockwork mechanism that drives it is concealed in the chair.
$1,500–$2,000

LI LA, 1900
This is a lithographed tinplate hansom cab with a hand-painted tin driver and two seated female passengers. A standing dog is featured on the front platform of this clockwork toy.
$1,000–$2,000

WHAT TO LOOK FOR:

- ◆ original boxes with colorful, lithographed paper labels increase the value of the toy

- ◆ company logos—"E. Lehmann" (the E. stands for Ernst, the name of the company founder)—are usually easy to find

With all the competition in the marketplace, Lehmann developed imaginative mechanisms in its toys to help them stand out. Friction wheels and coil springs were used to animate toys in a truly unique way. The inventory expanded to include buses, cars, a variety of animals pulling carts, cabs, and moving figures. Close to 90 percent of the company's products were exported. The production often reflected the times and traditions of the country. The toys were also clearly marked and easily identified.

From 1895 to 1929, many Lehmann toys poured into the United States. Only during the years of World War I did the flow stop. In 1951, the company relocated to Nuremberg, where it still produces a wide range of toys.

The toy and box feature the name of the toy, logo, and company. The original box adds significant value to these toys.

INSIDER'S TIPS

Look out for repaired or replaced wind-up mechanisms, as these will decrease the value of the toy.

HALLOH RIDER ON CYCLE, 1900
Made of lithographed tin, this toy comes complete with its original box.
$3,000–$5,000

Louis Marx & Company

Louis Marx was born in 1896 to German immigrant parents living in Brooklyn, New York. As a young man, Marx displayed great ambition and intelligence. After finishing school at age 15, he was introduced by a family friend to Ferdinand Strauss, who offered him a job as an office/errand boy at his mechanical toy company (*see page 116*).

Recognizing Marx's potential, Strauss put him in charge of his East Rutherford, New Jersey, factory in 1916. In addition to running the factory, Marx began exploring a variety of different manufacturing possibilities, especially volume manufacturing for the retail stores operated by the company. Marx's ideas met with total resistance from Strauss and his board of directors, and in 1917, Marx left the Strauss firm. A few years later, the idea of mass production became the formula for success for Marx's own company.

Marx enlisted in the Army in 1917 and rose to the rank of sergeant. At the end of World War I, he went into business with his brother David; they served as agents between toy manufacturers and wholesalers. In the booming post-war economy, the brothers' business prospered, as the demand for toys skyrocketed. Louis Marx now began to analyze more closely how toys were produced and came back to his idea of mass production.

(*Continued on page 113.*)

BUCK ROGERS 25TH CENTURY ROCKET SHIP, 1930s
This spaceship is made of lithographed tin and activated by a clockwork mechanism. It is shown with its original box.
$1,000–$2,000

WHAT TO LOOK FOR:

◆ simple actions
◆ early toys are all tinplate
◆ logo and company name on toys

When the toy is wound, sparks should appear if the flint is still intact.

INDUSTRIAL-AGE TOYS
1910s–1930s

The United States entered World War I in 1917 as an untried player on the global stage, but emerged from it as an undisputed world power. Ironically, a decade stained by the bloodiest war in history also gave rise to such comic geniuses as Charlie Chaplin and Mack Sennet and saw the maturing of a medium that would entertain billions around the world: motion pictures. Sennet's first Keystone Comedy films premiered in the 1910s, and instantly inspired toymakers like Schoenhut and Manoil to add Keystone Cop roly-poly toys to their lines of World War I toy soldiers.

The economic boom of the 1920s was accompanied by an unprecedented loosening of social mores, epitomized by the short-skirted, Charleston-dancing flapper. Automobile production skyrocketed during the period. Toy manufacturers responded with a huge array of toy cars of all models, shapes, and sizes. The aviation craze triggered by Charles Lindberg's solo, nonstop flight across the Atlantic in 1927 was celebrated by toymakers with new lines of cast-iron planes bearing the name "Lindy" on their wings.

Bust followed boom, as the stock market crash of 1929 ushered in the Great Depression. While President Franklin Roosevelt ably steered the country through the worst economic time in its history, it was not until the start of World War II in 1939 that the American economy began to fully emerge from its decade-long trauma. Like the lavish film musicals of the day, with their images of Hollywood wealth and splendor, the runaway toy success of the 1930s, Parker Brothers' "Monopoly," clearly reflected the concerns and fantasies of a Depression-era generation.

It was also during the depths of the Depression that the great Disney dream machine began to dominate the world of children's entertainment through both films and toys. Walt Disney had created several popular comic characters, and in order to finance his projects, Mickey Mouse and friends were licensed out to a variety of manufacturers. Such licensing deals helped fuel Disney's film business, and kept many a toy company in the black. The box office and licensing success of *Snow White and the Seven Dwarfs* set the pattern for future Disney triumphs. Toy companies like Ingersoll Watch and Lionel had enormous success producing Disney products and helped make Mickey Mouse the global icon that he is today.

American Flyer
and George Borgfeldt & Company

AMERICAN FLYER TANK CARS, 1930s

Shown with their original boxes, the car on the left is #4010 and reads "AF–Air Service"; the one on the right is #4010 with side ladders and top fill cap. Value range is for the car and its box; without the box, the value would be significantly reduced.

$600–$900 each

AMERICAN FLYER TRAIN SET, 1930s

The set, typical for the time period, consists of locomotive #4019 with a 0-4-0 wheel configuration, painted maroon, together with three coaches marked "Hamiltonian." The brass trim on the windows is lithographed.

$500–$700

BORGFELDT MAGGIE & JIGGS ON PLATFORM, 1920s

These lithographed tin, clockwork, comic-character toys have their original box. The figures stand on platforms attached to the wheels by a thin band. (Their value without the box would be significantly reduced.)

$1,500–$2,500

William Britain Ltd.
and Buddy "L" Manufacturing Company

BRITAIN WILD WEST #152 SETS, 1930s

A British company's interpretation of Native Americans and cowboys.

$200–$300 per set

BUDDY "L" RAILWAY EXPRESS TRUCK, 1930s

Buddy "L" was known for its large, sturdy, pressed-steel vehicles, like this open-cab express truck.

$800–$1,200

BUDDY "L" INTERNATIONAL HARVESTER, 1930s

This large, pressed-steel truck with spoke wheels and an enclosed cab has "International Harvester" painted on its open cargo section.

$2,000–$3,000

J. Chein & Company
and Daisy Manufacturing Company

CHEIN MECHANICAL AQUAPLANE, 1930s

This colorful, lithographed, tinplate seaplane features pontoons, a prop blade, and wind-up action.
(The value range given here would be less without the box.)
$300–$600

CHEIN MECHANICAL MERRY-GO-ROUND, 1930s

The colorful, lithographed, tinplate Playland toy features children seated on horses. The value range is for the toy and its original box.
(The value range given here would be less without the box.)
$700–$1,000

DAISY SUPERMAN KRYPTO RAYGUN, 1930s

This pressed-steel projector pistol is able to flash pictures on a wall. It is complete with original filmstrips and box.
$400–$600

EFFanBEE
and Gibbs Manufacturing Company

EFFANBEE COMPOSITION
BOY (left), c. 1930
This doll features brown molded hair
and blue sleep eyes and is dressed
as a boxer with leather gloves.
$100–$300

EFFANBEE SKIPPY DOLL
(right), c. 1930s
This doll has painted features and is
dressed in a sailor outfit.
$200–$400

EFFANBEE PATSY-JOAN (left),
c. 1930s
This is an all-composition doll with
sleep eyes, printed dress, hat and an
original bracelet.
$200–$400

EFFANBEE PATSY (right),
c. 1930s
This is an all-composition doll with
molded hair, painted facial features,
and a blue, polka-dot dress.
$200–$400

GIBBS HORSE-DRAWN CART,
c. 1920s
Made of wood, paper, and metal,
this pull-toy has animated
movement when drawn across
the floor.
$200–$500

A.C. Gilbert Company and Gund

GILBERT ERECTOR SETS #7, 1940s

These sets include an instruction manual, spoke metal wheels, a motor, a front hood, running boards, and rubber tires to assemble a truck. All pieces are contained in a wooden box.

$300–$400

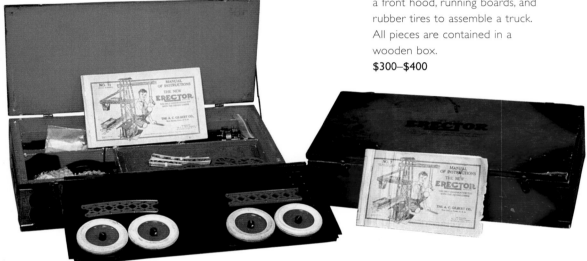

GUND POODLE, 1940s

The poodle is a typical Gund piece with a vinyl head and plush body that is stuffed with cotton and festively dressed.

$40–$60

Ideal Toy & Novelty Company and Ingersoll Watch Company

IDEAL SHIRLEY TEMPLE DOLLS, 1934–1939

These dolls show the various looks and outfits with which they came. The doll in the middle is wearing an outfit from Shirley's first movie, *Stand Up and Cheer.*

$300–$600 each

INGERSOLL MICKEY MOUSE WRIST WATCH, 1933

This Mickey Mouse watch comes with the original box and features a leather band with metal, die-cut Mickey Mouse figures. Collectors will pay a premium for watches in the original boxes and in good working condition. The World's Fair sticker increases the value of the item.

$800–$1,200

INGERSOLL MICKEY MOUSE ALARM CLOCK, c. 1930s

Features a pie-eyed Mickey with movable hour and minute hands.

$200–$300

Keystone Manufacturing Company and Kilgore Manufacturing Company

KEYSTONE RAPID-FIRE, TRI-MOTOR AIRPLANE, 1930s

This pressed-steel airplane features three nickel propellers, disc wheels, and an elaborate pulley system that turns the propellers when the plane is pulled across the floor.
$600–$800

KEYSTONE "RIDE 'EM" DUMP TRUCK, 1940s

This pressed-steel riding toy with a seat is 25 inches (63.5 cm) long.
$200–$300

KILGORE "OWL, SLOT IN BOOK," c. 1920s

This cast-iron mechanical bank is operated by placing the penny in the slot, causing "Blinkey's" eyes to roll down and back into place as the penny is deposited into the bank.
$300–$500

Kingsbury Manufacturing Company and Knickerbocker Toy Company

KINGSBURY U.S. MAIL VAN, 1910

This early mail van with spoke wheels and driver is made of pressed steel. The words "U.S. Mail" are stenciled on its sides.
$300–$500

KNICKERBOCKER PINOCCHIO AND JIMINY CRICKET, 1940s

These figures are from the 1941 animated Disney film *Pinocchio*. Made of composition, with hand-painted features, they are shown complete with their hats, which are often missing.
Pinocchio: $1,000–$1,500
Jiminy Cricket: $800–$1,200

KNICKERBOCKER DONALD DUCK, 1940s

This cloth figure is one of Disney's original five characters. He has a felt hat and bow tie.
$300–$500

Lehmann

RAD CYCLE, 1900
This tinplate clockwork toy is both lithographed and hand-painted. A woman with a large-brimmed hat is in the car and a gentleman is driving the cycle. It is priced with its original box, as shown. (Its value is considerably less without the box.)
$3,000–$6,000

MASUYAMA RICKSHAW, 1900
This lithographed, hand-painted, tinplate rickshaw toy is activated by a clockwork mechanism. The original box adds considerably to the toy's value.
$2,000–$4,000

Lionel Manufacturing Company

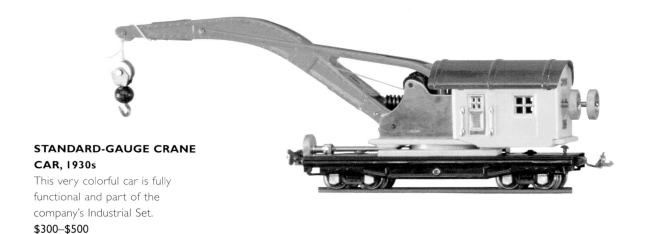

STANDARD-GAUGE CRANE CAR, 1930s

This very colorful car is fully functional and part of the company's Industrial Set.
$300–$500

390E LOCOMOTIVE AND TENDER, 1930s

This rare, two-tone green engine features copper domes and a 2-4-2 wheel configuration, with a distinctive orange side stripe. It is part of the Build-A-Loco series.
$1,500–$2,000

Louis Marx & Company

MARX MERRY MAKERS, 1920s
This lithographed, clockwork, tinplate toy is the rare version with the marquee. It also has its original box.
$1,000–$2,000

BUSY MINERS, 1920s
This lithographed, tin, clockwork toy depicts a miner on a coal wagon traveling into a mine shaft. The box is original, which adds considerably to the toy's value.
$200–$300

ROADSIDE REST SERVICE STATION, 1920s
This battery-operated, lithographed, tinplate toy features a roadside stand with two stools and die-cut figures at the counter. There are two gas pumps with electric globes, a car and lift, an oil pump and a tin oil can. The battery box is behind the station. It is mounted on a green base.
$800–$1,200

Metalcraft Corporation
and A. Schoenhut Company

METALCRAFT ST. LOUIS DELIVERY TRUCK, 1920s

This pressed-steel truck with disc wheels is painted black and green, with the company name on the side panels.

$300–$600

SCHOENHUT WOODEN CIRCUS SET ACCESSORIES, 1920s

This set features a pair of clowns, a jointed lion, a ladder, two chairs, and two circus barrels. These pieces either came with the circus set or could be purchased separately.

$300–$500

SCHOENHUT WOODEN PIANO, c. 1920s

This toy upright piano has 15 keys, a pair of candle sconces, and a bench.

$300–$600

Arcade Manufacturing Company

FURNITURE MOVING VAN,
c. 1928

A large-scale, cast-iron delivery truck painted green with gold trim. The vehicle features five nickled disc wheels and is 13³/₄ inches (35 cm) in length.
$1,500–$2,500

YELLOW CAB, 1930s

A cast-iron toy which features disc wheels. Car has "Yellow Cab" company name stenciled on the side door.
$500–$700

RED BABY, 1923

This cast-iron International dump truck features a nickel driver and winch, rubber wheels, and decals on the doors.
$600–$900

CULTI-VISION FARMALL TRACTOR, 1940s

This tractor is made of cast-iron. The nickel driver holds an extended steering column.
$2,000–$4,000

STAKE TRUCK, 1931

An International cast-iron stake truck with silver-trimmed radiator, decals on both doors, and rubber tires with spoked metal wheels.
$300–$500

TRACTOR, 1929

This tractor is made of cast-iron with original chain tracks and a plated driver. The trademark decal indicates that it was licensed by the Caterpillar Tractor Company.
$300–$500

Tootsietoy and Gebrüder Bing

TOOTSIETOY BABY-GRAND PIANO, 1920
This painted metal piano, shown with its colorful box, would fit in a doll's house.
$100–$200

BING RACING BOAT, 1910
This hand-painted tinplate boat with a seated figure has a clockwork mechanism.
$600–$800

BING TRAIN CAR, 1910
This tinplate, lithographed, "Old Dutch Cleanser" boxcar is a fine example of the type of advertising used to decorate toys.
$700–$900

(Continued from page 96.)

Marx proposed new methods of mass production that would save manufacturers money and create higher profits for wholesalers. As middlemen, the brothers stood to gain on both fronts. Soon, Louis was entertaining the notion of becoming the world's leading maker of toys.

In 1919, Marx began to turn his dream into reality. He used his savings to obtain old dies from his former employer, Strauss, and rented space in Erie, Pennsylvania. He started out slowly, with jobbing work from Strauss and his own Girard Model Works. Louis's mass-production methods proved so successful that he was soon producing more than half of both their lines and was able to place his logo on Strauss toys. That is why it is often difficult to accurately identify Marx toys today.

By 1928, toy companies were struggling to keep up the interest in their product lines. Marx decided to reintroduce one of the oldest toys around—the yo-yo. It is said that he sold millions! It was all part of his strategy of mass-production volume selling to supply the novelty stores, chain stores and five-and-dime stores.

This strategy allowed his company to weather the Depression and provided an opportunity for Marx to build his empire. As toy manufacturers around the country continued to crumble, Louis Marx was there to buy them out at a bargain price. It could be said that his yo-yo profits fueled his ambitions, as he began to acquire companies in America and Europe. Marx always insisted on keeping costs down. He believed in mass producing toys that reflected current events. They were popular with his customers.

The company continued to delight American children with competitively priced toys until it went out of business in 1979.

DRUMMER BOY, 1930s

This figure is made of lithographed tin, depicts a drummer boy in a parade outfit, and is activated by a clockwork mechanism.
$500–$800

WONDER CYCLIST, 1940s

This figure is made of tin and depicts a young boy riding a three-wheeled tricycle. The wind-up clockwork mechanism drives the trike and rings a bell at the same time.
$400–$800

Schuco

This German toy company, famous for the quality of its wind-up toys, began in Nuremberg, Germany, in 1912, when Heinrich Muller and Heinrich Schreyer teamed up to produce mechanical novelties. Muller had previous work experience with Bing, and that experience gave the new company an immediate advantage in the marketplace.

Schuco quickly established itself as one of the leaders in the wind-up toy category, but its rise to success was halted by the onset of World War I. After the war, Adolph Kahn took over from Muller and pushed the production of the company to new heights.

In the mid-1920s, the company created the Tricky Yes-No Bear, with its unique tail-lever feature. This simple creation became hugely popular not only with the children's market, but with adults, too. This realization prompted Schuco to take the adult market more seriously, and the company began to create bears that doubled as perfume bottles, compacts, and purses.

During the next 50 years or so, the company became known for the wind-up mechanisms in their automobile sets, character toys, and motorcycles. Schuco ceased operating in 1970.

JUGGLING COWBOY TOY, 1940s

This toy consists of a tin body dressed in brown chaps. When wound, the cowboy juggles the balls.
$1,000–$1,500

The toy features a tin face.

The toys are marked on the feet with the company name.

PIG WITH SUITCASE, 1940s

This enchanting wind-up toy is shown complete with its original packaging.
$800–$1,200

YES-NO MONKEY, 1930s

Dressed in a felt bellhop uniform, this monkey has a mohair face. It measures 13½ inches (34 cm).

$300–$600

Mohair is a durable material that comes from the Angora goat.

GREEN YES-NO MONKEY, 1930s

A smaller, green monkey dressed in a bellhop uniform and measuring 8½ inches (22 cm).

$200–$400

WHAT TO LOOK FOR:

- marked "Germany" or "U.S. Zone-Germany" on cars from the 1930s to the 1950s. Other markings are reissues
- company name and logo

ALSO WORTH COLLECTING:

TPS

This Japanese toy maker, also known as Tokyo Playthings, Ltd., is best known for its three-finger logo. TPS mass produced mechanical, lithographed, tinplate toys that were not of the highest quality, but which were very colorful and appealed to younger children. The company continued to supply the American market with playthings through the 1970s.

Strauss Manufacturing Corporation

Ferdinand Strauss, an Alsatian immigrant, founded this corporation in New York City at the turn of the 20th century. He began by commissioning manufacturers in Germany to produce mechanical tin toys and importing them to America. Once the toys arrived in New York, Strauss printed his name next to those of the German manufacturers prior to distribution.

The onset of World War I in 1914 affected the importation of toys to America. Strauss reacted quickly and gathered a group of investors to provide the backing for his own manufacturing company in America. He focused his toy line on mechanical tin toys with lots of action. His creations were very popular, and by the late teens, his designs earned him the title "Founder of the Mechanical Toy Industry in America." To retain control over the sale and distribution of his creations, he opened retail stores in four New York City railroad terminals.

Strauss continued to control the manufacturing and retail sale of the pieces he was producing through 1927, when he sold his manufacturing interests. Though his company ceased trading in 1940, Ferdinand Strauss always retained a presence in the toy world by consulting for other toy manufacturers and supporting new ventures within the industry. He also served as a catalyst and mentor for the great toy manufacturer, Louis Marx (*see pages 96 and 113*).

KNOCK-OUT PRIZE FIGHTERS, 1920s
Captilizing on the popularity of boxing, this colorful, lithographed boxing toy is activated by a clockwork mechanism.
$200–$400

The figure is removable and often missing on this toy.

ALABAMA COON JIGGER TOY, 1920s
This toy (a product of its time, of course) is made of lithographed tin and activated by a clockwork mechanism.
$200–$500

WHAT TO LOOK FOR:

- ◆ early mechanical toys
- ◆ simple mechanisms with limited motion
- ◆ company name located on the toy

Unique Art Manufacturing Company

In 1945, the Unique Art Manufacturing Company of Newark, New Jersey, published an advertisement which appeared in several newspapers and magazines, claiming that it had been in business since 1916. However, its real history is unclear. Nowadays, the company has a reputation for manufacturing innovative, quality wind-up toys, but the products it produced between 1916 and 1945 were very similar to the popular toys made at the time by Marx, Strauss, and other giants of the toy industry. It seems likely that Unique's Merry Juggler, Charlie Chaplin, Jazzbo-Jim, and Ham & Sam were pirated.

However, Unique's finest moment came in late 1945 with the production of Li'l Abner and His Dogpatch Band, a wind-up toy that proved to be the company's best seller and one which remains very popular with collectors today. But Unique's success was fairly short-lived, and the company ceased trading in 1952.

RAP & TAP IN A FRIENDLY SCRAP, 1940s
This boxing toy is made of lithographed tin and consists of a pair of wooden figures with tin arms and legs that fight when the key is wound.
$200–$300

JAZZBO-JIM, 1940s
This toy features a dancer on the roof next to a young boy playing the violin. The toy is activated using a clockwork mechanism.
$300–$500

TOY TRAINS

Collecting toy trains is an activity with many facets and many practitioners. Collectors focus on American, German, or British trains; wind-up, steam, or electric trains; and trains of different sizes. Trains are also distinguished by their size or scale, known as the gauge, and by their wheel configuration. Gauge represents the distance between the left and right wheels of a particular train or between the inside rails of train track. Standard or 2-gauge is $2^1/_8$ inches (54 mm); 1-gauge is $1^7/_8$ inches (48 mm); 0-gauge is $1^3/_8$ inches (35 mm); S-gauge measures $^7/_8$ inch (22.6 mm); and OO/HO-gauge is $^5/_8$ inch (16.5mm). Wheel configuration indicates the distribution of a locomotive's wheels. A train with a 4-6-2 configuration, for example, has four front wheels, six in the middle, and two at the rear.

It is important to remember that Lionel manufactured a multitude of train sets, especially after World War II, and there are many sets with their original boxes available on the secondary market. Trains from this period are highly desirable, however, and despite the large numbers available, collectors will still pay a premium for items that are in the best condition and come in their original boxes.

Most train sets made after World War II required space to set up the track and create villages for the train to travel through. Today, most people do not have the space for them, so the trains have either been disposed of, passed down over the generations, or stored away in attics or basements. If they are still around, they might make an annual appearance during the Christmas holidays or when Dad becomes nostalgic for the toys of his youth.

Just like other collectibles, excessive heat or damp condition can ruin a train set and damage its box. If you display your collection, make sure you do so out of direct sunlight and in a dry environment. Should your set or collection require any sort of repair or restoration to get it running, seek out a train professional who is knowledgeable about the engine types you possess. He or she will advise you correctly.

American Flyer

William Hafner of Chicago, Illinois, decided to venture into the toy manufacturing business in 1900. In the beginning, his company—the Toy Auto Company—focused on the production of clockwork automobiles. Hafner's creations reflected the advances in technology during those years, and clockwork mechanisms became the consistent component in all the pieces he manufactured. But the company struggled with the production and distribution of its products. In 1904, the name was changed to the W.F. Hafner Company.

Facing mounting financial troubles, Hafner entered into a partnership with Wiliam Coleman, a Chicago hardware store owner, in 1910. They focused the business on the production of clockwork trains and renamed it American Flyer. Four years later, Hafner formed a rival company, called Overland Flyer, to compete with the original company he had founded 14 years before.

American Flyer began experimenting with different products to compete with other manufacturers of the time. In 1928, in addition to the successful train line, the company designed four different styles of mechanical airplanes, the *Spirit of Columbia*, *Lone Eagle*, *Spirit of America*, and *Sky King*. But in 1931, the company dropped the airplanes from its line and refocused on the production of trains, gradually establishing itself as one of the leaders in the toy train market. The trains continued to be popular until the mid-1930s.

WHAT TO LOOK FOR:

- train cars and locomotives are always marked with the company name
- some cars and locomotives appear to be of lesser quality than Lionel trains, often made from lightweight materials, with low-quality paint or lithography

CROSSING SIGNAL, 1930s
This working signal is activated as the train approaches. Train accessories are valuable additions to collections.
$100–$300

AMERICAN FLYER LOCOMOTIVE, 1930s
This standard-gauge locomotive has a 4-4-2 wheel configuration, with copper pipes and accents on the boiler of the engine.
$700–$900

In 1938, the company was bought by the A.C. Gilbert Company (*see page 181*), better know for its Erector Sets. Gilbert made changes to the American Flyer production of trains. After World War II, the company introduced S-gauge railroad models, but these met with little success. The Lionel Corporation, its major competitor, bought out American Flyer in 1966.

STEAM LOCOMOTIVE, 1920s

This engine features a 4-4-0 wheel configuration and showcases the brass boiler typical of all steam toys from this time period.
$400–$800

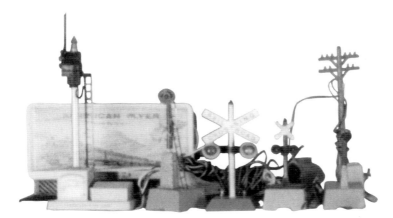

AMERICAN FLYER ACCESSORIES, 1920s

American Flyer accessories complete a collection and realistically accent a train layout.
$50–$300

ALSO WORTH COLLECTING:

Ives Trains

Ives trains were first introduced in 1903 and continued until the company fell on hard times and went into bankruptcy reorganization in 1928. American Flyer and Lionel jointly shared control of the ailing company while they managed to produce trains under the Ives name until 1932. American Flyer relinquished its control of the company, and in 1933, Ives was taken over by Lionel. Trains were manufactured with Lionel markings, and Ives was phased out, ending the glorious reign of a great American toy manufacturer.

Lionel Manufacturing Company

Joshua Lionel Cowen was born in New York City on August 25, 1877. An inventive and enterprising youth, Cowen started working in his teens for the Acme Electric Lamp Company in Manhattan, assembling battery lamps. He found himself in the heart of a technological free-for-all as electricity was incorporated into everyday life.

By the turn of the century, Cowen began to experiment with battery-operated lamps in his spare time. A local merchant approached him one day and asked him to create a whimsical window display to attract the public. His first effort produced the Electric Express, a showpiece featuring trains powered by a dry-cell battery wired to the track. It was a grand departure from the wind-up, steam-powered, and motorized vehicles of the time.

The succcess of Cowen's window display was due in no small part to the advances in transportation that were transforming America at the time. Railroad tracks were crisscrossing the country, and trolley cars or streetcars were becoming a staple in every major city. New York City, in particular, had developed an elaborate transportation system of electric-powered streetcars. This became the model for Cowen's displays the following year. Once again, his displays were a huge hit. The orders started coming in from stores as far away as Rhode Island, and Cowen found himself much in demand.

In 1903, he set up the Lionel Manufacturing Company. The company started out producing store displays featuring trains and trolley cars, but five years later, the company realized a larger market for children's toys. It was in this mass market that the company could produce trains with movable working parts that captured the imaginations of children of all ages. In 1909, the company added the tag line "The standard of the world" to all their promotional advertising.

While every other major toy train manufacturer around the world was producing trains with steam engines or wind-up clockwork mechanisms, Cowen continued to perfect the electric train. He understood electricity and realized it would become the power of the future. In 1918, the company was renamed the Lionel Corporation, and by 1920, it had become one of three major American producers of model electric trains and accessories.

WHAT TO LOOK FOR:

- boxes are all marked, and some include graphics
- trains and cars are all marked with the legend "Lionel Lines," and are numbered to indicate the date manufactured
- Lionel trolley cars are particularly rare, as only a limited number were produced
- Lionel trains use a third rail

PASSENGER SET 1930s
This set features a locomotive with a 2-4-2 wheel configuration and includes a coal car and three passenger cars.
$800–$1,200

The company continued to grow and expand the line of engines, cars, and accessories. By 1931, Lionel took over the financially failing Ives Company. Lionel took great pride in the trains it produced, which mirrored the streamlined trains of the day.

Lionel continued to be prosperous until the mid-1950s, when Cowen sold his interest in the company and retired. He died at the age of 85 on September 8, 1965. A year later, the company he founded and led for nearly 60 years was sold to General Mills, which resumed limited production of Lionel trains in its Mount Clemons, Michigan, facility.

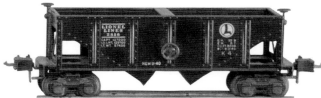

DONALD DUCK RAIL HAND CAR, 1930

This toy features a long-billed Donald Duck with Pluto peering out of a lithographed doghouse. It is clockwork-activated and shown complete with its original box.
$800–$1,200

COAL CAR, 1930s

A typical coal car included with most train sets of the era is shown here. It features locking couplers on both ends as well as the Lionel Lines logo.
$30–$60

INSIDER'S TIPS

Look out for repainting. Fakes are sometimes artificially distressed.

There are companies making boxes today in the style and design of the boxes produced in the 1930s and 1940s.

This area of collecting is vast, so collectors should seek out knowledgeable dealers.

STANDARD-GAUGE "BLUE COMET" PASSENGER SET, 1930s

This set features a #400E locomotive with a 4-4-4 wheel configuration and nickel trim. It includes a tender, and passenger cars #420 "Faye," #421 "Westpal," and #422 "Temple."
$6,000–$8,000

FACT FILE

PRESSED-STEEL TOYS

Pressed-steel toys continue to be popular with collectors today and consistently show yearly increases in value. Condition is a major factor in the value of items in this area of collecting. If the item and its miscellaneous parts are in original condition and come with the original box, a collector will pay a premium for it.

Though steel can be found in early toys as parts or structure pieces, it was not until the 1900s that toy companies began to utilize this material for the production of entire toys. Companies like Buddy "L" or Keystone used heavy-gauge pressed steel for riding toys and oversized trucks and cars.

In the early 1960s, Tonka was the last company to utilize pressed steel in the production of its toys before they, too, changed over to plastics in the 1970s.

Pressed-steel toys are vulnerable to damp and wet conditions—these will result in paint loss and rusting. Once these occur, it is difficult and costly to do the work needed to restore the toy to its original condition.

The collectibles market for this area mirrors America's fascination with driving machines. As the trucks, cars, and industrial vehicles were rolling off the assembly line in Detroit, Michigan, the toy companies were fighting for the rights to replicate the designs for the toy market. Oversized vehicles—especially fire trucks, delivery vans, and riding toys—have continually been sought out by collectors of all ages.

My partner Greg and I were called on to assist a woman in Palm City, Florida, who was going through some family items stored in her garage. Her father, who had lived in Pennsylvania, had passed away 10 years earlier, and our client had all his possessions packed up and shipped to Florida, where they remained untouched. Our job was to wade through and select items we felt would be worth consigning. After discovering several wonderful treasures, our journey led us to a room where she stored her father's toys, and before my eyes was a late 1920s Steelcraft fire engine that was in good condition, complete with ladders and company label. We put the toy up for auction, and collectors across the country wanted more information about it. When all was said and done, the toy sold to a collector in Iowa for $850—not bad for something hiding in the garage.

Buddy "L" Manufacturing Company

Founded by Fred A. Lundahl in 1910, the Moline Pressed Steel Company began by producing steel fenders for International Harvester trucks. The International Harvester contract provided the company, based in Moline, Illinois, with an abundance of work. The story goes that one day, around 1916, Lundahl, bored with the monotonous production of fenders, and keen to make something special for his new-born son Buddy, gathered some scrap metal from the plant and fashioned a miniature dining table and chairs. He continued to build scale toys as the young boy grew. To celebrate his son's fourth birthday, in 1920, his father presented him with a reduced-scale, open-bed pickup truck, an exact, scaled-down version of the International Harvester truck for which he manufactured fenders.

Young Buddy was thrilled with the toy, but it was the reaction from the neighborhood children that sparked Mr. Lundahl's creative mind to produce other trucks and consider the possibilities of marketing his creations. The quality, craftsmanship,

and attention to detail helped propel this neo-toy maker into the spotlight. Starting out with a limited line, he produced samples of trucks and a steam shovel to use as demonstrations during his presentations to F.A.O. Schwarz in New York and Marshall Field's in Chicago. Both stores reacted positively to his line by placing huge orders for a fall delivery.

Buddy "L" toys made their debut in September 1921, just in time for the Christmas season. The company continued to produce truck parts, but now expanded to include a toy division. By the end of 1923, the toy division led the company in sales. The demand for Buddy "L" toys facilitated the complete transition of the company from truck parts to the exclusive production of toys. The line grew to include steamrollers, cranes, and cement mixers. By 1926, the company had established sales offices throughout the country and decided to answer consumer demand by releasing a staggering 29 different car and truck designs.

CONCRETE MIXER, 1930s
Made of pressed steel this toy features an

upright boiler, mixing drum and green water tank.
$3,000–$4,000

WHAT TO LOOK FOR:

- trucks marked, usually on the sides of the vehicles, with company logo and legend "Buddy 'L' Express Line"
- sturdy, well-built, and durable trucks and cars
- well designed, with close attention to detail
- oversized vehicles in the early production were over 20 inches (50.8 cm) in length

In 1930, the company changed its name from the Moline Pressed Steel Company to the Buddy "L" Manufacturing Company. Mr. Lundahl's nickname for his young son Buddy became immortalized as a permanent namesake for one of America's favorite, quality-made, pressed-steel toys. Up to this point, the basic design element was based on the International Harvester mold. Advances in technology and industry during this decade made possible the use of pressed-steel wheels and real rubber tires. The most dramatic change took place around 1935, with the addition of electric headlamps to the cars and a total redesign of the entire truck line. At this time, the toys were made large enough and strong enough for a child to ride on. This new line featured removable saddle seats on some of the trucks, as well as advertisements of the period. A Wrigley Chewing Gum advertisement on the sides of the trailer of the Railway Express truck was particularly popular.

After the death of Fred A. Lundahl, the company was bought by J.W. Bettendorf, but he struggled to maintain a streamlined operation during the Depression and was unable to a keep the company profitable. As a result, the company was dissolved by a court order in 1939.

ROUNDHOUSE AND TURNTABLE, 1930s

This useful accessory was made of pressed steel and featured engine sheds and tracks attached to a turntable.
$800–$1,200

This is a clear example of the use of a company logo on toy packaging.

The turntable can be moved to line up the track to one of the three stations.

SHELL OIL TRUCK, 1940s

This early truck is made of pressed steel and shown complete with its original box.
$300–$500

Keystone Manufacturing Company

This company developed out of a partnership formed by brothers Ben and Isidore Marks. The Marks Brothers Company began in 1911 as a major supplier of human-hair doll wigs and celluloid doll heads to American doll manufacturers. Over the next decade, the company prospered and added a vast array of other playthings to their product lines.

At the 1919 New York Toy Fair, the brothers introduced a new moving-picture machine that was greeted with great enthusiasm. This success prompted their decision to purchase the American Pictograph Company of Manchester, New Hampshire, in 1924. The combined companies were renamed the Keystone Manufacturing Company and relocated to Boston, Massachusetts.

Toy manufacturers of the day were quick to recognize new consumer markets. Keystone was well placed to take advantage of the rising popularity of the new entertainment medium.

Keystone started with the production of motion-picture toys featuring Charlie Chaplin and Tom Mix films. Their Keystone Movie Graph machines were a big hit, as children were able enjoy the "movies" at home.

Eager to take advantage of the prosperous American economy of the time and aware of their ability to take advantage of trends, Keystone noticed the increase in the number of toy autos being produced by their competitors. Keystone needed to establish itself with products that separated their toy autos from other manufacturers. The company decided to approach the Packard Motor Company and ask for permission to recreate and market trucks modeled after the popular Packard design. The request was granted, and the Keystone Packard Truck included the popular radiator design and logo.

WATER TOWER TRUCK, 1940s
The pressed-steel fire toy features a removable child seat, a hand siren and a hand lever with real pump action.
$500–$700

A fine example of the company's logo used on its toys.

The new truck made its debut in 1925, with Keystone advertising its special features. Each truck had a 22-gauge, cold-rolled steel body, nickel hubcaps and radiator cap, a see-through celluloid windshield, front cranks, headlamps, signal arms for "stop" and "go," steering capabilities, and for 50¢ extra, rubber tires.

The Packard Truck was so successful that Keystone's new product line came to rival the market leader, Buddy "L." One advertising campaign even guaranteed that a 200-pound (90 kg) man could stand on the toy without damaging it. All of their efforts paid off with a growth in sales and increased market share.

This popularity helped Keystone weather the era of the Depression. Manufacturing slowed but did not hinder the creative powers of the design staff. Striving to stand out in the market, Keystone released a Siren Riding Toy in 1934. This featured a saddle seat in the bed of the toy and handlebars in front for steering. The public's overwhelming response pushed the designers to create a new, sturdy, and affordable riding toy. Two years later, Keystone released a new creation, the Ride 'Em Mail Plane. The toy was 25 inches (63.5 cm) long and sturdy enough for a small child to ride. Affordably priced at $2.00, the Ride 'Em plane was yet another major success for the company.

The Keystone Manufacturing Company went out of business in 1957.

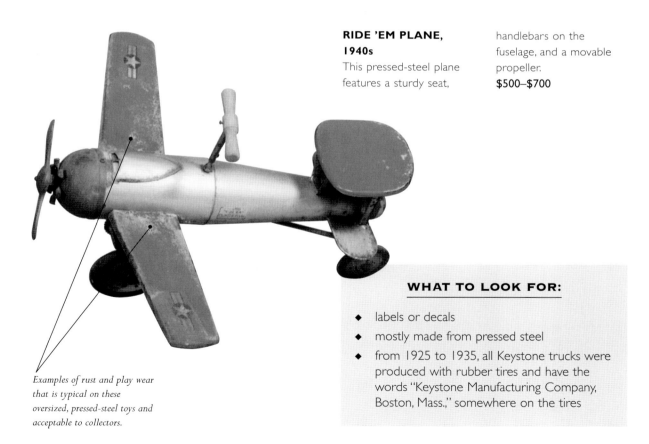

Examples of rust and play wear that is typical on these oversized, pressed-steel toys and acceptable to collectors.

RIDE 'EM PLANE, 1940s
This pressed-steel plane features a sturdy seat, handlebars on the fuselage, and a movable propeller.
$500–$700

WHAT TO LOOK FOR:

◆ labels or decals
◆ mostly made from pressed steel
◆ from 1925 to 1935, all Keystone trucks were produced with rubber tires and have the words "Keystone Manufacturing Company, Boston, Mass.," somewhere on the tires

Metalcraft Corporation

During the first half of the 20th century, a number of American manufacturing companies assisted the government by producing supplies and tools for the troops overseas as part of the war effort. Metalcraft was one of these. Based in St. Louis, Missouri, the company began life in 1920 as the Measuregraph Company, making dies, stamps, and tools for the troops still in Europe after World War I. As the demand for these materials subsided, the company had to reorganize its output. The company changed its name to Metallic Industries and decided to venture into manufacturing playground equipment and sidewalk toys like scooters, wagons, and tricycles.

The success of a teeter-totter toy called the Teeter-Go-Round earned the company membership in the Toy Manufacturers of America after only one year in the toy business. This early recognition helped to push the company's design team to develop more than a dozen different toys for the next year, including such popular items as the Taxi-Plane, the Winsum-Coaster, and the Jackrabbit Racer. However, after an initial boom, sales began to decline.

In response to this decline, the company renamed itself the Metalcraft Corporation. Now, it needed a new product to capture the buying public's interest.

In 1927, Charles Lindbergh had just successfully completed his transatlantic flight from New York to Paris. This international event caught the attention of the media around the world, and manufacturing companies scrambled to capture the rights to produce a Lindy airplane toy.

Metalcraft obtained the rights to manufacture a *Spirit of St. Louis* pressed-steel airplane kit. Once again the company had struck gold. Each kit contained one basic airplane with a variety of parts, making any number of airplane style options possible. This made the kit very popular, as the variety it offered captured children's imaginations for hours. The kits sold by the thousands, but the novelty soon began to wear off, and by 1928, Metalcraft went back to full production of its staple sidewalk toys.

The company began to search for another concept that would duplicate the tremendous success of the Lindy toy. Looking around the marketplace, Metalcraft realized that though price had caused a decline in the popularity of cast-iron toys, Buddy "L" pressed-steel vehicles were still the most popular toys on the shelves. With their facilities already producing steel sidewalk toys, there had to be a way to manufacture toys with the quality of Buddy "L," but at a cheaper price. Metalcraft decided to produce a

HEINZ DELIVERY TRUCK, 1940s
This truck is made of pressed steel and features advertising decals and electric headlights.
$300–$500

scaled-down version of a steel truck which carried advertising on its panels. In order to keep the price down, the pieces had to be manufactured in large volume. Metalcraft obtained initial contracts with Kroger Stores, the Jewel Tea Company, and Coca-Cola. Once more, the company had found a niche in the marketplace, and sales grew to such an extent that the trucks became Metalcraft's premium products, outselling their sidewalk toys.

Metalcraft also produced other products that became popular at drugstores and grocery stores. These included painted, pressed-steel folding chairs and a four-wheeled, 32 x 16 inch (81.3 x 40.6 cm) coaster wagon. The wagon—sold to customers who presented a store with a fully punched card for the purchase of a dog food called Doggie Dinner plus 99¢—became Metalcraft's most popular item. By 1932, Metalcraft was proud to announce that it had produced over a million "business leaders," as it affectionately referred to its trucks.

Always trying to stay on top of technology, Metalcraft began experimenting with battery-operated trucks. The company took a gamble and began mass producing the trucks as part of its premium line. Unfortunately, customers rejected the new toys, leaving Metalcraft with huge unsold inventory. More agents were hired to spur sales, but

the addition of new employees caused Metalcraft to raise prices at a time when toy manufacturers around the country were slashing prices to maintain a competitive edge. The company struggled along for a couple of years, but sales steadily declined. In 1937, Metalcraft stopped production for good and closed its doors. The company known for its great ideas was unable to reinvent itself one last time.

TOWING AND REPAIRS TRUCK, 1930s
This truck features a tow bar, disc wheels, an enclosed cab, and an open body with advertising decals.
$300–$500

COCA-COLA TRUCK, 1940s
This truck has rubber wheels and 10 glass bottles, and features early advertising decals for Coca-Cola.
$1,000–$2,000

WHAT TO LOOK FOR:

◆ trucks with advertising
◆ disc wheels on early trucks
◆ sleek, art deco cars and trucks

Smith-Miller

Founded in 1945, just after the end of World War II, this Santa Monica-based company specialized in the manufacture of exact replicas of existing trucks and tractors using cast-metal and aluminium. They also had a second-tier product line offering more affordable toys which were not exact replicas. The higher-priced toys, like the Lumber Truck or Aerial Ladder Truck, ranged from $6.95 to $27.85. They all featured the slogan "Cost more because they give more," which helped sell the toys at a time when realism in toy production was at its height.

Competition with more established companies like Hubley and Buddy "L" inspired Smith-Miller designers to emphasize pinpoint accuracy in their recreations. As a result, the company was able to hold its own in an incredibly competitive market for about 10 years.

But Smith-Miller toys, or "Smitty Toys," as they were also known, became the victims of poor timing in a competitive toy automotive market. The onset of the Korean War affected the use of metal, and this, in turn, created shortages for manufacturers who had to limit production. Coupled with the increased use of plastics, this contributed to the demise of the company. In 1954, Smith-Miller officially closed its doors.

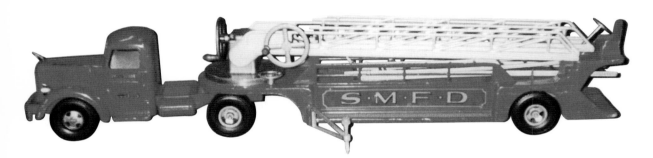

WHAT TO LOOK FOR:

- toys made of cast-metal or aluminum
- exact replicas of working Mack trucks
- the last year of productions were changed to an Auto-Car diesel design with opening doors and steering wheels that actually moved
- the smaller series of toys made by the company range in size between 11 and 14 inches (27.9 and 35.5 cm), while the larger replicas range between 17 and 30 inches (43.1 and 76.2 cm)

AERIAL LADDER TRUCK, 1950
This truck has a die-cast Mack cab and a separate trailer body with an extension ladder that can rise to 4 feet (1.25 m). The ladder sits on a revolving base. The toy measures 36 inches (91 cm) in length.
$700–$900

INSIDER'S TIPS

Collectors will pay a premium for toys in good condition with all their original parts and box.

This view of the undercarriage focuses on the steering mechanism employed by Smith-Miller.

The logo and trademark of the company are shown here: "Famous Trucks in Miniature."

ST. LOUIS F.D. TRUCK, 1940s

This true-to-life fire truck comes equipped with 10 extension ladders.
$800–$1,200

TRUCK, 1950s

Here is an example of a 14-wheeler truck hauling a platform made of metal and wood. The hubcaps of the wheels all have the initials "SM" on them, while the truck's design is very basic.
$200–$500

Steelcraft

During the 1920s, airplanes shared the spotlight with a short-lived but distinctive airship, the zeppelin. A number of toy companies seized the opportunity to create toys that emulated the *Graf Zeppelin*, the *Los Angeles*, and the *Akron*. Such companies as Marx, Strauss, and Dent manufactured their airships in lead, iron, and tin. Steelcraft's version was, as its name implies, made of pressed steel. Steelcraft was an offshoot of the J.W. Murray Manufacturing Company which branched out from its traditional product line of stamped metal body parts for the automotive industry and introduced its first line of all-steel toys in the mid-1920s. The production of the toys was coordinated at the Murray-Ohio manufacturing plant, located in Cleveland, Ohio.

Steelcraft concentrated production on pull-toys and pedal cars. The pedal cars were pressed steel, modeled after full-scale GMC trucks; all had open cabs and averaged 26 inches (66 cm) in length. Later, in 1926, the company changed the design style to imitate the life-size Mack trucks that were also gaining in public popularity. The quality and craftsmanship of the Steelcraft products provided stiff competition for Buddy "L" and Keystone, which also produced pressed-steel toys. Steelcraft's reputation for quality reached retail giants J.C. Penney and Sears, and both requested their own "house brands" of pressed-steel toys. "Little Jim Playthings" became J.C. Penney's brand, and "Boycraft" became the brand for Sears. Steelcraft continued to manufacture toys and pedal cars up to the outbreak of World War II. After the war, the company focused on pressed-steel pedal cars and the manufacturing of bicycles.

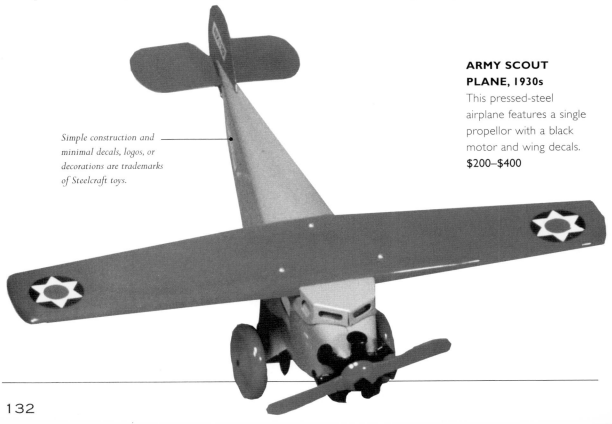

Simple construction and minimal decals, logos, or decorations are trademarks of Steelcraft toys.

ARMY SCOUT PLANE, 1930s

This pressed-steel airplane features a single propellor with a black motor and wing decals.
$200–$400

WHAT TO LOOK FOR:

◆ pedal cars are modeled after full-scale GMC trucks

◆ toys usually have disc wheels with rubber treads

CADILLAC PEDAL CAR, 1940s
Among Steelcraft's child-size cars was this Cadillac with black fenders and running boards. The car features a windscreen, a chrome grill, ornament headlamp, steering wheel and white upholstered seat.
$1,000–$3,000

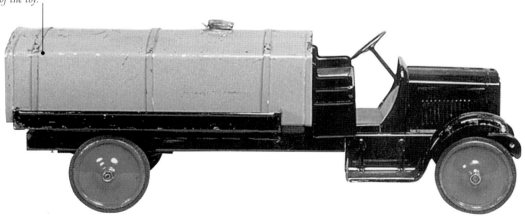

Minor paint loss and rust on the tank can reduce the value of the toy.

TANK TRUCK, 1930s
This pressed-steel truck features a filler cap on the top of the tank. It also has an open cab and disc wheels with solid rubber tires.
$500–$700

Toledo Metal Wheel Company

Organized in 1887 by Frank E. Southard in Toledo, Ohio, this company began by manufacturing wire wheels for manufacturers of baby carriages. Mr. Southard eventually became general manager and president of the company and expanded its offerings to include go-carts, velocipedes, baby carriages, bicycles, sleds, steering coaster wagons, and doll vehicles.

With a fever for toy automobiles sweeping the U.S. in the early 1900s, the Toledo Metal Wheel Company continued to grow, and by 1918 had established itself as the country's largest manufacturer of children's pedal cars, with sales representatives in many states. The company was known for the fine craftsmanship and attention to detail in all the products it manufactured. It also became an innovator in its field with the introduction of adjustable rubber pedals and "no dead-center driving gear" that allowed children to start pedaling from a stationary position, while other manufacturers' pedal cars needed to be push-started.

In 1925, Toledo introduced the Bull Dog and Blue Streak brands of large, indestructible, pressed-steel toy trucks, with designs based on the life-size Bulldog Mack trucks common on the highways at the time. The company faced stiff hometown competition from similar products like the American and Giant brands of trucks manufactured by the American-National Company, and the Sampson trucks made by the Gendron Wheel Company. It is thought that after 1925, American-National and the Toledo Metal Wheel Company consolidated production or that Toledo produced the American-National line, because the two companies' trucks were identical, except for the names and logos on the toys.

Whatever the truth of the matter, the Toledo Metal Wheel Company ceased production in 1930.

ROAD CAR, 1920s
This car is made of sheet metal and features chrome headlights, a hood ornament, and wheel hubs. The car is 46 inches (117 cm) long. **$2,000–$3,000**

WHAT TO LOOK FOR:

- Bull Dog trucks have oval decals on the sides of the service bed and on the front featuring a standing bulldog and the words "Bull Dog"
- some early trucks have an oval and diamond decal with a lightning bolt and the words "Blue Streak"
- a few rare trucks feature a rectangular Blue Streak decal with fancy border artwork
- "Toledo" on the nameplate attached to the top of the radiator
- black rubber tires marked "Juvenile Federal Rubber Co., U.S.A." are found on Bull Dog trucks
- trucks sport a hand-cranked noisemaker at the front

FACT FILE
PLUSH TOYS

Plush toys provide collectors with warm and happy memories of childhood. Not surprisingly, this area of collecting is very emotionally charged. Collectors will pay a premium for a plush toy that is accompanied by old photographs of the toy and its original owner.

Most early plush toys are bears or animals made of mohair, the wool of the Angora goat. Mohair is a very durable natural fiber that requires little maintenance. A gentle brushing will remove surface dust and keep the toy looking its best. If a toy is more heavily soiled, it is best to seek out the advice of a professional before attempting any extensive cleaning.

As synthetic fibers became a cheaper alternative to mohair in the 1950s, manufacturers began turning out synthetic plush and mass-produced bears and animals. The large output of cheaper plush toys has lowered their value on the secondary market.

Plush toys are subject to insect attack. The best way to eliminate bugs that may be inside your plush toy is to place it in a zipper freezer bag and store it in the freezer overnight. This will eliminate anything that may have taken up residence inside.

Whether you have mohair or synthetic plush toys, store them out of direct sunlight to prevent fading. It's also important to keep them in a stable environment—if you store or display a plush toy in a spot that is too dry, fibers may become brittle, while excessive humidity will promote the growth of mold, which can damage the toy.

An apricot-colored, 1904 Steiff bear named "Teddy Girl" with a center facial seam measuring 18 inches (45.7 cm) holds the record for a bear sold at auction. It sold at Christie's in South Kensington, London, on December 5, 1994, for $171,600. The reason it sold for such an aggressive price was a combination of excellent condition and provenance. The bear had belonged to a British Army officer, Colonel T.R. Henderson. The story goes that from a very young age, he became inseparable from the bear, traveling everywhere with it. He later became instrumental in promoting the organization Good Bears of the World. The new purchaser of "Teddy Girl" was Japanese businessman Mr. Sekiguchi, who bought it for his newly opened Izu Museum in Japan. He received international publicity for the purchase, and "Teddy Girl" resides there with other bears, plush toys, and amusements.

Character Toy and Novelty Company

The teddy bears and plush character toys manufactured by this American company, based in South Norwalk, Connecticut, turn up all over the United States today. The success of the Character Toy and Novelty Company can be credited to two New Yorkers, Caesar Mangiapani and Jack Levy. Mangiapani expanded the line of toys to include a wider variety of animals, particularly teddy bears. He was responsible for the designs that captured the imaginations of children everywhere. Levy, who joined the company after World War II, managed the sales end of the business and can be credited with getting its product into every major department store across the country.

Since the United States was going through a post-war boom when the company began in the late 1920s, and more babies were being born than in any other period of history, the bears and toys of the Character Toy and Novelty Company were in great demand. In the 1930s and 1940s, the company was able to secure a licensing agreement with Walt Disney, and they made Mickey, Donald, Goofy, and Pluto toys, along with characters from the movies *Song of the South* and *Bambi*. Levy retired in 1960, but the company continued for over 20 more years with Mangiapani at the design helm until his death in 1983.

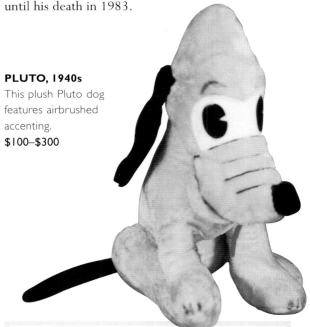

PLUTO, 1940s
This plush Pluto dog features airbrushed accenting.
$100–$300

WHAT TO LOOK FOR:

- bears from 1920 have a cloth manufacturer's label sewn into the left ear that reads, "Character Designed by Character Novelty Co. Inc., So Norwalk Conn"
- early bears are fully jointed, while later bears have no joints.
- a felt red tongue and white felt circles behind the eyes are marks of the baby-faced bears
- some noses were made of metal
- early bears have a music box encased in their tummies that plays the tune "Toy Maker's Dream"
- no stitched claws; sometimes claws were airbrushed on paw pads
- high forehead, shaved muzzle, and large ears
- kapok stuffing in early bears

INSIDER'S TIPS

These bears are often confused with the Knickerbocker bears from the same time period. These bears have lots of personality and were mass produced using cheap materials. The value of the early mohair bears is slowly rising; however, to be valuable, they must be in very good condition.

Gund

Still run by descendants of an original employee, Gund holds the distinction of being one of the oldest American stuffed-toy manufacturers that remains in business today.

Founded by Adolph Gund in 1898 in Norwalk, Connecticut, the company began by manufacturing belts, necklaces, novelties, and handmade stuffed toys. Little did Gund realize how answering a customer's request for a stuffed bear would forever alter the future of his company. In 1906, he purchased a quantity of plush and began producing teddy bears in four sizes, ranging from 10 to 16 inches (25.4 to 40.6 cm). He followed up with rabbits for Easter, and also experimented with other animals. In 1910, Gund presented its first line of stuffed animals. The public response was overwhelming, and the company continued to focus on the production of stuffed toy animals.

In 1915, a new janitor, Jacob Swedlin, was hired. Swedlin was the oldest of seven children and took the job to help support his family, newly arrived in the United States from Russia. Swedlin's hard work and determination earned him a promotion, and within three years, he had become head of the cutting department. His ambition and hard work did not go unnoticed. Adolph Gund selected Swedlin, to be his personal assistant. This promotion provided Swedlin with the necessary exposure to learn the everyday running of the Gund company.

After 27 years of business, the original Gund company was dissolved in 1925, and the assets of the company were taken over by Jacob Swedlin. Jacob and two brothers, Abraham and Louis, reorganized the company and continued to revolutionize the industry. Swedlin is credited with developing the use of machines to cut the patterns for stuffed toys more accurately and efficiently. Under his guidance, Gund

These eyes are typically Gund.

The spaced single stitching on the pads is a sure way to identify your bear as a Gund.

TEDDY BEAR, 1920s
This early example of a mohair Gund bear has the characteristic eyes and round, cupped ears used in the production of bears at the time.
$400–$500

was also the first company to utilize foam rubber and synthetic materials in the manufacture of its stuffed toys.

In 1940, the company moved to New York City, where it remained until 1973, when it relocated to Edison, New Jersey. Today, the privately owned company is still run by descendants of Jacob Swedlin, and they continue to produce bears and stuffed toys for the next generation of collectors.

PLUSH DOG, 1930s
The dog has floppy ears and googly eyes that were popular features of Gund plush toys.
$50–$75

The spaced single stitching and eyes identify the pup as a Gund.

MONKEY, 1940s
Gund was known for innovations such as using a combination of materials on animals like this monkey, which combines a plush body with plastic features.
$50–$150

IDENTIFICATION

- ◆ no tags on bears or toys prior to the 1940s
- ◆ from 1940 to World War II, Gund toys featured tags which stated, "A Gund Product, A Toy of Quality and Distinction"
- ◆ after World War II, a stylized logo was used on which a "G" appeared as a rabbit with ears and whiskers
- ◆ if the label shows a New York City address, the bear was produced between 1940 and 1956
- ◆ in 1956, the factory moved to Brooklyn, New York, and the address reflected this through 1973
- ◆ from 1960 to 1987, the logo was a straight block type that features a bear's head above the letter "U"
- ◆ since 1987, the name "GUND," set in capitals, has indicated a toy manufactured by the company

Ideal Toy & Novelty Company

The very first teddy bear was created in 1903 in Brooklyn, New York, by Russian immigrant inventor Morris Michtom and his wife Rose. The inspiration for the now universally beloved plush toy was an incident depicted in a *Washington Post* cartoon, in which President Theodore Roosevelt refused to shoot a bear cub during a hunt in Mississippi. Rose handcrafted soft, jointed versions of the cartoon cub and displayed them in the storefront window of the Michtoms' toy shop. The bears quickly became a huge hit in the neighborhood, prompting the Michtoms to establish the Ideal Toy & Novelty Company to meet the overwhelming demand for the new toy sensation.

Legend has it that Rose wrote a letter to President Roosevelt asking for permission to use his name, "Teddy," for the advertising of their new product. She named it Teddy's Bear and hoped the president would be flattered by the compliment. The legend continues that the president wrote back to the Michtoms, giving his blessing on the name and adding that he was doubtful it would add anything to its popularity. How wrong he was! Eventually, the "'s" was dropped, and the world took the "teddy bear" to its heart.

Ideal earned the distinction of being the first American toy manufacturer to mass produce bears, which remained its main product until the 1930s. By then, comic-character toys were becoming very popular in the United States. The company obtained the rights to produce toys of characters like Mickey Mouse, Popeye, and Dopey. In addition,

SOLDIER, 1930s
Ideal made a wide range of dolls in its line, including this composition soldier with painted eyes, uniform, and hat.
$100–$300

CAMPBELL'S SOUP GIRL, 1930s
Another Ideal doll was this Campbell's Soup doll, dressed in a red and white uniform.
$100–$300

composition dolls and, later, plastic dolls were added to the product line.

There were no permanent labels placed on the bears during manufacture, so exact identification of the early bears can be difficult. But the bears were produced in a distinctive style that seasoned collectors have come to recognize. Dolls are usually marked on the back or under the hairline on the back of the neck.

WHAT TO LOOK FOR:

- triangular-shaped bears' heads
- early bears have fabric or horizontally stitched noses in a triangular shape
- toys and dolls are marked with company logo (in chronological order, left to right)

COLLECTOR'S STORY

We were doing appraisals for the *Antiques Roadshow* in Louisville, Kentucky, a few years ago when a couple approached me with several items that had been in the family for some time. As is often the case, they were curious about the collectible value their items might have had. They produced a copy of a color plate from a book called *More About Teddy B. and Teddy G: The Roosevelt Bears,* by Seymour Eaton, published in 1907. The book, together with an early Ideal bear, had belonged to the woman's great-grandmother. She presented me with a photograph of her great-grandmother, taken at Christmas with the bear and book in her lap. The old sepia-tone photograph was dated 1907 and corresponded with an inscription inside the book, "Elva M. Rabuck of Louisville, KY. Christmas 1907."

The bear featured beautiful, short, clipped mohair, cupped ears, boot-button eyes, a cloth nose, a barrel-shaped body, a humpback, and a triangular-shaped head, all characteristic of the Ideal bears of the early 20th century. The overall condition of the bear, photograph, and book made the package very attractive to any collector. My opinion was that its value was $3,000 to $3,500, which astounded the woman— she had found these items in the attic after Elva had passed away.

About a year after the appraisal, the woman contacted me to help her sell the items. She felt it was time to let them go and hoped the new collector would better appreciate their historic value. The entire package sold at an Internet auction through TreasureQuest Auction Galleries, Inc. (www.tqag.com), for $4,000!

Knickerbocker Toy Company

MICKEY AND MINNIE MOUSE DOLLS, 1930s
These dolls are made of and cloth and feature composition shoes together with their original paper tags.
$1,000–$3,000 a pair

to Knickerbocker, which also became the name of their new company.

The company first produced lithographed paper-on-wood blocks, as well as a variety of wooden puzzles and educational toys. After relocating to New York City around 1922, the company expanded its line to include stuffed dolls, animals, marionettes, and stuffed bears. The jointed, mohair bears could be distinguished from others on the market by their use of felt, embroidery, or metal noses.

Around the same time, Walt Disney was busy developing a new form of entertainment—animated short films. His first film, *Steamboat Willie,* featured Mickey Mouse. Mickey was already a popular comic-strip character featured in newspapers across the country, but now, audiences could both see him move and hear him talk. By the mid-1930s, Mickey, Minnie Mouse, and Donald Duck were household names. The Knickerbocker company, now established as a major American toy manufacturer, recognized the popularity of Walt Disney's characters. It approached Disney with the idea of reproducing his creations in composition, cloth, and plush. The company was granted licenses from Disney, and the popular characters, along with teddy bears, began to dominate the production line. These are truly some of the finest examples of early Disney characters around.

Knickerbocker bears from the 1920s and 1930s have been increasing in value in recent years as more and more collectors recognize the craftsmanship that went into their production.

The Knickerbocker Toy Company was founded around 1869 by a family of Dutch immigrants, originally named Van Whye, who settled in Albany, New York, in the mid-1800s. At this time, the predominantly English and French population of New York State used the term "knickerbocker" to refer to the early Dutch settlers who had populated much of the region before the arrival of the English. The Van Whyes officially changed their family name

During the 1930s, Knickerbocker produced a bear called Winston, the Good-Luck Bear. Legend has it that a mother presented the bear to her daughter, who was having trouble conceiving a child. The mother instructed her daughter to keep the bear on the bed to bring her luck. Within a year, the daughter happily gave birth to her first child. The Knickerbocker Toy Company could not guarantee similar results for everyone, but the story earned Winston the nickname "the Fertility Bear."

Between the 1930s and the 1960s, the company expanded its reach, manufacturing a variety of licensed toys and collectibles including Raggedy Ann and Andy, Holly Hobbie, Nancy and Sluggo, Hanna-Barbera characters, *Sesame Street* characters, and Smokey the Bear. The Knickerbocker bear business was also very strong during this time period, and the company came up with several slogans that appeared on the labels with the company's logo. "Animals of Distinction" was in use during the 1940s, and "Joy of a Toy" in the 1960s. These slogans also appeared on the packaging.

The 1980s saw Knickerbocker taken over by the Lionel train company (*see pages 121–122*), after which a complete reorganization took place. Applause, a division of Knickerbocker at the time, took over production of Raggedy Ann and Andy and made a few design changes to the face of this classic American folk doll, including stitched facial features with painted eyes, nose, and smile. The Lionel company filed for bankruptcy in 1984, and the production of Knickerbocker toys was discontinued.

In 1990, Louis and Tammy Knickerbocker (surprisingly, no relation to the original family) resurrected the tradition of producing high-quality collectibles at an affordable price. Today, the L.L. Knickerbocker Company produces a wide range of dolls and collectibles.

IDENTIFICATION

If a bear is not marked, it can be difficult to positively identify the manufacturer, country of origin, or production date. We do know Knickerbocker bears were mass produced between 1920 and 1960, and Smokey the Bear was about the only bear manufactured during the 1970s. Here are a few pointers that may help identify your bruin as a Knickerbocker and date its manufacture.

- between 1920 and the 1930s, the bears had black, metal, stitched noses and glass or tin eyes; they had large cupped ears set wide apart on a round head; they were fully jointed, with small oval feet that had velveteen or felt pads

- in the 1940s, they had long mohair bodies and short mohair or velveteen muzzles; they were fully jointed and had glass eyes; during this time, the "Animals of Distinction" tag was used

- the 1950s saw the use of acrylic plush with glass or plastic eyes; vinyl faces and ears had painted features; only the heads were jointed; the tag read "Animals of Distinction. Made in the USA."

- in the 1960s, the bears were made exclusively of plush, and all had plastic eyes; the "Joy of a Toy" tag was used during these years

MOHAIR BEAR, 1940s
This small, non-jointed, mohair bear features the

Knickerbocker company tag on its tummy.
$200–$300

Steiff

Margarete Steiff was born in 1847 in Giengen, a town in Germany's Black Forest. As a child, she suffered from polio, but even though she was confined to a wheelchair, she did not allow her infirmities to dampen her industrious spirit. She became an accomplished seamstress who took remnant pieces of felt material to make animals for the children in the neighborhood. The first one she made, a felt elephant pincushion, was so popular that she began to produce them in quantity.

With the help of her nephew, Richard, Margarete Steiff established the Steiff company in 1877, devoted to the production of mohair animals and bears. Richard convinced Margarete that a joined bear should be the focus of the product line, which was first presented at the Leipzig Toy Fair in 1903. Richard had observed the grizzly bears at the Stuttgart Zoo and thought a mohair version would be a prime product. The bears' acceptance was mixed, and they were even ridiculed by some as "stuffed misfits." However, at the conclusion of the fair, an American confectioner from New York ordered 3,000 bears on the spot. By 1908, close to a million Steiff bears had been sold.

Today, Steiff continues to produce a variety of plush and mohair animals, but it is the bear that dominates the company's current production and the international secondary collector's market.

MOHAIR BEAR, 1920s
This bear is fully jointed and has a button in the ear, a stitched nose, elongated limbs, and felt pads.
$2,000–$3,000

INSIDER'S TIPS

The most valuable and vulnerable part of the bear is the nose or muzzle area. If there has been any restoration or damage to this area, the value is affected.

The pads should be felt and the nose should be hand-stitched. A horizontal nose stitching indicates an early bear.

There are many books, articles, and collectors that have information on these collectibles. Seek out as many as possible for further information.

Contact the Steiff Club for more information (see page 213).

WHAT TO LOOK FOR:

◆ a button in the left ear of the bear or animal will determine its age
◆ if a chest tag is present, the animal's name will be printed on it

The desirability of Steiff bears, animals, and character dolls continues to increase among collectors the world over. Yet prized items still turn up in unexpected settings like garage sales and flea markets. During a taping of the popular PBS/WGBH television series *Antiques Roadshow*™, a collector approached my table with a bear she wanted to have appraised.

She had acquired it five years earlier from a dealer who knew that the bear was rare but did not realize how its value would increase over time.

The white mohair Steiff "Rod" bear came complete with a set of X-rays that revealed its metal rod joints. The bear has a sealing-wax nose, is fully jointed, and measures over 20 inches (51 cm) long. The collector had focused her collection on unique Steiff bears and animals and was truly attracted to the "Rod" bear. The white color and rarity of this type of bear make it a wonderful addition to any collection of bears. My estimate of the bear's value was somewhere between $20,000 and $30,000. As you can imagine, the collector was more than a bit surprised!

FELT DONKEY, 1915
This donkey on wooden wheels features shoe-button eyes and a leather saddle.
$800–$1,200

Button in the ear.

Chest tag.

TEDDY BABY MOHAIR BEAR, 1940s
This small teddy is shown complete with chest tag and button in the ear. It measures 3 inches (8 cm).
$1,500–$3,000

IDENTIFICATION

Although Steiff toys have always had chest tags, the Steiff logo has been used at distinct times over the years. The following details will help you determine the exact age of any Steiff animal:

Dates	Logo Used
1904–1905	embossed elephant with upright trunk
1905–1909	blank button
1905–1940	**STEIFF** printed in raised letters with a trailing underline on the final F
1946–1947	silver-blue, dull blank button
1948–1960	silver button with "Steiff" in raised script
1960–1976	silver button with *Steiff* in incised script
1977–Present	brass button with *Steiff* in incised script

POST-WAR TOYS
1940s–1960s

The Japanese bombing of Pearl Harbor on December 7, 1941, united all Americans in the defense of freedom at home and in war-torn Europe and Asia. At the end of the war, in 1945, the United States emerged not only victorious but as the most powerful nation on Earth. Although millions around the world jubilantly celebrated the return of peace, it was a peace overshadowed by the new and awful specter of the atom bomb.

The ten years after the war's end witnessed the introduction of a host of new products and inventions, among them the mobile phone, the frozen TV dinner, the bikini, and Tupperware. As it did on all other aspects of life, the war had a tremendous impact on the toy industry, causing manufacturers to suspend production of many toy lines due to wartime restrictions on the use of lead. With lead once again plentiful, toymakers like Heyde, Britains, and Barclay resumed production of toy soldiers, with a new focus on victorious Allied regiments.

The end of World War II also led to the creation of a much bigger market for toys. Young men returned from the battlefields eager to start new families.

Throughout the late 1940s and 1950s, it was the toy manufacturers who had to mobilize to meet the growing demand for toys and playthings triggered by the post-war "baby boom."

Television, introduced widely in the early 1950s, spawned a host of characters that quickly became fodder for the toy industry. Perhaps reflecting the fears of a nuclear age, monster and science-fiction themes became very popular in the 1950s—in films, on TV, in books, and in toy stores. What seemed like fantasy in such 1950s movies as *Destination Moon* and *Forbidden Planet* became thrilling reality at the end of the following decade, when on June 20, 1969, Neil Armstrong and Edwin (Buzz) Aldrin achieved the impossible by walking on the moon.

The new space age presented great opportunities for the toy industry. Japanese companies, in particular, such as Cragston, Yonezawa, and Linemar, began to produce a variety of wind-up and battery-operated robots, space guns, and space vehicles. These colorful, mass-produced toys were made of lithographed tin, had a simple movement or sparking action, and came in lithographed boxes.

Fisher-Price

SQUEAKY THE CLOWN #777, 1958

This brilliantly colored circus toy features a bobbing head that squeaks, a red wood nose, a green plastic collar, and rotating arms.

$200–$400

MICKEY MOUSE DRUMMER #476, 1941

This pull-toy has movable wooden arms, mallets that beat the metal-topped, fiber drum, a wood base, and wheels.

$300–$400

GOLD STAR STAGECOACH
#175, 1954

This stagecoach has two galloping horses that make realistic hoofbeat sounds as the driver sways from side to side. On top of the coach are a luggage rack and two lithographed mail pouches, which are often missing. This is one of the all-time classic, horse-drawn vehicles made by Fisher-Price.
$500–$700

PETER PIG #479, 1959

This cute pull-toy has "oink-oink" sound, a wooden beanie, vinyl ears, and a twirling plastic tail.
$50–$100

DONALD DUCK XYLOPHONE
#177, 1946

When pulled along, this paper-on-wood Donald moves his arms and strikes the keys of the xylophone with his mallets.
$300–$400

Smith-Miller
and Toledo Metal Wheel Company

**SMITH-MILLER MOBILOIL
TANKER, 1940s**
This tanker has a die-cast cab and
pressed-steel, enclosed tank body
with rubber tires and spoke wheels.
$100–$300

TOLEDO CADILLAC, 1940s
This pressed-steel pedal car has been
restored to its original splendor.
This is one type of piece on which
collectors do not mind restoration.
$1,000–$2,000

Ohio Art

SAND SIFTER, *c.* 1950s
This tinplate sand toy is decorated with lithographed scenes of children at the seaside. Sand toys were a staple of Ohio Art.
$25–$75

TOP, *c.* 1950s
This colorful tinplate top has a lithographed scene of cowboys and horses. Mechanical tops provided children with hours of enjoyment. Like sand toys, they are popular collectibles today. Their value depends on their condition and the quality of the lithography.
$50–$100

Dinky Toys

HEINZ 57 VARIETIES BEDFORD VAN, 1961–1965

This 1:43 scale, die-cast metal vehicle features advertising on the side panels that makes it a crossover collectible, appealing to collectors of toys and collectors of advertising items.

$50–$100

WEETABIX GUY VAN #514, 1950s

This 1:43 scale, die-cast metal van also features advertising. It was distributed only in the United Kingdom, where the brand of breakfast cereal is a favorite, yet it also appeals to American collectors.

$50–$100

JAGUAR XK120 COUPE #157, 1954–1962

This popular, 1:43 scale, die-cast metal sports car was manufactured in a variety of colors, including green, yellow, red, turquoise, cerise, and yellow-gray. However, the white version is worth twice as much as the others.

$50–$100
$100–$200 white version

AUSTIN COVERED WAGON
#413, 1950s
This 1:43 scale, die-cast metal industrial vehicle was a popular staple in the Dinky toy line. This example is shown with its original box.
$40–$60

SPRATT'S GUY VAN #514, 1950s
This 1:43 scale, die-cast metal example has regional advertising that Dinky was keen to include on its trucks and vans. The local advertising appealed to children and helped promote the featured companies.
$100–$200

FODEN FLAT TRUCK #902, 1950s
Like all Dinky toys, this truck—a 1:43 scale, die-cast metal version of the trucks often seen on highways or near construction sites—exhibits accurate detail and includes a spare tire.
$100–$200

Corgi

JAMES BOND ASTON MARTIN DB5, 1960s

This metallic gold car has a red interior, clear windows, a working roof hatch and ejector seat, a bullet shield, and guns. The figure is often missing from this toy, which decreases its value.

$75–$100

PATATES FRITES VAN #411, 1950s

This van features advertising on both side panels and a pull-down side, as shown on the box above.

$50–$75

THREE MINIS (top) AND THREE MORRIS MINORS, 1950s

This group of vehicles illustrates the variety in the Corgi lines. Each exact car or van would be painted a different color to keep production costs down and increase the possible variations in the marketplace.

$20–$40 each

CHITTY CHITTY BANG BANG, 1960s

This toy features a metallic copper body, a dark red interior, spoked wheels, a black chassis with silver running boards, and a hand brake. The toy is shown in its original packaging, which increases its market value.

$100–$300

PAIR OF COMMERCIAL VEHICLES, 1980s

Examples of late-model Corgi toys, these delivery vans feature ads for Rice Krispies and Budweiser Beer.

$20–$40 each

Character Toy and Novelty Company

DONALD DUCK, 1940s
This long-billed, plush character toy features simple, applied eyes, beret, and company tag showing near the leg.
$200–$300

BAMBI, 1940s
The wide-eyed deer features the same simple, applied eyes as Donald Duck, while the company's tag is attached to its ear.
$200–$300

Manoil Manufacturing Company, Inc., and Barclay Manufacturing Company

MANOIL MOTORCYCLE RIDER #52, 1940s

This toy features a grass base with the number 52 attached to the back wheel.

$20–$50

MANOIL HAPPY FARM FIGURES, 1940s

Part of the Happy Farm series, these cast figures were made to be very colorful to contrast the brown color used for soldiers. Included from left to right are #41/13 Farmer Carrying Pumpkin, #41/38 Girl Picking Berries, #41/16 Watchman Blowing Out Lantern, and #41/33 Woman with Butter Churn. All figures are marked with the numbers and an "M" in a circle.

$10–$50 each

BARCLAY COWBOYS

Cowboy #18 features a figure holding a gun in the air. It is paired with Cowboy #18A, which has both hands in the air.

$10–$30 each

Schuco

A GROUP OF MONKEYS, 1930s

The tumbling monkey (left) has a tin body dressed in felt and tumbles when wound.
$200–$300

The walking monkey (right front) has a tin and mohair body, wears red felt pants, and walks when his clockwork mechanism is wound.
$100–$200

The bellhop monkey (right rear) is a stuffed animal with glass eyes in a felt uniform.
$100–$200

CLOWN JUGGLER, 1940s

The wind-up toy features a tin body with a black and yellow felt suit, orange hair, and a black hat. When wound, it juggles the balls. It is shown here with its original box.
$400–$600

DONALD DUCK, 1940s

This long-billed, clockwork-activated Disney character is made of lithographed tinplate and sports his trademark blue sailor's cap and jacket.
$200–$400

STUDIO 1050 RACE CAR, 1940s

This sporty, tinplate race car is a great example of the line of wind-up race toys that Schuco manufactured. It features a functioning steering wheel and rubber tires.
$200–$400

MONKEY VIOLINIST, 1940s

This animated wind-up monkey has a tin body, face, and violin and a cloth outfit. The box is original and adds considerably to the toy's value.
$200–$300

Unique Art Manufacturing Company

LI'L ABNER AND HIS DOGPATCH BAND, 1945

This wind-up, lithographed, tinplate toy features four characters from the popular comic strip. When the toy is wound, the characters spring into action, performing as an ensemble. The box is original.
$400–$700

G.I. JOE AND HIS JOUNCING JEEP, 1940s

This wind-up, lithographed, tinplate toy has its original box. Without the box, it would be worth substantially less.
$200–$400

Wolverine Supply & Manufacturing

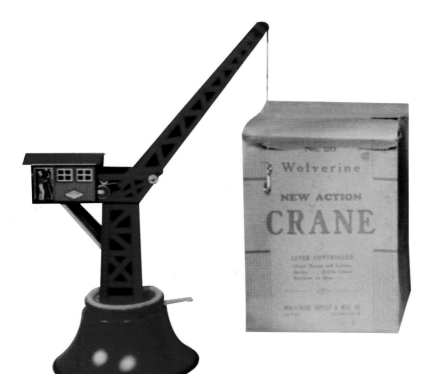

WOLVERINE NEW ACTION CRANE #420, 1920s

This large, lithographed, tin crane has a moving bucket, swivel base, and crane operator. It is shown complete with its original box.
$300–$500

WOLVERINE DRUM MAJOR, 1940s

This lithographed, tinplate soldier in full parade dress plays his drum when wound.
$200–$300

Wyandotte Toys

HUMPHREY MOBILE, 1940s

This toy features Humphrey, the famous comic character, riding an outhouse-shaped motorbike which is activated by a clockwork mechanism.

$300–$500

RABBIT ON MOTORCYCLE, 1940s

This very colorful, tinplate, lithographed toy features a bunny driving a motorcycle with a sidecar. The toy is activated by a clockwork mechanism.

$100–$200

TOY SOLDIERS

Toy soldiers have been popular since they first appeared in Germany in the 1700s. They are ingrained in our cultural history, reflecting the bravery and heroism of generations of fighting men. They appeal not only to young boys and old soldiers, but also to antique collectors, historians, and war-game players of every generation.

At first, these soldiers were flat figures made of lead. It was British toy maker William Britain who perfected the technique of hollow casting in the 1890s and became the dominant figure in the field. The use of lead, the development of various casting styles, and the definite style patterns established by the companies who manufactured these toys help to differentiate and brand the manufacturers around the world.

Over the years, the companies featured in this Fact File produced many sets of toy soldiers, representing many different regiments. Collectors today tend to focus on specific regiments. Doing research on the regiments, as well as on the techniques and colors used by each company, is very helpful when it comes to identifying toy soldiers found in flea markets or garage sales. Boxed sets, especially those made by European companies, are particularly prized. American toy soldiers were mass produced, and their lack of quality and craftsmanship is evident in their appearance and lack of popularity in the secondary market.

Special attention needs to be taken when storing toy soldiers, because hollow-cast lead figures will disintegrate if they are stored for extended periods in a dry, hot environment. Also keep the figures out of direct sunlight to ensure the paint does not fade. The loss of even a piece or two from a boxed set can be painful for a collector, as such a loss seriously detracts from the set's value on the secondary market. Collectors will pay a premium only for complete sets in very good condition and in their original, intact boxes.

Several different companies produced a variety of regiments. Most of the toy-soldier shops have closed, but collectors can find plenty of books to study. Armed with that knowledge, they can search the Internet for the batallions in which they have interest.

William Britain Ltd.

This venerable company had humble beginnings in the United Kingdom as a family business run from a suburban home at Lambton Road, Hornsey Rise, North London. The patriarch of the family, William Britain, possessed entrepreneurial skills and an unshakable faith in the free-enterprise opportunities of Victorian London. The company's early business in the 1840s centered on the production of mechanical tin toys, manufactured and distributed from home. There were two major factors that contributed to the overall success of the business: The first was having a surname that fitted in well with the chauvinistic Victorian English trade, and the second was being blessed with a large number of children, all of whom were enthusiastic about their father's venture.

Early toys featured clockwork mechanisms that were key- or coin-operated. They included a walking bear, a Chinese man pulling a rickshaw, and a kilted Scotsman drinking a bottle of whiskey. The figures' clothes were designed, cut, and sewn by the female members of the family, while the boys worked on constructing the toys and mechanisms.

From the 1880s into the early 1890s, the production of tin mechanical toys became increasingly costly, thus making them harder to sell. William Britain observed that foreign companies, like Heyde, Mignot, Heinrichsen, and Allgeyer, were the ones that dominated the U.K. tin toy market and felt that is was time to expand the scope of the family business to include lead soldiers.

His sons, Alfred and William Jr., helped their father to formulate a plan of attack. They determined that the process used by Heyde in Dresden, Germany, and Mignot in Paris, France, was the best place to start. They used a master model based on an accurate military print and created a plaster mold from which a two-piece brass mold was produced and snapped together. When boiling liquid lead was poured into the mold, it created a lead figure. The brilliant stroke of genius that separated Britain's soldiers from the rest occurred one afternoon late in 1892, when William Jr. was under the cherry tree in the garden, experimenting with pots of boiling metal. He discovered that by placing tiny air holes at the top of the head of a figure's mold, it allowed him to 'tip some of the molten metal out again in a quick upside-down motion, resulting in the development of the first-ever

JAPANESE CAVALRY SET #135, 1940s
This set features five pieces in a box designed by F. Whisstock.

$400–$600

Sets with original boxes are more desirable to collectors and command higher prices.

hollow-cast soldiers. The secret of success relied on the temperature of the metal coupled with the speed of the process.

William Jr. perfected his process and in 1893 produced a model of a Life Guard—the household cavalry of the Queen—consisting of a mounted figure with fixed arms that carried a thin strip of tin for a sword. This simple creation became a direct competitor of the solid-cast lead soldiers already on the market. The hollow-cast pieces were more economical to produce, resulting in a lower price for the consumer. William's younger brother Fred, the salesman of the family, set out to convince the conservative-minded British storeowners that Britain's lead soldiers were worthy of being sold alongside the Heyde and Mignot pieces. Fred persuaded Albert Gamage, a draper's assistant who opened shop in 1878, to carry a small number of the hollow-cast lead figures. Gamage's became one of London's leading stores and the perfect selection to carry Britain's line. The success Gamage had with the lead soldiers prompted other store owners to place orders, and the family could hardly keep up with domestic demand. By the end of the 19th century, Britain had established itself as a market leader.

WHAT TO LOOK FOR:

- ◆ lightweight, hollow-cast lead figures
- ◆ a hole at the top of each figure's head
- ◆ finely finished figures that have great attention to detail in the uniforms
- ◆ figures on horses not removable
- ◆ the only moving part on some figures is the sword arm that goes up and down

As time marched on, domestic sales turned into international sales. Two world wars, minor battles, and skirmishes around the globe provided the company with endless opportunities to manufacture soldiers that reflected world events. The soldiers always featured great attention to detail and were produced with the correct uniforms. When World War II ended, the production of lead toy soldiers was slow to restart, due to the government's restrictions on lead for the home market. The only toy soldiers available at this time in the U.K. were for export. By 1949, however, normal production resumed, and the company still produces its toy soldiers today.

CAPE TOWN HIGHLANDERS SET #1901, 1940s

The set consists of eight pieces, including the slope officer.

$400–$600

It was the fine attention to detail in the uniforms and outfits of the soldiers that set them apart from the competition.

Heyde

Georg Heyde founded his toy soldier company in Dresden, Germany, right after the Franco-Prussian War of 1870, in which Bismarck's armies conquered Paris, awarding Prussia a stunning victory and providing fresh current events for the toy soldier industry to mirror. Heyde was regarded as one of the leading manufacturers of full-rounded, solid figures in Germany during the late 19th and early 20th centuries. Very little is known about Georg Heyde himself because his factory and all the company records were destroyed along with the rest of Dresden in the British and American bombing raids of February 1945. One thing is certain, though: Hyde's legacy lives on in each and every soldier set manufactured by the company.

When Georg Heyde began his business, he studied the competition to better decide his course of action and what we would call today his business model. It was not so much what the competition was doing but how they were doing it that interested him. At the time, soldier manufacturers were producing sets with all the figures in the exact same pose. One set would all be marching while another would all be firing rifles. Heyde created sets with soldiers in numerous postures. No other maker manufactured figures in such a variety of poses. His soldiers all did something, and each one was different. This set his company and its toys apart from those of other manufacturers. The company also produced non-military figures, like their farm series. This flexibility enabled the Heyde company to turn out millions of figures, much to the delight of children at the time and collectors today.

Whether it was the Boxer Rebellion in China; the Spanish-American, Russo-Japanese, or Greco-Turkish War; or the uprising against the Germans in Southwest Africa, Georg Heyde would rush out appropriate sets of figures in time for the Christmas holiday demand. Sometimes, existing figures were adapted to fit the occasion, and other times, new figures were commissioned.

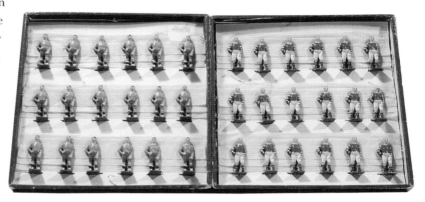

SOLDIER SET, 1940s
This boxed set of Heyde lead soldiers from the same infantry comes in a hinged box.
$100–$300

WHAT TO LOOK FOR:

- if the box is present, look for the founder's initials in gold
- figures without boxes are difficult to identify, because they are not individually marked
- Heyde infantry step forward with the right foot
- company logo

Manoil Manufacturing Company, Inc.

The United States became known as the "Land of Opportunity" at the turn of the 20th century as families traveled huge distances to escape oppression in their home countries and establish themselves on American soil. One such family was the Manoil clan, who arrived in New York City in the early 1900s.

In 1927, Jack Manoil started a novelty and metal-lamp manufacturing business at 34 West Houston Street in Manhattan. At first, the company was called Jack Manoil Manufacturing, but the name changed a year later when older brother Maurice joined as co-owner. The Man-O-Lamp Corporation continued to manufacture lamps for the next six years. In July 1934, the company changed its name yet again, to the Manoil Manufacturing Company, Inc., and shifted its focus from lamps to toys.

The company's first toy line in 1934 consisted of four die-cast cars that were 4 inches (10.1 cm) in length, a pair of sedan coupes, and a die-cast wrecker. Jack employed the creative assistance of Walter Baetz, a Moravian from Canada, who ultimately became the company's longtime sculptor and designer. Working together, the two brought a greater diversity to the toy line. In 1935, they introduced the Manoil lead soldiers. The platoon of lead soldiers became popular, and the company constantly looked for ways to perfect their molds in order to increase the structural soundness of the castings and eliminate the possibility of air bubbles. Subtle changes in manufacturing caused variations in some of the soldiers from year to year. In 1937, the company moved to Brooklyn, New York. Maurice handled the business end of the operation,

RUNNING FIGURE, 1930s
A slush-cast figure pulls a cart of wooden wheels.
$20–$50

FIREFIGHTER, 1930s
This figure, made of slush-cast metal, is a typical Manoil design.
$40–$100

WHAT TO LOOK FOR:

◆ soldiers have a distinctive jauntiness
◆ the Manoil company encircled "M"

IDENTIFICATION

◆ early 1930s soldiers have a concave underbase

◆ 1940s Manoil soldiers are more jaunty and on the portly side

◆ late 1940s and 1950s soldiers are more realistic and leaner-looking

◆ pre-World War II soldiers are marked "M" and numbered between 1 and 169; post-World War II items are marked "M" and numbered between 170 and 224

◆ composition items are marked "MC" and numbered 1, 2, 3, 3a, and 4

◆ Happy Farm series of lead figures are marked "M," 41/, and another number ranging from 1 to 41

while Jack took the reins as creative director of the toy line.

In June of 1940, Waverly, New York, became the new home for Manoil Manufacturing. At its peak, the company employed 225 people. The move to Waverly proved to be an excellent decision; the new location provided the company with better access to the railroad line, which made shipments easier and more affordable. But success did not last long. The threat of another world war prompted the United States government to prohibit the use of lead in the manufacturing of toys. The regulation stated: "No lead toys can be fabricated after April 1 (1942) and the quantity of lead used during the first quarter of 1942 must be restricted to 50 per cent of the amount used in either the 3rd or 4th quarter of 1941." Toys made from other strategic materials continued to be manufactured until June 30, 1942.

The Manoil Manufacturing Company, Inc., responded to this mandate by temporarily shutting down production with the onset of hostilities, but resumed a limited production of sulfur-based, fine-grained, composition soldiers in January 1944. However, the toys proved to be brittle and ultimately unsuccessful, and production was terminated by the year's end.

Despite this setback, the end of the war brought about a rejuvenation of the company. Manoil began offering several new lines of soldiers, as well as the popular new Happy Farm series, which reflected life in rural America. Despite the popularity of the new creations, distribution began to decline, and the company was forced to move back into a smaller location. In 1953, the company became known as the Jack Manoil Specialty Company, and it finally went out of business after Jack Manoil's death in 1955.

ALSO WORTH COLLECTING:
Barclay Manufacturing Company

Participation and victory in World War I in Europe gave the American people a feeling of community, unity, and purpose. In the years immediately following the conflict, things military were popular with people of all ages. In 1923, Leon Donze and Michael Levy established the Barclay Manufacturing Company in Hoboken, New Jersey, to produce toy soldiers and take advantage of this popularity.

The recently ended war gave a tremendous boost to the sales of the company's various lines of soldiers, and within five years, Barclay had become the largest American producer of toy soldiers. In the 1930s, the company added jeeps and a variety of other military vehicles and personnel to its still-popular product line.

Barclay soldiers are marked "U.S.A." In some cases, the soldiers and their boxes are also marked with the company name. Early soldiers had tin helmets, but after consumer complaints that the helmets came off, the company incorporated the helmets into the die-cast designs and painted them silver.

The company ceased production in 1971. This 1930s bugler figure by Barclay has a value of **$25–$50**.

To fully understand the history of die-cast toys, we must venture back to the tiny, tinplate "penny toys" of the 1840s. These toys were so named because they were sold for the price of a penny, though sometimes they were a ha'penny or a tuppenny. This meant that even the poorest child could have at least one toy to play with. Penny toys of the early 20th century were slush-cast or hollow-cast and were made by pouring hot liquid metal into a mold. The liquid was then drained through holes in the top and bottom of the toy. It was a similar technique to that employed by the lead soldier manufacturers. After World War I, casting techniques improved, and an American company called Tootsietoy emerged as the leader and innovator in this area. Tootsietoy manufactured automobiles, planes, trains, and doll-house furniture, as well as doll houses, and was responsible for changing the material used to make these items from lead to mazac, a zinc-based alloy that was more durable and lighter than lead. Tootsietoy was careful with its pricing and kept things cheap in true "penny-toy" tradition.

In 1934, Dinky was the most popular toy maker in Britain. In fact, its products were so popular that the company's success developed and expanded the market, inspiring others to join in the competition for customers' money. This competition resulted in an abundance of toys being manufactured, providing collectors today with a huge variety of vintage toys to search out at flea markets and garage sales.

The popularity of these two companies led many others to manufacture automotive toys using similar designs and styles. Many of these new companies were based outside America and Britain, opening up the market to international competition. Competition was so fierce that all notable companies made sure their vehicles were marked somewhere with their company name. This makes identification today much easier; even vintage toys can be easily identified.

Die-cast toys are durable but can be susceptible to fading if they are exposed to direct sunlight. It is essential to keep them in a stable environment, because excessive moisture or dryness will damage the vehicles and the original paintwork.

The overall popularity of die-cast toys has been increasing. These toys easily fit the bill for collectors looking for affordable collectibles that are easy to display and store.

Corgi

The story of the famous Corgi brand of toy vehicles starts in Germany with Philip Ullman, the head of Tippco, a German toy manufacturer. In 1933, Ullman moved to Great Britain and began working as a subcontractor for other toy makers. In 1936, he set up his own company, Mettoy, for which he created a line of lithographed tinplate cars, aircraft, and other vehicles. Based in Northampton, the company expanded, and in 1946 ventured into the production of large-scale, die-cast models. Consumers reacted positively to the products, and soon, demand forced the company to build larger facilities. In 1948, a 14-acre (5.6 hectares) factory was built near Swansea in Wales which has remained

the company headquarters since that time.

One of the new lines manufactured at the new facility was called Castoys. These vehicles were slightly smaller than the other vehicles the company manufactured, and Castoys remained popular through the early 1950s. During the late 1950s, Dinky Toys (*see pages 170–171*) was making great strides in the die-cast marketplace, and Mettoy needed to devise a line that could be competitive in that sector of the market. The hard Welsh dog breed, the corgi, lent its name to the new line of die-cast vehicles. The name Corgi was selected for three reasons. First, it was short and catchy; second, the corgi is a Welsh breed; and finally, the dog was—and

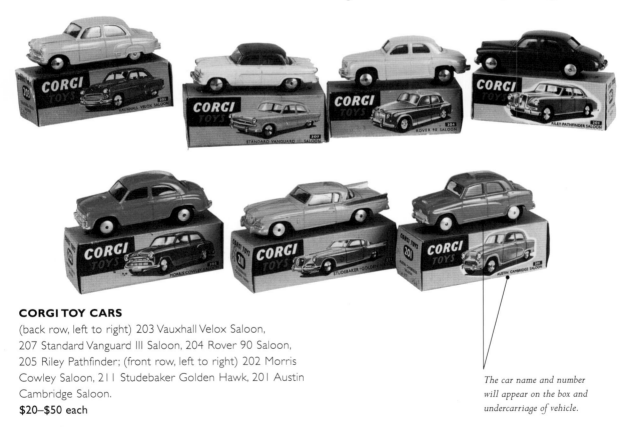

CORGI TOY CARS

(back row, left to right) 203 Vauxhall Velox Saloon, 207 Standard Vanguard III Saloon, 204 Rover 90 Saloon, 205 Riley Pathfinder; (front row, left to right) 202 Morris Cowley Saloon, 211 Studebaker Golden Hawk, 201 Austin Cambridge Saloon.

$20–$50 each

The car name and number will appear on the box and undercarriage of vehicle.

remains—a favorite of Britain's royal family. Relaunching their line of smaller vehicles, firmly based on the Castoys idea, Corgi established a new benchmark for quality, particularly in the casting of the toys. Toolmakers required to make the new dies came from Germany. The innovative packaging for the new line of Corgis was designed to be attractive and eye-catching.

As the years progressed, Corgi continued to innovate and remained competitive in the marketplace. In 1959, it added spring suspension to its vehicles, and in 1964, it launched its most popular and famous toy—a replica of James Bond's Aston Martin DB6. The car had been made popular in the film *Goldfinger*, so Corgi packed as many features and devices into the toy as possible to emulate the car in the movie. These included a front machine gun, a rear bulletproof shield, and an ejector seat. Corgi's designers worked long and hard to ensure all of these special features would work flawlessly, and the toy, introduced in November 1965, was awarded "Toy of the Year" by the National Association of Toy Retailers. Over the next three years, the Corgi James Bond Aston Martin was extremely popular, selling over three million cars.

Corgi continued to manufacture die-cast toys and established a variety of film and television tie-in vehicles following in the footsteps of the successful James Bond car. In 1966, Corgi's Batmobile became the top-selling toy-vehicle model of all time, reaching five million cars sold and helping to keep the company competitive. In the 1970s, Corgi introduced Wizzwheels, a line of die-cast vehicles designed to compete with America's craze for Hot Wheels.

Since then, Corgi has continued to grow, with new models regularly introduced into one of the most competitive toy markets of all.

BATMOBILE, 1960s
The car features a black body and front chain cutter, a rear hook, and both Batman and Robin figures.
$80–$200

The figures are usually missing, so when both accompany the toy, collectors are more likely to snap it up.

MAGIC ROUNDABOUT PLAYGROUND, 1970s
A complete play set with train, roundabout, figure, and original box.
$70–$200

Dinky Toys

The history of die-cast metal vehicles really begins in turn-of-the-century Liverpool, England, where Frank Hornby received a patent for the world's first metal construction set in 1901, and called it Meccano. The success of his new toy was immediate and widespread, so he decided to start a company named after his invention, and Meccano Ltd. was born.

Meccano was soon acquired by the expanding arm of Hornby's construction empire. Early Meccano sets consisted of ½-inch (1.2-cm) wide tinplate strips, as well as wheels and rods that could be connected to holes in the strips to create working models. The sets were later improved when tinplate strips were replaced by nickel-plated steel. In 1926, the company introduced red-and-green colored metal strips.

Meccano is also credited with creating a spring-driven locomotive in 1915 that in turn inspired Frank Hornby to develop a completely separate line of toys—Hornby trains. The trains became popular in England from the 1920s onward, and as the railroad line grew, Hornby introduced a range of track accessories to complement the train sets. The early accessories are lithographed tinplate, but by 1931, lead figures were introduced as part of the Modelled Miniature series. The next step was to add die-cast lead vehicles, and in 1933, Hornby was responsible for introducing to the world a line of die-cast cars known as Dinky Toys. The name is believed to have come from a friend of one of Frank's daughters, and is believed to be a diminutive of the Scottish word "dink" that means neat or fine. The company continued to flourish and grow even after Frank Hornby's death in 1936.

Following the example of Tootsietoy in America, Dinky stopped using lead in 1937 and adopted injection-mold processes using a magnesium and zinc alloy called mazac. Dinky discovered the importance of keeping the mazac mixture free of contaminates. A toy made with the alloy should be indestructible, but impurities introduced to the mixture cause a chain reaction, resulting in problems with the molding process. These problems compromised the quality of the toys and resulted in distorted vehicles with minor cracks—some simply crumbled into pieces.

DINKY TOY SET #24, 1930s

This assortment of seven luxury vehicles and an ambulance showcases popular car designs of the day.

$200–$400 (for the set)

An original box insert is shown here, listing both the parent company, "Meccano," and the subsidiary, "Dinky Toys."

Having received multiple consumer complaints about the quality of Dinky's toys, the company tried to be very careful with the alloy mixture. It continued to produce a variety of vehicle series until 1941, when toy production stopped and the manufacturing of war supplies took over.

When the war ended, toy production resumed slowly. With no time to design a new line, Dinky had no choice but to reissue a selection of pre-war vehicles, this time using thicker axles, a perfected method of creating the alloy mixture that was virtually contaminate-free, and a toned-down palette of colors. As the decade progressed, Dinky introduced a variety of successful new toy lines, including Supertoys, Guy Series, and a range of commercial, racing, sports, and military vehicles.

The mid-1950s saw a new look in the production of Dinky

Toys. A more vibrant color palette added more luster to the line and signaled a return to pre-war production vitality. But the retooling and marketing of the new line took its toll, and a liquidity crisis in 1964 forced the board of Meccano Ltd. to sell Dinky to Triang, its main competitor. Dinky Toys continued to be made by Triang for another 15 years.

DINKY TOYS, 1940s
This assortment of die-cast industrial vehicles, complete with boxes, features a police van, a Philips truck, a crane truck, and a pair of vans.
$40–$80 each

IDENTIFICATION

◆ pre-war vehicles have thin axles and smooth, unridged hubs, are finished in primary colors, and often display metal fatigue

◆ post-war vehicles have thicker axles and ridged hubs and are finished in drab colors

WHAT TO LOOK FOR:

◆ company markings on the boxes and on the undersides of the vehicles

◆ all vehicles have open windows

INSIDER'S TIPS

To maintain the condition of your die-cast collectible, keep it in moderate temperatures out of direct sunlight, and handle it carefully. This should ensure the longevity of your piece.

Hot Wheels

Hot Wheels became a popular brand for the mega-giant toy manufacturer Mattel. However, the company itself had very humble beginnings. In 1945, working out of a garage workshop in El Segundo, Calilfornia, the original founders, Harold Matson and Elliot Handler, created the name Mattel by combining letters of their last and first names. The company began producing picture frames, though Elliot had a side business for doll furniture made from picture-frame scraps. His relative success put more focus on the company's toy output.

Poor health forced Matson to sell his shares in the new company to Handler and Handler's wife Ruth. The success of their doll furniture made way for a line of musical toys. In 1955, the Handlers revolutionized the way toys were marketed by buying 52 weeks of advertising on the new *Mickey Mouse Club* TV show: the first time toys had been advertised on a year-round basis. In conjunction with the company's sponsorship of the show, a child-size Mouse Guitar was introduced, and Mattel had another industry sensation on its hands.

Four years later, lightning struck again with a toy inspired by Ruth's observation of her young daughter playing with cutout paper dolls. Ruth created a three-dimensional doll that girls could use to act out their dreams. The doll was named Barbie, after Ruth's real-life daughter. Since her introduction, over one billion Barbie dolls have been sold, making her the best-selling fashion doll in almost every major global market, with worldwide annual sales of $1.5 billion.

CLASSIC '32 FORD VICKY #6250, 1969–1971
A U.S.-made, customized 1932 Ford Victoria toy, this piece has a metal chassis, a plastic interior, an exposed metal engine, a smooth black roof, and red-striped tires.
$20–$50

WHAT TO LOOK FOR:

- cars made between 1968 and 1977 have red stripes on the tires
- in 1969, blister packs were introduced and are still used today; cars in their original blister packs have a higher value
- the 1968, the VW with metal chassis and exposed engine was produced in a very small quantity in metallic blue, metallic green, and enamel green; these have a value in the $700–$1,000 range
- in 1969, the VW Beach Bomb, with two surfboards mounted through the back window was discontinued; it is the rarest-ever Hot Wheels car, and if found, has a value in the $4,000–$7,000 range

As the 1960s progressed, so did the toy lines at Mattel. Barbie and friends were popular with little girls but what the company wanted was a toy that had the same popularity with boys. In 1968, it discovered the answer—Hot Wheels. Despite the fierce competition in the die-cast market, Mattel introduced its line as "the fastest metal cars in the world." The designers at Mattel discovered that their use of a special torsion-bar suspension and a low-friction wheel bearing had given them a competitive edge. The 16 original Hot Wheels models were an instant success, with their California styling and Spectra flame paint colors all contributing.

In 1998, Hot Wheels celebrated its 30th anniversary and reached a milestone when the two-billionth car was produced. That's quite something for a company that started in a garage workshop.

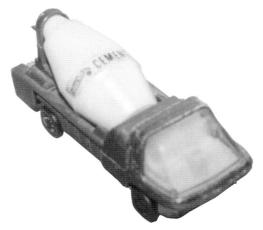

**CEMENT MIXER,
1970–1972**
The concept for the design of this truck was by Ira Gilford and features a metal chassis with a plastic truck bed and barrel that should have the Hot Wheels logo. The vehicle was made in a variety of colors, but white enamel is the rare color.
$20–$40,
$100–$200 white

**FIRE ENGINE #6454,
1970–1972**
The vehicle has a detachable trailer and should have a ladder. The loss of the ladder, a common occurence, cuts the value of the vehicle in half.
$10–$20

**MOVING VAN,
1970–1972**
This truck has the Hot Wheels logo on the side panels, a swivelling cab, and a rear trailer door that opens.
$20–$60

Lesney Matchbox

Leslie Smith and Rodney Smith first met as schoolboys, and then lost touch with each other, only to meet again in 1940, when both were serving with the British Royal Navy. The two men shared a dream of owning their own businesses, and once World War II was over, they achieved their goal together. On June 19, 1947, they formed Lesney Products, the name being a combination of their first names— "Les" from Leslie and "ney" from Rodney.

The partners started out slowly, making pressure die-cast products for industrial use. In 1953, they introduced a novel line of small die-cast replicas of real-life vehicles and registered the trade name Matchbox. They coined this name because they had created boxes for their cars based on the design of Norvic Safety Match boxes.

The company did well with its die-cast vehicles, and in 1969, it introduced Superfast models to compete with the hugely successful Hot Wheels cars. In the 1970s, a new line of vintage vehicles, called Yesteryears, was introduced. The new line was an instant success. By 1978, the company was on top of the world; at the peak of its success, it was producing millions of toys a week.

The late 1970s brought many market changes. Matchbox suffered a fire and a flood which destroyed much of its factory in Rochford, England. Competition became an increasing problem for the firm and finally led to bankruptcy on June 11, 1982. The firm was taken out of receivership when Universal International of Hong Kong purchased it. Ten years later, in 1992, Tyco bought Universal, and the Matchbox brand was transferred to Tyco Toys. In 1997, Mattel took over Tyco Toys and currently owns the Matchbox brand.

LESNEY MATCHBOX SERIES GIFT SET G-5
This set features nine Army vehicles, together with its original box.
$100–$300

WHAT TO LOOK FOR:

◆ logo and company name on boxes
◆ undercarriage of the car carries the logo and company name

The undercarriage of a Matchbox car provides collectors with details on the vehicle.

Tootsietoy

Some of the earliest premium, or gift-with-purchase, toys were created by Tootsietoy, an offshoot of the Dowst Brothers Company, which in 1876 launched the highly successful *National Laundry Journal*. In 1893, Samuel Dowst visited the World's Columbian Exposition in Chicago and was struck by one of the exhibits, a typesetting machine called the Linotype. One of the things the new machine did was make possible the mass production of slogan buttons or pins, and it occured to Dowst that such items would make ideal premiums to help sell his magazine. The brothers first produced political giveaways and lead collar buttons, but by the turn of the century, they had begun to see the real potential of the premium market. To meet rising demand, they increased their production lines. In 1906, the Dowst company had great success with a miniature version of a Ford Model T. Over 50 million were sold. This success led to the production of many other vehicles, including a limousine with free-turning wheels, a Ford touring car, and a matching Ford pickup truck.

In 1922, the Dowst company introduced a line of metal doll furniture. That same year, the prospering toy division was named Tootsie, after the grand-daughter of one of the brothers. The Depression had a serious effect on the fortunes of the company,

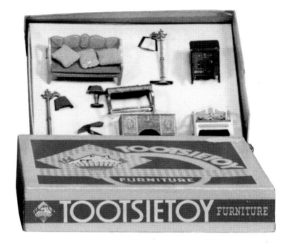

FURNITURE SET, 1930s

The quality and variety of the Tootsietoy line are evident from the graphics of the box top and the die cut insert inside the box.

$400–$700

but the appeal of their toys and low prices kept the firm competitive. Such products as the Tootsie Toy Speedway, the Airport Set, and a variety of car designs helped maintain customer interest, and the company survived the lean years. It even ventured into science fiction by producing a whole set of Buck Rogers spacecraft, called Flash Blast Attack Ships and Venus Duo-Destroyers.

WHAT TO LOOK FOR:

- logo usually on the bottom or underside of the toy
- small, colorful, metal toys cast in a mold; zinc replaced lead in the mid-1930s; lead toys are heavier, a useful indicator of the age of a piece

INSIDER'S TIPS

Look out for repainting or chipped paint on collectibles. This will significantly reduce the value of the piece.

If the paint has the appearance of being wet or too bright, chances are that it is not original.

CHARACTER TOYS

The popularity of character-based toys was linked to the widespread appeal of the comic strips that ran in the funny pages of most major newspapers across America in the early 1900s. The strips were written in serial format, and people became interested in the antics of their favorite comic characters. Toys were produced and distributed by companies like Borgfeldt, which was responsible for the Felix the Cat wind-up toy, and Marx, which manufactured a wide variety of Walt Disney character toys.

While manufacturers quickly learned that comic characters could generate huge profits, the owners of the rights to the characters began to realize the power of their properties. In the early 1930s, a young Walt Disney was trying to raise money to finance his new movie venture, and he allowed just about every company that approached him to use the images of his original five characters: Donald Duck, Mickey and Minnie Mouse, Pluto, and Goofy. This resulted in a market saturated with Disney creations, from Donald Duck bread wrappers to Mickey Mouse watches made by the Ingersoll Watch Company. But saturated or not, the funds that were raised helped finance the first full-length animated feature film ever made—*Snow White and the Seven Dwarfs*—which opened in 1937. The movie was a big success, and some toy companies such as Lionel, Knickerbocker, and Character Novelty clamored for permission to produce toys based on characters in the film.

For a time, Disney dominated the market. However, as film—and later, television—became popular, new studios sprang up, and with them came a whole range of new characters. Howdy Doody, Bugs Bunny, Charlie McCarthy, and Mortimer Snerd became sought-after characters in the toy market. Companies began to produce new toys, from wind-up and friction toys to marionettes and ventriloquist dummies, all in the characters' likenesses.

There is no doubt that character toys have always been popular—indeed, a large percentage of Disney profits are generated by its licensing activities. But for collectors, the central appeal of character toys is in the nostalgia they evoke for a time gone by.

Character toys are what I classify as crossover collectibles. A Mickey Mouse wind-up toy, for example, appeals to both collectors of wind-ups and collectors of character toys.

George Borgfeldt & Company

Although George Borgfeldt was not a toy maker, he made a significant contribution to the American toy business. He was a pioneer in toy licensing, which is a major part of the toy business today. In 1881, Borgfeldt created a wholesale importing business in partnership with brothers Marcell and Joseph Kahle. Borgfeldt died in 1903, but the firm Borgfeldt & Company acquired exclusive rights to a variety of copyrighted toys and subcontracted their production. The toys were marked with the company's "Nifty" logo, a smiling moon face which became the company's trademark.

By the late 1920s, Borgfeldt & Company owned the copyrights to Felix the Cat, Maggie & Jiggs, and Creeping Buttercup. In the late 1930s, the company became one of the first in America to represent Margarete Steiff (*see pages 143–144*) and started to import her mohair bears. Borgfeldt's expertise with comic characters coupled with Steiff's quality products opened the door to a collaboration which climaxed when they brought the newly popular Mickey Mouse to life in a plush incarnation.

In addition to comic-character toys, Borgfeldt & Company also distributed the ever-popular tinplate

BARNEY GOOGLE RIDING SPARK PLUG TOY, 1920s
This famous comic strip duo is made of lithographed tin, this toy is activated by a clockwork mechanism.
$500–$700

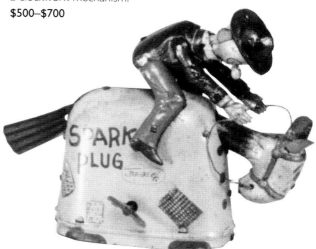

wind-up Toonerville Trolley and Highway Henry. These products continue to captivate collectors today. The firm finally closed its doors in 1962.

ALSO WORTH COLLECTING:

EFFanBEE

This popular American doll company was started in 1913 in New York City by Fleischaker and Baum. At the time, doll manufacturing in America was still quite a young industry, and many companies looked to the European makers to create their products. Effanbee decided to specialize in baby dolls; however, by 1915, the company had produced over a hundred other varieties. The dolls were all marked on the back or under the hairline with the name of the company, and sometimes with the name of the doll. The early pieces were made with human hair.

effanbee

Ingersoll Watch Company

In 1880, two brothers from Michigan named Ingersoll—Robert, age 21, and Charles, age 15—started the Ingersoll Watch Company in New York City. They created a pocket watch design and presented it to the Waterbury Clock Company, which produced 12,000 of them, each with a price tag of $1.50. Three years later, the brothers created another watch that sold for $1.00, and by 1895, production of their new design hit 15 million.

In 1899, their pocket watch captured the attention of Symond's, a London shop, which placed a million-dollar order. This prompted a new advertising slogan: "Ingersoll—the watch that made the dollar famous." The success of the company continued into the new century. In 1922, the Waterbury Clock Company bought out the Ingersoll brothers' company but continued to do business using the name of Ingersoll-Waterbury Company.

A decade later the new company struck a deal with Walt Disney to produce a wristwatch that featured Mickey Mouse on the face and three little mice chasing each other on the second-hand dial. The watch came in a cardboard case that featured the popular Disney characters of 1933, including Mickey and Minnie Mouse, Pluto the Pup, and Clarabelle the Cow. The watches were a huge success, and the company continued production, adding images of Donald Duck, the Big Bad Wolf, and the Three Little Pigs. Novelty alarm clocks were also added to the line. The Ingersoll company ceased production in 1944.

MICKEY MOUSE WRISTWATCH, 1950s
This watch has its original box and insert. Mickey's design and the overall graphic style help date the watch.
$200–$400

MICKEY MOUSE WRISTWATCH, 1930s
The chain-link, wind-up watch features Mickey Mouse and comes with the original box.
$200–$800

WHAT TO LOOK FOR:

◆ on the 1933 watch, Mickey Mouse wears yellow gloves, and the word "Ingersoll" is printed on the face

◆ in 1934, the watch was also marked "Made in the USA"

◆ in 1938, the words "© W.D. Ent." were added

INSIDER'S TIPS

Look for watches complete with cardboard case and watch fob.

Most watches were overwound and are nonfunctioning today, but this should not affect the overall value of the piece.

Look for repairs or repainting on the boxes of the early watches.

NOVELTY TOYS

Toy makers are constantly on the lookout for new ideas and designs in the hope of creating the next breakout toy sensation—the runaway bestseller that becomes a national obsession and shakes up toy markets around the world. Unfortunately, only a small percentage of toys ever attain the cult collectible status of such classics as the Daisy BB gun and the A.C. Gilbert Erector Set.

These toys fall into what I call the novelty category because of their originality and because they do not necessarily fit into other categories of collectible toys. While not necessarily an obvious fit in this category, Wyandotte toys have been included here because they came from an unusual source—the All Metal Products Company, which specialized in automotive parts, dustpans, and basket trays—and because Wyandotte products had such a huge impact when they were introduced.

The toys in this category appeal to a special band of collectors who actively seek them out. In the wider world of toy collecting, these toys are usually regarded as an occasional passing fancy.

It has been my experience as I travel around the country doing appraisals that novelty toys are less popular than other categories of collectible toys. One reason, I think, for this lack of popularity is that novelty toys like the Daisy BB Gun were used heavily, often neglected or abused by their owners, and then discarded. Those that turn up in good condition are indeed sought after by collectors, but their popularity never quite matches that of toys in other categories. It's worth remembering, though, that markets fluctuate and people's tastes and collecting habits change. In order to be a successful collector, one must keep up with trends and changing conditions that affect the "collectability" of an item.

Novelty toys need to be looked after and conserved in the same way as other toys—carefully. Keep them safe, clean, dry, and away from direct sunlight and excessive heat, and your novelty toy collectibles will give you years of enjoyment. Keep Erector Sets in their original boxes, and if you have the original instructions, hang on to them. They only increase the value of your set.

Daisy Manufacturing Company, Inc.

The Daisy Manufacturing Company can trace its roots back to the Plymouth Iron Windmill Company in Plymouth, Michigan, which manufactured windmills for the farms of the Midwest and Great Plains in the early 1880s. As sales began to decline, the company decided to develop new products to attract new customers. In 1886, company inventor Clarence Hamilton came up with a revolutionary new item: a combination of metal and wire, vaguely resembling a gun, that could fire a lead ball using compressed air. During a demonstration, the then-president of the company, Lewis Cass Hough, gave the gun a try and enthusiastically exclaimed, "Boy, that's a daisy!" The name stuck, and the very first Daisy BB guns went into production. The first ones were given away as premiums to farmers when they purchased a windmill; later they were sold as toys. In the first year, 86,000 were sold. The guns were so popular that on January 26, 1895, the directors agreed to change the company name to the Daisy Manufacturing Company, Inc.

In the late 1920s, the funny papers and their comic-strip characters were becoming a significant part of American popular culture. Daisy latched onto a futuristic comic hero named Buck Rogers, whose adventures as a spaceman in the 25th century were popular with both adults and children. The strip, which began in 1929, generated toys and premiums from several companies. Daisy capitalized on the science-fiction craze by creating several versions of Buck Rogers's Atomic Detonator Pistol.

Sensing that comic characters were useful as marketing tools, the company then turned to a cowboy who first appeared in the comic pages in 1935 as Bronc Peeler. By 1938, the character had evolved into Red Ryder, the company's most popular creation. The Daisy Red Ryder, coveted by every young American boy, became a household name. More than nine million Red Ryders were sold.

The Daisy company has maintained continuous production since that time. Based in Rogers, Arkansas, since 1958, today Daisy is considered the world's oldest and largest manufacturer of air guns, ammunition, and accessories.

HANDGUN #80, 1930s
The metal toy pistol shown here has the company name and logo incised into the handle.
$200–$400

WHAT TO LOOK FOR:

- early guns are marked "Daisy Mfg. by Iron Wind Mill Co. Plymouth Mich. Pat. Apd. For"

- later guns are marked "Daisy Mfg.," along with a name, a single letter, a combination of letters and numbers or a number and model, e.g., No. 121, Model 40

- names of some of the Daisy guns include Bull's Eye, Dewey, Hero, Dandy, and Atlas

- every Daisy product has the name of the company and patent information somewhere on the item

A.C. Gilbert Company

Born in 1884, Alfred Carlton Gilbert entered Yale University Medical School at age 20 and helped support himself by performing magic shows. In 1908, Gilbert established the Mysto Magic Company with John Petrie, a machinist who had a mutual interest in magic and manufactured magic props. By 1909, they were manufacturing boxed sets of magic equipment for the wholesale trade. Gilbert took care of sales and promotion, while Petrie produced the magic sets.

In 1911, Gilbert bought out Petrie and changed the direction of the company, turning his sights toward engineering and construction toys. His new Erector Sets were the first-ever American construction toys equipped with moving parts and motors. Introduced at the toy fairs of 1913, Erector Sets became an instant success, thanks in part to Gilbert's marketing savvy. He immediately initiated a media blitz with a series of ads in local and national magazines. The success of the new line was also due to the public's interest in construction during a major building boom in America. Originally priced from $1.00 to $25.00, Gilbert's new line of toys was awarded a gold medal at the Panama Pacific Exposition in 1915 and went on to sell more than 30 million units over the next 40 years.

In 1916, Gilbert's company underwent major changes: It was renamed the A.C. Gilbert Company and moved to a five-block complex in New Haven, Connecticut. New products were also launched,

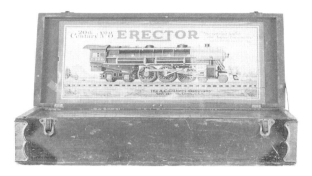

ERECTOR SET NO. 8, 1940s
This set features a super locomotive and a New York Central tender. The box (above) is original.
$800–$1,200

including a line of pressed-steel cars and trucks and a line of educational scientific toys.

In that same year, Gilbert became the first president of the Toy Manufacturers of America, an organization set up by him to further the interests of American toy manufacturers after the embargo on German products was lifted following the war.

By 1938, Gilbert had taken over the American Flyer Corporation, relocating the entire operation from Chicago to New Haven. He redesigned the look and packaging of the trains, but retained the American Flyer name. Gilbert's magic helped revive sales, and American Flyer once again competed with Lionel Trains, the market leader at the time.

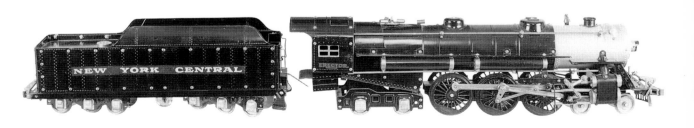

Wyandotte Toys

Located in Wyandotte, Michigan, the All Metal Products Company was formed by George Stallings and William F. Schmidt in 1920. Although the partners had originally intended to produce automobile parts, they decided instead to focus on the manufacture of guns and rifles. Toys produced by All Metal were marked and labeled Wyandotte Toys. In nine years, the company expanded production of their streamlined wheeled toys to include pressed-steel airplanes, automobiles, racers, mechanical toys, musical tops, pressed-steel dustpans, baskets, trays, and playhouse toys, many of which sold for a dime during the Depression.

The 1930s proved to be the best decade for the company, and by 1935, Wyandotte had distributed over five million toy guns worldwide. It was during this decade that the company produced its large pressed-steel automobiles with a fine enamel finish and battery-powered lights. Over the next two decades, the company underwent many management changes and reorganizations, including the acquisition of the Hafner Train Company in 1950. After plastic toys became all the rage in the mid-1950s, All Metal was not able to keep up with the times, due to poor corporate leadership. The company filed for bankruptcy on November 6, 1956.

LA SALLE SEDAN, c. 1930

The sleek design of the red, pressed-steel vehicle shown here features white rubber tires. The simplicity of the art deco style is illustrated in the fenders and in the slopes and curves throughout the toy.
$300–$400

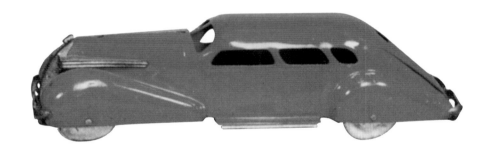

CRANE TRUCK, 1940s
This pressed-steel industrial vehicle has rounded tenders, a front bumper, and rubber tires.
$200–$300

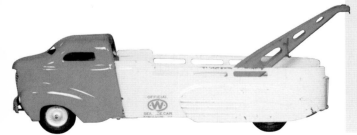

WHAT TO LOOK FOR:

♦ streamlined designs and futuristic features
♦ round fender crowns, concealed headlights in the fenders, or "teardrop" wheel covers
♦ the label or box top will be marked "Wyandotte Toys"
♦ the company slogan, "Wyandotte toys are good and safe," is also featured on many of the company's products

BATTERY-OPERATED TOYS

Battery-operated toys, especially those with elaborate or multiple movements, have been very popular among collectors over the years. Early examples of battery-operated toys were made entirely of tinplate or metal. It was during the later 1950s that manufacturers slowly began introducing plastic parts. This transition from metal to plastic aids in dating the toy: The more plastic used in a toy's construction, the newer it is.

Collectors of this category of toys need to pay special attention to the battery chamber, which is susceptible to corrosion. Check to make sure that there is no corrosion, but also be sure that the chamber has not been replaced, as both those factors will reduce the value of the toy.

Mass-produced, battery-operated toys had rudimentary wiring that shorted out easily, causing some of the actions to malfunction. Since these toys were played with heavily and their original boxes were quickly discarded, collectors now look for toys in good working condition with their original boxes. Such items will always command higher prices.

Condition, however, is not the only factor affecting the value of battery-operated toys. The number of actions a toy perfoms is also a key consideration. Most battery-operated toys perform two simple actions over and over again. Because toys that perform three or more actions are relatively rare, collectors will pay a premium for them.

It is important to remember not to store batteries in the toy. Always remove them when the toy is not in use. Keep the toys out of direct sunlight to ensure that the paint does not fade and the finish does not become dull.

If a toy has a hand-held battery chamber with controls, the toy dates from the early 1950s. Internal battery chambers on toys are typical for toys made in the late 1950s and 1960s.

I grew up in the 1960s, when battery-operated toys were really popular. Now that my generation has some disposable income, we account for the majority of battery-operated toy collectors today. I have a close friend and fellow toy collector who shares her toys with her two sons; she focuses on collecting the toys she remembers from her childhood and teaches her boys to distinguish between "Mommy's toys" and their toys. The boys are a pair of new collectors in training! It is never too early or too late to start collecting.

ALPS

The distinctive logo of this Japanese company (*see "What to Look For" box below*) makes its toys easy to identify. ALPS made battery-operated mechanical toys, and the company produced some of the better-quality Japanese toys throughout the post-war years. Many of its toys had multiple actions; for example, a convertible car would not only move forward and back, but the top would also roll down and go back up. This ingenuity ensured the toys' popularity, and for a time, they were in great demand.

However, despite their success, ALPS abandoned toy making some time in the early 1970s to become a manufacturer of consumer and industrial electronics. The company remains in the electronics business today.

GRANDPA BEAR, 1950s

This plush gray bear sits on a tin rocking chair mounted on a colorful floor base. Grandpa Bear is able to smoke his pipe as he rocks.
$200–$400

MUSICAL MARCHING BEAR, 1950s

This musical bear has a remote control. It consists of a plush upper body, fabric pants, and tin lithographed shoes.
$200–$400

Note the hand-held battery chamber and toy control.

WHAT TO LOOK FOR:

◆ quality-built, battery-operated toys
◆ battery-operated toys that perform multiple actions
◆ company logo

Cragston

Cragston was a U.S.-based toy marketing and distribution firm that specialized in importing mechanical and battery-operated toys made in post-war Japan. The company focused on toys with multiple actions and made sure its company name appeared on the highly decorated boxes in which they were sold. It is believed that the company's name was derived from a combination of the owners' names. They continued to operate through the mid-1960s.

The toys manufactured by this company are more sophisticated and detailed than the battery-operated toys made by other companies. A combination of factors—the more complicated actions of the toys, the attention to costuming detail, and the fine lithography on the toys and boxes—help set this company apart from the rest.

MR. FOX THE MAGICIAN, 1950s

Mr. Fox stands on a colorful lithographed base. When activated, this battery-operated toy performs the popular disappearing rabbit trick.

$200–$400

Since the boxes were usually disposed of, finding a toy with the box is a bonus for collectors.

WHAT TO LOOK FOR:

◆ multiple-action toys
◆ highly decorated boxes
◆ company name on box

ALSO WORTH COLLECTING:

Bandai

Based in Tokyo, this Japanese toy maker started production in 1950, focusing on the manufacturing of toy mechanical vehicles, primarily those that were battery-operated. Over 50 years later, this powerhouse of Japanese toy making has become Japan's largest and most successful manufacturer of toys. Bandai is best known for manufacturing its line of Mighty Morphin' Power Ranger action figures and accessories.

Linemar

Linemar was established in the 1950s as a manufacturing and import subsidiary of the successful American toy manufacturer Louis Marx & Company (*see pages 96 and 113*). The company was responsible for overseas manufacturing and distribution relationships involving the importation of mechanical and battery-operated toys from Japan. Marx was able to secure several important character licenses, such as Popeye and the Flintstones, and had the toys made in Japan to keep the cost down. This meant huge profits when the toys were sold in the United States. Linemar continued to produce a variety of character toys until it went out of business in the 1960s.

R-35 ROBOT, c. 1950s

This metallic-blue, lithographed tin toy has elaborate graphics on its chest and a cylindrical head with light-bulb eyes. The battery box has colorful, lithographed robot images on it. **$700–$1,400**

The battery chamber for this toy doubles as the control box and features great graphics.

TINPLATE POPEYE AND OLIVE OYL PLAYING BALL, 1950s

The lithographed tin clockwork figures toss the ball back and forth when the toy is wound. **$1,000–$1,500**

This early, tinplate, wind-up toy from Linemar comes with this odd-shaped box.

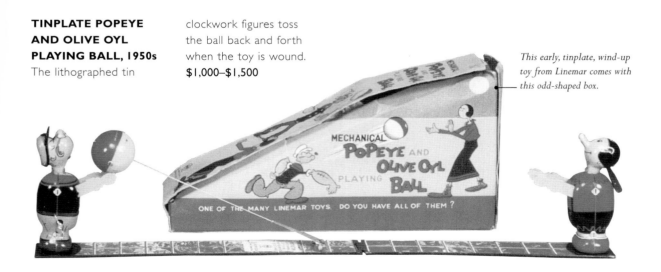

SMOKING SPACEMAN, 1950s
Colored dark gray, this tinplate robot has eyes that light up and a mouth that emits smoke. The batteries are housed in the toy's legs.
$800–$1,200

WIMPY MECHANICAL TRICYCLE, 1940s
This colorful, lithographed tin toy features Wimpy seated on a tricycle that is operated by a clockwork mechanism.
$300–$600

ALSO WORTH COLLECTING:
Linemar Wind-up Toys

The mechanical toys produced by Linemar include a variety of licensed character toys that performed multiple actions when the toys were wound. The packaging was always colorful and eye-catching. As demand now starts to exceed supply, these toys are increasing in collectability and value. The Disney characters are the most popular, followed closely by Popeye and his crew and the Flintstones from prehistoric Bedrock.

"Made in Japan"

Prior to World War II, toys manufactured in Japan were usually marked "Japan." At the end of World War II, the United States occupied Japan (from 1945 to 1952) and helped rebuild its battered economy, which depended heavily on the manufacture and export of novelties, ceramic items, and toys. To satisfy export requirements, such products had to be marked "Occupied Japan." This requirement ended with the occupation on April 28, 1952. Toys made after that date were marked simply "Made in Japan." But due to the relatively short time in which they were produced, "Occupied Japan" toys have become collector favorites.

However, just to complicate matters, certain items made during the occupation may only have been marked "Japan," while the boxes in which they were packed were marked "Occupied Japan"; this is because the toys were already in production when the new labeling requirements were introduced.

Only the boxes were relabeled to expedite shipping.

The generic label "Made in Japan" most often appears on wind-up toys, friction toys, and battery-operated toys. The golden years of Japanese toy production indisputably were the 1950s and 1960s, when a fantastic array of tin mechanical toys powered by inertia, friction motors, clockwork, or batteries were produced by the million. These toys flooded the American market and dominated the marketplace. The tin cars made during this period provide a history of vehicles in miniature and are eagerly sought after by collectors today. Some of the best space toys and robots were manufactured in Japan during the 1960s and illustrate the worldwide fascination with space travel.

A company logo may accompany the "Made in Japan" label. The most common of these are Nomura, Yoshiya, Ichida, Horikawa, Shudo, Bandai, ALPS, Linemar, Masudaya, and Aoshin.

GROUPING OF "MADE IN JAPAN" ROCKET SHIPS, 1960
This group includes three large-scaled, tin lithographed rockets, each designed with great detail and featuring extensive graphics.
$200–$300

WHAT TO LOOK FOR:

◆ toys usually marked "Made in Japan" or "Japan"

◆ simple tinplate, wind-up, or battery-operated toys

Plastic is an entirely synthetic material derived from petroleum. It is pliable and easy to mold when soft, and hardens quickly. It is the perfect material for manufacturing durable and safe toys. Plastic was first used in toy production after World War II, and came to dominate the industry in the 1970s.

For the purposes of this book, plastic toys means those manufactured during the later part of the 20th century. The toys in this category have survived partly because of the lack of attention paid to them by their owners, perhaps because they were thrown in a drawer on Christmas Day and forgotten. But they were also introduced at a time when collectors were becoming more sophisticated in their habits. Many people saved the packaging and took better care of their toys. The result is that a vast supply of plastic toys in great condition is available to collectors at affordable prices.

The best rule of thumb in this area of collecting is to collect whatever you are attracted to, and look for the first or last in a series. Generally, collectors pay more for the first and last of a series. Only time will tell how this market will mature.

In the case of *Star Wars* plastic action figures, those made after the 1977 release of the original film are more popular with collectors and always generate a higher price than toys from the sequels and prequels. When the hype builds for the next installment to be released, new collectors enter the arena looking for older toys to add to their collections. When the hype cools, so do collectors' appetites.

Collectors need to be mindful of the millions of dollars spent on advertising to push the action figures from the latest Hollywood blockbuster. In some cases, the toys fare better than the movie, or they both bomb and the toys end up on the clearance shelf, only to be resurrected years later in the secondary market. An example is Disney's *Rocketeer*. The movie did poorly, catapulting the licensed products into the clearance aisle. Today, some of the action figures from the film are selling for more than original retail prices because so few were bought at the time. They become desirable for collectors because of the "movie bomb" factor.

Hasbro, Inc.

Textile remnants, pencil boxes, and school supplies were the first products sold by this family-owned company, founded in 1923 by two Polish immigrant brothers, Henry and Helal Hassenfeld. Hassenfeld Brothers, which would eventually become Hasbro, Inc., was an immediate success, and by 1939 had annual sales of $500,000.

Henry's son Merrill took over as president of the company in 1943, and three years later, he added toys to the firm's product line. Doctor and nurse kits, wax crayons, and paint sets were introduced, and by the late 1940s, Hassenfeld Brothers posted annual sales figures of $3 million. The company continued to grow, experiment, and expand its toy lines to satisfy the interests of a growing children's market.

In the 1950s, the company developed an American popular culture icon, Mr. Potato Head, which holds the distinction of being the first toy ever advertised on television. In 1964, the firm introduced G.I. Joe, which became one of the most successful toys ever marketed in America. This new market of boys' action figures won widespread popularity. Keeping things in the family, Merrill's son Stephen joined the company to oversee production.

During the 1980s, Hasbro acquired Glenco Infant items, Knickerbocker Toy Company, Milton Bradley, Playskool, and Child Guidance products that included Tinkertoys and some Ideal games. Also during this decade, the company was renamed Hasbro, Inc., with sales topping the $1 billion mark.

The combined business deals of the 1980s provided a springboard for the company and brought with them a greater level of profitability, allowing Hasbro to continue to make more acquisitions. In 1991, Hasbro took over the Tonka Corporation, which included Kenner and Parker Brothers, providing the company with an impressive array of classic brands

that include Tonka Trucks, Monopoly, Nerf, Easy-Bake Ovens, Clue, and Play-doh, producing over $3 billion in sales yearly by the late 1990s. The company continues to follow the vision firmly established by the Hassenfeld brothers back in 1923.

G.I. JOE ACTION FIGURES, 1960s
This ever-popular action figure for boys comes with a wide range of outfits and accessories. Pictured here are a military policeman, an action sailor and an explorer. **$75–$125 each**

IDENTIFICATION

◆ markings on toy and box:
   1923–1968: Hassenfeld Brothers
   1968–1985: Hasbro Industries, Inc.
   1986–Present: Hasbro, Inc.

Kenner

This company's famous name lives on even after multiple corporate takeovers, mainly because its products have worked their way into the very fabric of American popular culture. The company was founded in 1947 by three brothers, Al, Phil, and Joe Steiner, who named it after Kenner Street in Cincinnati, Ohio. It's first big hit that year was Bubbl-Matic, followed in 1955 by the cultural icon known as Play-doh. Despite its takeover in 1967 by General Mills, Kenner continued to expand its line of toys under its own name.

In 1977, lightning struck in the form of a movie called *Star Wars*. Having secured the licensing rights, the company fell behind in toy production and could not fill the voluminous orders for the Christmas season. That Christmas shopping season in 1977 marked the debut of the "it" toy, the yearly phenomenon that turns rational parents into consumer maniacs. Facing a huge potential loss, Kenner devised a plan to issue chits or IOUs to be redeemed when the toys became available. With little other choice, the public bought into the plan, and Kenner was able to make good on all the chits by February of 1978. Between 1977 and 1984, over 300 million *Star Wars* toys were manufactured.

In 1985, General Mills acquired Parker Brothers and merged it with Kenner to create Kenner Parker Toys, the fourth-largest toy company at that time. Three years later, General Mills sold Kenner Parker to the Tonka Corporation. That association ended in 1991, when Hasbro acquired the Kenner name and legacy.

WHAT TO LOOK FOR:

- logos and markings on toys and box:
1947–1967:	Kenner
1967–1985:	Kenner became a division of General Mills
1988–1991:	Kenner became a division of Tonka

- 1991–Present: Kenner became part of the Hasbro toy empire

- *Star Wars* toys made since the film's 1977 release are desirable and popular with collectors; the better the condition the higher the value

TUSCAN RAIDER, GAMOREAN GUARD, AND AT-AT DRIVER, 1990s
These plastic action figures represent secondary characters from the *Star Wars* empire of toys that defined popular culture at the end of the 20th century.
$10–$75 each (depending on condition)

INSIDER'S TIPS

The collecting of Star Wars toys has been hyped by the media, TV shopping channels, and trade shows at which the actors make appearances. The hook here is the "limited edition." But do not be taken in by these greedy marketing tactics. You should collect what you like, and if you are looking for action figures, then be sure to do your homework. Be aware of the misrepresented claims of outrageous prices for items in the marketplace. Believe in what you know and not what you are told. Kenner manufactured a variety of Star Wars toys, and it is important to be able to identify the rare items from the more common ones. The following is a list of the large Kenner action figures that were only produced for three years, along with their estimated values.

STAR WARS FIGURES, CHARACTER & HEIGHT	VALUE UNBOXED	VALUE BOXED
Ben (Obi-Wan) Kenobi – 12 inches (30.5 cm) White robe with black collar, brown robe with hood, brown boots, and yellow lightsaber	$100–$200	$200–$400
Boba Fett – 13.5 inches (34.3 cm) Swing-up "range-finder," green cape, rifle, backpack, rocket, two Wookiee scalps, and belt	$100–$200	$200–$400
Chewbacca – 15 inches (38 cm) Crossbow rifle and bandolier with 16 removable gray plastic inserts	$50–$100	$100–$300
C-3PO – 12.5 inches (31.8 cm) No clothes or accessories	$40–$60	$100–$200
Han Solo – 12.5 inches (31.8 cm) Black pants, white shirt, black vinyl vest, boots, pistol, holster, and gold plastic medallion on red ribbon	$250–$350	$400–$700
IG-88 – 15 inches (38 cm) Brown bandolier with four red grenades, pistol, and rifle	$200–$400	$500–$800
Jawa – 8 inches (20.3 cm) Brown hooded robe, X-shaped bandolier, and rifle	$50–$150	$200–$400
Luke Skywalker – 12 inches (30.5 cm) Tan pants, white shirt, white boots, belt, grappling hook on string, and blue lightsaber	$200–$300	$200–$400
Princess Leia – 12 inches (30.5 cm) Fiber hair held in original bun style by two plastic rings, white stockings, white plastic shoes, blue plastic comb, and brush; a hairstyle booklet also originally came with this figure	$100–300	$300–$400
R2-D2 – 7.5 inches (19 cm) Back panel opens to hold two removable "circuit boards"	$50–$100	$100–$300
Stormtrooper – 12 inches (30.5 cm) Rifle can be secured to waist of figure with black thread loop	$100–$200	$200–$400

FOREIGN PACKAGING:

The Kenner small action figures were marketed in foreign countries by several different companies:

Palitoy	United Kingdom
Meccano	France
Harbert	Italy
Glassite	Brazil
Lili-Lily	Mexico
Popy	Japan

The artwork on the foreign packaging may vary. However, all the manufacturers used blister cards, except in Japan, where a boxed *Empire* series was released. Only Palitoy's line rivaled the graphics used for the United States packaging. Foreign figures complete with packaging and in similar condition have a value about 25 percent higher than their U.S. counterparts.

POPULAR-CULTURE TOYS
1970s–1990s

The many shocks of the 1970s included the killing of 11 Israeli athletes by Palestinian terrorists at the 1972 Munich Olympic Games, the Watergate scandal and the resulting resignation of President Richard Nixon in 1974, and the Iranian hostage crisis of 1979. But if the 1972 Olympics were marred by bloodshed, the 1976 Olympics in Montreal were marked by perfection: Nadia Comenici's string of perfect 10s— a first in Olympic history. On the toy front, G.I. Joe became the first popular action figure for boys, and Hot Wheels rolled off the assembly line by the millions. Also during this decade, new and stringent child-safety regulations were first introduced, forcing some toy companies out of business altogether.

As more American households became equipped with TV sets, toy manufacturers realized the power of the medium and began targeting the growing audience of children watching Saturday morning cartoon shows. Companies like Hasbro, Kenner, and Mattel all used the medium to successfully get the word out about their new toy lines as well as information on new clothing and accessories made specifically for toys like G.I. Joe and Barbie.

Toy companies were well aware of the value of accessories to their bottom lines and encouraged young consumers to keep adding such items to their collections. Today, some accessories for G.I. Joe and Barbie are more desirable to collectors than the figures themselves.

During the last years of the century, action films created a huge market for action toys, tying the fortunes of the toy industry ever more closely to Hollywood blockbuster movies. *Star Wars*, for example, with its sequels and prequels, has generated an entire empire of spinoff toys and products—one of the largest such collections in the history of film and film-based toys. The introduction of "limited edition" and "collector's edition" toys stoked collectors' enthusiasm for certain popular items.

The battery-operated toys that had been popular in the 1960s were overtaken during this period by electronic games. Early games, like Pac-Man, were played on the family TV set; later versions required a hand-held device. And as the 20th century drew to a close, early American tinplate and cast-iron toys could finally be classified as antiques, having reached the requisite age of 100!

Lesney Matchbox

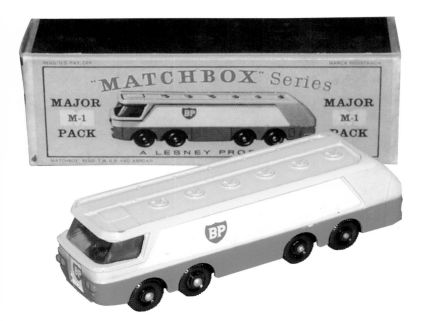

BP TRUCK, 1960s
This die-cast vehicle bears the familiar logo of British Petroleum and is shown with its original box.
$50–$100

ATLANTIC PRIME MOVER c. 1960s
The die-cast truck shown here is painted orange and features a spare tire in the bed of the truck and a trailer hitch to haul other Matchbox accessories. It is shown with its original box, which significantly adds to the value of the toy. Matchbox items without boxes are less valuable. This item sold at Christie's South Kensington in May of 2001 for $2,000. The market is stronger in the United Kingdom than in the United States for these toys.
$600–$800

INTERNATIONAL COMBINE HARVESTER, 1970s

This tiny harvester is an accurate rendition of a real one, but it has suffered the plight of most playthings. It has chips on the front that affect its value.
$5–$10

PONTIAC FIREBIRD, 1970s

This sporty and flashy car has several paint flakes, as often happens on cars that are not looked after correctly.
$5–$10

TIPPER CONTAINER TRUCK #47, 1970s

This industrial vehicle has a working dump bed and is marked on the undercarriage with the company's logo.
$10–$20

Hot Wheels

AUBURN #843, 1975

This car is part of the Flying Colors set, a line of 25 new cars in a brand new palette introduced in 1975. It is in its original blister pack with its colorful cardboard backing.
$20–$50

DOOZIE #31, 1977

This model was first introduced in 1977 and is a copy of a 1931 Duesenberg Dual Cowl Phaeton. This car is shown in a blister pack with original graphics on the card.
$20–$50

DUAL-LANE CURVE PAK #6477

This pack includes a curved, banked track for side-by-side, figure-8 racing, and two cars.
$20–$30

TORENO #6260, 1969–1971

This concept car was made in the U.S. and designed by Ira Gilford. It features a metal chassis and engine, a lift-up hood, red-striped tires, and clear plastic windows.

$10–$40

CUSTOM AMX #6267, 1967–1971

Based on the American motors AMX, this model has a metal chassis, a white plastic interior, a lift-up hood revealing a metal engine, clear windows, and red-striped wheels. Pink or purple paint adds $100 to the value.

$50–$75

CUSTOM CORVETTE #6215, 1968–1971

The metalic light-green car features a metal chassis, a plastic interior, red-striped tires, and a lift-up hood. The car was made in a variety of colors.

$100–$300

ROCKET-BYE-BABY #61816, 1971–1972

Designed by Bob Lovejoy, this Hong-Kong-made concept car has a metal chassis, a metal rocket on the roof, red-striped tires, a blue-tinted windshield, and pop-out engine covers. Almost all the metal rockets are tarnished but can easily be cleaned.

$40–$100

Linemar

ROBOT, 1950s
This battery-operated tinplate toy has a hand-held control that doubles as a battery chamber. It is shown in its original box
$200–$400

JOE THE XYLOPHONE PLAYER, 1960s
This amusing, lithographed, tinplate and cloth toy is activated by a clockwork mechanism. The box is original.
$100–$300

POP UP OLIVE OYL SQUEAKER TOY, 1950s
This interesting toy, made of composition with a tin-wire body frame, wears a red and black outfit and holds a colorful umbrella. It includes a neck tag that reads "Push Me Down and I'll Pop Up." Shown with its original box.
$1,000–$1,500

Linemar and ALPS

LINEMAR MECHANICAL GOOFY, 1950s

This lithographed tinplate Goofy wearing a colorful outfit is activated by a clockwork mechanism. It is shown with its original box, which adds greatly to its value.
$400–$800

ALPS TELEVISION SPACEMAN, 1960s

Here is a combination of television and science fiction, merged to produce a battery-operated toy that has a higher value when it comes with its original box.
$400–$800

TPS

MECHANICAL SKATING CHEF, 1950s

This lithographed tinplate toy depicts a chef wearing cloth pants and an apron, in a comical position holding a tray of food. Activated by a clockwork mechanism, he skates across the floor. The original box has colorful graphics.
$300–$500

MECHANICAL CIRCUS CYCLIST, 1950s

The comic toy shown here features an elaborately made-up clown riding on a tricycle that is made of tinplate and cloth. When wound, the bell rings, and the toy moves across the floor. It is shown with its original box.
$300–$400

Cragston

SPACE MAN, c. 1950
This lithographed tinplate astronaut is dressed in a spacesuit. It has battery controls and its original box.
$1,500–$2,500

SAM THE SHAVING MAN, 1960s
This lithographed, tinplate and plastic, battery-operated toy goes through the motions of shaving. The box is original.
$300–$500

"Made in Japan"

**APOLLO LUNAR MODULE,
1970s**
This battery-operated *Eagle*
spacecraft has the NASA logo.
It is lithographed tin with plastic
parts and has its original box
$200–$400

**APOLLO-Z SPACECRAFT,
1970s**
This battery-operated moon
traveler toy is made of lithographed
tinplate with a plastic, see-through
bubble shield. The box is original.
$100–$300

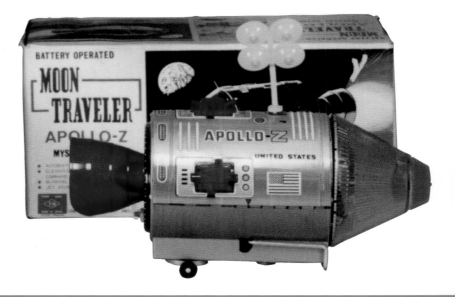

DOCKING ROCKET, 1970s
This large, battery-operated toy has elaborate graphics and great action.
$100–$200

INTERPLANETARY ROCKET, 1970s
This battery-operated space toy, a combination of lithographed tin and plastic, features great graphics.
$100–$300

GROUP OF THREE ROBOTS, 1970s
These complicated, battery-operated robot toys are made of lithographed tin and plastic. From left to right: Gear Robot, Space Explorer, and Mars King—all shown with their original boxes.
$200–$400 for group

"Made in Japan"

JUNK PILE, 1960s
This tinplate car is painted and features "Junk Pile" on the hood of the vehicle. Here is an example of a vehicle toy that was dented on its floorboards and made to represent a junk car.
$20–$40

DUMP TRUCK, 1960s
Here is a red and yellow tinplate dump truck with plastic windows that features a tipping action and wheels that roll.
$40–$60

HIGH-LIFT LOADER, 1960s
This bulldozer is a lithographed, tinplate friction toy that features "Jones Construction, Arlington, VA" on the side of the vehicle.
$40–$60

SPARKING TANK, 1960s
Made of lithographed tinplate, this friction toy moves slowly, and if the flint is working properly, a spark will be generated near the gun.
$40–$60

CADILLAC, 1960s
This friction car is a detailed reproduction of the real car with the fin-tail, rear-fender design. This is a great crossover collectible, because it appeals to car collectors and collectors of friction toys.
$50–$100

SUBMARINE #571, 1960s
This tinplate, battery-operated toy is a fine example of simplicity in design. The top portion of the vessel opens to reveal the battery chamber that powers the back propeller.
$75–$120

Kenner

**SPEEDER BIKE VEHICLE,
1995–1996**
This vehicle and figure is from the
"Power of the Force" series of toys.
It is shown with its original green box.
$20–$40

**LUKE SKYWALKER (left)
AND DARTH VADER (right),
1995–1996**
The two main *Star Wars* protagonists
were sold with their lightsabers
in multilingual packaging for a
European audience.
$10–$50 each

**IMPERIAL AT-ST TOY,
1995–1996**

Toys derived from the *Star Wars* movies were a global sensation. This is the European version of the Scout Walker from the "Power of the Force Series," with its original multilingual box.
$20–$40

Hasbro, Inc.

PBS/WGBH *ANTIQUES ROADSHOW*™ GAME, 2001

This is my personal game. You might think that being a collectibles expert, I would not have even opened the tin and would have been sure to keep all the game pieces intact. Well, games are meant to be played, and I have lost some pieces. This game is based on the popular public television show *Antiques Roadshow*™. The players have to guess which story and estimate are correct for the item shown on the card sitting on the easel.

$19.95

SCARLETT COUNTER INTELLIGENCE FIGURE #6507, 1982

This is a 3³/₄-inch (9.5 cm) figure from Series #1, Cobra. It holds the distinction of being one of the few female characters in the G.I. Joe series of action figures. Figures without the blister pack are considerably less valuable.

$50–$150

TOY COMPANIES: A QUICK REFERENCE GUIDE

This easy-access guide to every company mentioned in this book provides valuable information about the materials used and the types of toys produced by the major toy manufacturers. It will be an especially useful tool when you are out and about in the marketplace, adding to your toy collection.

 ALPS quality, battery-operated toys with multiple actions; always feature the distinctive company logo **pages 184, 199**

 American Flyer toy locomotives and cars, often made from lightweight materials with low-quality paint or lithography; are always marked with the company name **pages 98, 119–120**

 Arcade Manufacturing Company cast-iron transportation toys; primarily cars, including Yellow Cabs; company name cast into toys; comic-character toys include Andy Gump Roadster #348 and Chester Gump Pony Cart **pages 72–73, 110–111**

 Bandai Japanese mechanical toys, primarily battery-operated, best known for Mighty Morphin' Power Ranger series **page 185**

 Barclay Manufacturing Company die-cast toys soldiers, early ones had real tin hats, many marked "USA" **pages 155, 166**

 Gebrüder Bing early tinplate transportation toys, powered by superior clockwork mechanisms, and decorated with detailed lithography; all toys feature the company logo **pages 42–43, 112**

 R. Bliss Manufacturing Company ornately designed, lithographed, paper-on-wood toys; simple and accurate representations of boats, trains, and carriages of the late 19th century; high-quality lithography with a variety of rich colors; colors may be faded and pieces missing, e.g. sailboats may lack masts **pages 33, 52**

 George Borgfeldt & Company early licensed-character toys, often marked with the company's "Nifty" logo; produced first-ever plush Mickey Mouse **pages 98, 177**

 William Britain Ltd. lightweight, hollow-cast lead soldiers; finely finished figures with great attention to detail in uniforms; each figure has a small hole in its head; figures on horses are not removable; only moving part might be the soldier's sword arm **pages 99, 162–163**

 George W. Brown Company toys made of tinplate with elaborate, hand-painted stenciling or decoration and simple designs; toys with a folk-art early Americana feel **pages 44–45, 52**

 Buddy "L" Manufacturing Company sturdy, well-built, pressed-steel trucks and cars, usually marked with company logo and legend "Buddy 'L' Express Line"; well designed with close attention to detail; some oversized vehicles in 20-inch (50 cm) range **pages 99, 124–125**

 Georges Carette & Cie. high-quality tinplate toys with great attention to accurate detail, working lights on automobiles, and sturdy mechanisms; always marked with the company logo **pages 45–46, 54**

 Character Toy and Novelty Company teddy bears and character plush toys; no stitched claws; high foreheads, shaved muzzles, and large ears; some with noses made of metal; some Walt Disney characters **pages 136, 154–155**

 J. Chein & Company lightweight, mechanical wind-up toys with colorful lithography **pages 92, 100**

 Corgi die-cast automobiles; all vehicles had plastic windows; all marked with the company logo on the underside and on the packaging **pages 152–153, 168–169**

 Cragston multiple-action, battery-operated toys; highly decorated boxes; boxes always feature the company name; all toys imported from Japan **pages 185, 201**

 Crandall simple wooden toys, sometimes featuring interlocking blocks and often packed in wooden boxes; some were gaily painted, giving them an aspect of folk art **page 34**

 Daisy Manufacturing Company, Inc. toy guns, particularly the BB gun, and character toys like the Daisy Red Ryder; all products marked with the company name **pages 100, 180**

 Dent Hardware Company highly detailed, quality, cast-iron automotive toys, mostly in the 4 to 12 inch (10 to 30 cm) category **pages 55, 74**

 Dinky Toys die-cast metal automobiles; all vehicles have open windows; company markings are on the underside and the packaging **pages 150–151, 170–171**

 EFFanBEE dolls—in particular baby dolls; early ones had human hair; all were marked with the company name on the back or under the hairline **pages 101, 177**

 James Fallows & Sons early tinplate toys, usually marked "IXL" on the underside; decorated with stenciling, embossed tin parts of vehicles or smokestacks of trains **pages 47, 55**

 Fernand Martin wind-up toys with elaborate and comical movements; figures have a wire outline for the shape of the body; figures dressed in cloth with expressive facial features; marked with company logo **pages 51, 93**

Fisher-Price wooden pull-toys; usually some kind of animal; all the early wooden toys produced by Fisher-Price are marked with the company logo and a product number **pages 35–36, 146–147**

 Gibbs Manufacturing Company simple platform pull-toys, usually featuring a circus animal; early toys were numbered and named, e.g., "No. 27 U.S. Mail" **pages 37, 101**

 A.C. Gilbert Company makers of the the Erector Set—the first American construction toy with moving parts and motors; also made pressed-steel automobiles and educational scientific sets **pages 102, 181**

 Gong Bell Manufacturing Company simple bell toys, with the bell typically an integral part of the overall design; bells were usually cast in one piece without a seam; early toys had J. & E. Stevens's cast-iron wheels; toys are often unmarked **pages 56, 75**

 Gund plush bears and other stuffed toy animals; from 1940, toys were usually tagged with the company name and assorted legends, including "A Toy of Quality and Distinction" **pages 102, 137–138**

 Hasbro, Inc. "Mr. Potato Head" and boys' action figures, primarily "G.I. Joe"; bought out many established toy companies, including Tonka and Parker Brothers; one of today's largest toy companies **pages 190, 208**

 Heyde solid lead soldiers; company name on the packaging, but soldiers not individually marked; infantry soldiers step forward with right foot **page 164**

 Hot Wheels fast-moving, die-cast metal toy automobiles; distinctive, low-friction wheel bearings; California styling; often in blister packs **pages 172–173, 196–197**

 Hubley Manufacturing Company primarily automobiles, service vehicles, and some airplanes; sturdy construction using heavy cast-iron; company name is usually cast into the toy in an inconspicuous place **pages 57, 76–77**

 Hull & Stafford tinplate toys made in halves and fastened with tabs; hand-painted and stenciled decoration in primary colors in thin paint; simple designs have the charm of folk art **page 48**

 Ideal Toy & Novelty Company plush toys and dolls; popularized the term "teddy bear"; bears have triangular-shaped heads, fabric or horizontally stitched triangular noses, and are usually marked with company name and logo **pages 103, 139–140**

 Ingersoll Watch Company comic-character watches and novelty alarm clocks with Mickey Mouse and other Disney characters on the face **pages 103, 178**

 E.R. Ives & Company tinplate and wooden clockwork toys and floor trains with a folk-art appearance; in 1910, introduced electric trains and accessories, but continuted to make mechanical trains; company merged with Lionel in 1930 **pages 58, 65–66**

 Ives Trains mechanical and electric trains and accessories from the early part of the 20th century **page 120**

 Judd Manufacturing Company cast-iron mechanical banks, many with moving parts **page 77**

 Kenner toys based on the *Star Wars* movies **pages 191–192, 206–207**

 Kenton Hardware Company cast-iron, horse-drawn vehicles like fire trucks, carriages, drays, and the Overland Circus, mostly with removable figures; many feature the company slogan, "The real thing in everything but size" **pages 58, 78**

 Keyser & Rex cast-iron mechanical banks **pages 59, 73**

 Keystone Manufacturing Company early motion-picture toys and pressed-steel automobiles, planes, and other vehicles that can be ridden; often decorated with labels or decals; 1925–1935, vehicles had rubber tires; often marked with the company name **pages 104, 126–127**

 Kilgore Manufacturing Company quality, cast-iron cap guns and automotive toys; often marked with the company trademark, "Toys that last" **pages 79, 104**

 Kingsbury Manufacturing Company cast-iron automobiles, fire trucks, airplanes, and delivery trucks; miniature versions of real-life vehicles **pages 80, 105**

 Knickerbocker Toy Company teddy bears and other plush toys, including comic characters licensed by Disney; often marked with the company name and legends "Animals of Distinction" and "Joy of a Toy" **pages 105, 141–142**

 Lehmann tinplate wind-up toys with colorful lithography; in paper boxes with a prominently positioned company logo **pages 94–95, 106**

 Lesney Matchbox small, colorful, die-cast automobiles; the company logo is usually found on the underside of the vehicles; distinctive packaging based on design of Norvic Safety Match boxes **pages 174, 194–195**

 Lincoln Logs wooden logs for building cabins, invented by Frank Lloyd Wright's son, John Lloyd Wright, in 1916; in 1943, purchased by Playskool; now owned by Hasbro **page 39**

 Linemar robots and other battery-operated, licensed-character toys, including Disney characters, Popeye, and the Flintstones; eye-catching, colorful packaging, all marked with the company name **pages 186–187, 198–199**

 Lionel Manufacturing Company early, electric model trains; all feature the legend "Lionel Lines" and are numbered to indicate the date manufactured; trains use a third rail; boxes are all marked with the company name **pages 107, 121–122**

"Made in Japan" simple, tinplate, wind-up or battery-operated toys marked "Japan," "Occupied Japan," or "Made in Japan" **pages 188, 202–203, 204–205**

 Manoil Manufacturing Company, Inc. lead soldiers; often have a distinctive jauntiness; normally marked with the company logo **pages 155, 165–166**

 Märklin high-quality, German, tinplate automotive toys, trains, and accessories; made with meticulous attention to detail; marked prominently with the company logo **pages 60–61, 67–68**

 Louis Marx & Company tinplate, wind-up toys with simple actions and colorful lithography; always marked with the maker's name **pages 96, 108, 113**

 McLoughlin Brothers mass-produced paper toys and games in colorful packaging **pages 59, 88**

 Metalcraft Corporation pressed-steel trucks and automobiles with wooden disc wheels and sleek art deco designs; many have advertising **pages 109, 128–129**

 Milton Bradley board games and puzzles marked with the company logo, date of manufacture, copyright, and patent date **pages 87–88**

 Ohio Art colorful, lithographed, tin sand toys, tops, climbing monkeys, and other toys marked with the company logo; in 1960, made and marketed "Etch A Sketch" **pages 69, 204**

 Parker Brothers paper soldiers, puzzles, and board games, including "Monopoly" **pages 53, 89–90**

 Pratt & Letchworth high-quality transportation toys; horse-drawn vehicles and passengers rendered with accurate detail to reflect the lifestyle at the close of the 19th century **pages 62, 81**

 W.S. Reed late 19th-century paper-on-wood toys similar to Bliss; transportation toys, blocks, pull-toys and mechanical circus toys **page 62**

 A. Schoenhut Company wooden dolls with carved limbs and steel joints; early circus sets with animals; figures and props were all wood; later versions include figures with porcelain heads and wooden bodies and limbs; wooden figures with glass eyes are rare and more desirable to collectors; dolls are usually marked "Schoenhut Toys Made in USA" **pages 38–39, 109**

 Schuco German, tinplate, wind-up novelty toys; also battery-operated automobiles and aircraft figural toys; marked with the company name **pages 114–115, 156–157**

 Shepard Hardware cast-iron mechanical banks with square coin traps; often have to be opened with a key **pages 63, 83**

 Smith-Miller trucks and tractors made of cast-metal or aluminum; accurate renditions of Mack trucks; opening doors and working steering wheels **pages 130–131, 148**

 Steelcraft good-quality pressed-steel trucks and pedal cars with disc wheels and rubber tires; modeled after GMC trucks **pages 132–133**

 Steiff plush and mohair animals and bears, usually with a tag or button on which the animal's name is printed; always marked with the Steiff logo, the contents and design of which indicate the age of the toy **pages 110, 143–144**

 J. & E. Stevens Company the first cast-iron toys manufactured in America; quality cast-iron mechanical banks, many with moving parts **pages 64, 82–83**

 Strauss Manufacturing Corporation early mechanical wind-up toys; simple mechanisms with limited motion; company name is on toys **pages 51, 116**

 Tinkertoys construction toys for younger children, packaged in a distinctive, cylindrical canister; introduced in 1914 or 15; boxes are marked with the company logo **page 40**

 Toledo Metal Wheel Company pressed-steel pedal cars, with adjustable pedals; "Bull Dog" trucks with decals; company nameplate is attached to top of the radiator grill **pages 134, 148**

 Tootsietoy small, colorful doll furniture and automobiles made of cast metal; company logo is usually found on the underside of the toys **pages 112, 175**

 TPS mass-produced, Japanese, mechanical, lithographed tinplate toys; very colorful but not always of the highest quality **pages 115, 200**

 Unique Art Manufacturing Company lithographed, tinplate wind-up toys; best known for 1945 "Li'l Abner and his Dogpatch Band"; usually marked with the company logo **pages 117, 158**

 Watrous cast-iron bell toys on bases with wheels; bells were cast in a single piece **pages 56, 84**

 Wilkins Toy Company cast-iron transportation toys; horse-drawn vehicles, trains, paddle boats, and carpet toys; automobiles often had vulcanized rubber wheels **pages 54, 85**

 Wolverine Supply & Manufacturing lithographed tinplate sand toys, marble toys, toy kitchens, and stores for girls; toys were marked with the company name **pages 70, 159**

 Wyandotte Toys produced a huge variety of toys, including guns and rifles, airplanes, automobiles, mechanical toys, and other playhouse toys; many have streamlined designs and futuristic features like concealed headlights and teardop wheel covers; all are marked with the company name **pages 160, 182**

USEFUL ADDRESSES

MUSEUMS WITH TOYS
United States

Antique Toy Museum and Gift Shop
2426 S. Outer Road
Stanton, MO 63079
Tel: 573-927-5555

Bauer Toy Museum
233 E. Main
Fredericksburg, TX 78624
Tel: 830-997-9394

Daisy Airgun Museum
114 South 1st Street
Rogers, AR 72756
Tel: 501-986-6873

Delaware Toy & Miniature Museum
P.O. Box 4053
Route 41
Wilmington, DE 29807
Tel: 302-427-8697
www.thomes.net

Denver Museum of Miniatures, Toys, & Dolls
1880 Gaylord Street
Denver, CO 80206-1211
Tel: 303-322-1053
Fax: 303-322-3704

Evanston Historical Society
225 Greenwood Street
Evanston, IL 60201
Tel: 847-475-3410

Islip Town Museum
963 Montauk Highway
Oakdale, NY 11769

Matchbox & Lesney Toy Museum
62 Saw Mill Road
Durham, CT 06422
Tel: 860-349-1655

Museum of the City of New York
5th Avenue and 103rd Street
New York, NY 10029
Tel: 212-534-1672
Fax: 212-534-5974

Nashville Toy Museum
2613 McGavock Pike
Nashville, TN 37214
615-391-3516
www.toytrains.citysearch.com

The National Toy Train Museum
300 Paradise Lane
Strasburg, PA 17579
Tel: 717-687-8976
www.traincollectors.org

Remember When Toy Museum
Box 226A
Canton, MO 63435

San Francisco International Toy Museum
2801 Leavenworth Street
San Francisco, CA 94133

Smithsonian Institution
Public Inquiry Mail Service
—MFC010
1000 Jefferson Drive SW
Washington, DC 20560
Tel: 202-357-1300

The Sterling Collection
Stone Castle
804 North Third Street
Bardstown, KY 40004

Strong Museum—Dolls, Toys, and Bears
One Manhattan Square
Rochester, NY 14607
Tel: 716-263-2700
www.strongmuseum.org

Sullivan-Johnson Museum
223 North Main Street
Kenton, OH 43326

The Toy and Miniature Museum of Kansas City
5235 Oak Street
Kansas City, MO 64112
Tel: 816-333-2055
www.umkc.edu/tmm

Washington Doll's House & Toy Museum
5236 44th Street NW
Washington, DC 20015

United Kingdom

Bethnal Green Museum of Childhood
Cambridge Heath Road
London E2 9PA
United Kingdom

The London Toy & Model Museum
23 Craven Hill
London
United Kingdom

The Toy Museum
42 Bridge Street Row
Chester, Cheshire
United Kingdom

AUCTION HOUSES
United States

Noel Barrett Antiques & Auctions
P.O. Box 300
Carversville, PA 18913

Bertoia Auctions
2141 DeMarco Drive
Vinland, NJ 08360
Tel: 856-692-1881
Fax: 856-692-8697
www.bertoiaauctions.com

Dunning's Auction Service
755 Church Street
Elgin, IL 60123-9302
Tel: 708-741-3483
Fax: 708-741-3589

Hake's Americana & Collectibles
P.O. Box 1444
York, PA 17405
Tel: 717-848-1333
www.hakes.com

Jackson's Auctioneers and Appraisers
James L. Jackson
2229 Lincoln Street
Cedar Falls, IA 50613
Tel: 319-277-2256
Fax: 319-277-1252

Henry Kurtz, Ltd.
163 Amsterdam Ave.
Suite 136
New York, NY 10023
Tel: 212-642-5904
Fax: 212-874-6018

Lewis & Lambright, Inc.
112 N. Detroit Street
LaGrange, IN 46761
Tel: 413-549-3775

Joy Luke Auction Gallery
300 E. Grove Street
Bloomington, IL 61701-5232
Tel: 309-828-5533
Fax: 309-829-2266

Mapes Auctioneers & Appraisers
1600 Vestal Parkway West
Vestal, NY 13850
Tel: 607-754-9193

Lloyd W. Ralston
173 Post Road
Fairfield, CT 06430
Tel: 203-255-1233

Skinner, Inc.
357 Main Street
Bolton, MA 01740-1104
Tel: 508-779-6241
Fax: 508-779-5144

Smith House (mail)
P.O. Box 336
Eliot, ME 03903
Tel: 207-439-4614

Sotheby's
1334 York Avenue
New York, NY 10021
212-606-7000
www.sothebys.com

Toy Locaters (mail)
5821 Diana Lane
Lake View, NY 14085
Tel: 716-627-5840

TreasureQuest Auction & Appraisals
2581 Jupiter Park Drive
Suite E5
Jupiter, FL 33458
Tel: 561-741-0777
Fax: 561-741-0757
www.tqag.com

Withington, Inc.
RD 2 Box 440
Hillsboro, NH 03244
Tel: 603-464-3232

United Kingdom

Christie's
85 Old Brompton Road
London SW7 3LD
United Kingdom
www.christies.com

Sotheby's
34-35 New Bond Street
London W1A 2AA
United Kingdom
Tel: 020-7293-5000
www.sothebys.com

Wallis & Wallis
West Street Auction Galleries
Lewes
East Sussex BN7 2NJ
United Kingdom
Tel: 01273-480208
Fax: 01273-476562

TOY ASSOCIATIONS

A.C. Gilbert Heritage Society
Jay Smith
1440 Whalley, Suite 252
New Haven, CT 06515
www.acghs.com

Action Toy Organization of Michigan
Michael Crawford
2884 Hawks
Ann Arbor, MI 48108
Tel: 734-973-1904

American Flyer Collector Club
Frank Hare, Ed.
P.O. Box 13269
Pittsburgh, PA 15243-0269
Tel: 412-221-2250
Fax: 412-221-8402

American-International Matchbox Collectors and Exchange Club
Bob Fellows
532 Chestnut Street
Lynn, MA 01904-2717
Tel: 617-595-4135
Fax: 617-595-4007

Association of Game & Puzzle Collectors
P.O. Box 321
197M Boston Post Road West
Marlborough, MA 01752
www.agca.com

Canadian Toy Collectors Society
91 Rylander Blvd
Unit 7, Suite 245
Scarborough, Ontario
MIB 5MS
Canada
Tel: 905-389-8047
www.ctcs.on.ca

Fisher-Price Collectors Club
Jeanne Kennedy
1442 N. Ogden
Mesa, AZ 85205
Tel: 480-396-2534
www.fpclub.org.

G.I. Joe Official Collectors' Club
Brian Savage
225 Cattle Barron Parc Drive
Ft. Worth, TX 76108
Tel: 800-772-6673
Tel: 817-448-9863
Fax: 817-448-9843
www.mastercollector.com

National Pedal Vehicle Association
Bruce Beimers
1720 Rupert NE
Grand Rapids, MI 49505
Tel: 616-361-9887

Ohio Art Collectors Club
18203 Kristi Road West
Liberty, MO 64068

Schoenhut Collectors Club
1003 W. Huron Street
Ann Arbor, MI 48103-4217
Tel: 734-662-6676

Steiff Club
P.O. Box 2829 Woburn,
MA 01888-9872
Tel: 800-830-0429

Toy Car Collectors Club
Peter H. Foss
33290 W 14 Mile Rd., #454
West Bloomfield, MI
48322-3549
Tel: 248-682-0272
Fax: 249-682-5782

Wheels of Fire—A Hot Wheels Club of Arizona
P.O. Box 86431
Phoenix, AZ 86431
Tel: 623-842-2680
www.azneighbors.com/466

REPAIR SERVICES

Frank Capozzi
6 Devon Road
Bethpage, NY 11714
Tel: 516-938-9765
—battery-operated, friction, and wind-up toys

Captain Bob's
9 Mohawk Drive
Hampden, MA 01036
Tel: 413-566-5109
—specializes in friction and wind-up toys

Imaginary Friends
P.O. Box 40601
Denver, CO 80204
Tel: 303-761-7234S
—Steiff bears and other stuffed toys

Chad Mapes Pedal Car Restoration
3216 Wayne Street
Endwell, NY 13760
Tel: 607-754-7952

Marc Olimpio's Antique Toy Restoration Center
P.O. Box 1505
Wolfeboro, NY 03894
Tel: 603-569-6739
—tin, iron, pressed-steel, and hand-painted toys

Randy's Toy Shop
165 N. 9th Street
Noblesville, IN 46060
Tel: 317-776-2220
www.randystoyshop.com
—celluloid, composition, battery-operated, and wind -up toys

Remember When Restorations
Mike Taylor
5545 Celestial Road
Dallas, TX 75240
Tel: 972-788-1411
Fax: 972-385-0779
www.rememwhen.com
—metal toys, pedal vehicles, cast-iron, pressed and pot metal

Samuelson Pedal Tractor Parts
234 1st Avenue East
P.O. Box 346
Dyersville, IA 52040
Tel: 319-875-6222
Fax: 319-875-6126
www.pedaltractorparts.com

Tin Toy Works
Joe Freeman
1313 N. 15th Street
Allentown, PA 18102
Tel: 610-439-8268

WEB SITES

www.bigredtoybox.com
—articles about action figures, dolls, toys, and collectibles

www.diecast.org
—news, reviews, and collector bulletin boards

www.ebay.com
—online auction site

www.mobilia.com
—automobilia toys

www.sothebys.com
—one of the best online auction sites

GLOSSARY

Animated toys Any playthings that simulate lifelike movements, whether powered or activated by spring, string, flywheel, rubber band, gravity, controlled movement of sand, gyroscopic mechanism, steam, electricity, or batteries.

Articulated The term describing a toy connected by joints that are sufficiently loose to allow movement in any direction.

Axle A metal rod joining two vehicle or wagon wheels.

Balance toys Toys counterweighted with pebbles or buck shot—like roly-poly toys—that constantly return to the same starting point when set in motion. Also includes early tin toys that were weighted above or below the toy and, when set in motion, maintained their equilibrium.

Balance wheel Most often seen on horse-drawn vehicles, it is a small rotating or stationary wheel normally attached to a front hoof or a shaft suspended between two horses that facilitates passage across the floor.

Black light An ultraviolet light that reacts with color pigments and chemicals used in paints and glazes. Often used to detect repainting of old toys.

Board games Games played on a specially designed card or fabric surface. The most common types of games involve players throwing dice and using counters to move across the board.

Carpet toys The Victorian term for toys that were played with on carpets.

Cast-iron toys Made of molten, gray, high-carbon iron, hand-poured into sand-casting molds; usually cast in halves, then mated and bolted or riveted as one. More elaborate versions incorporated interlocking, nickel-plated grills, chassis, bumpers, people, and other accessories.

Celluloid The original trade name for Pyroxylin, an early and highly flammable form of plastic used for making toys. Invented in the United States in 1869 by the Hyatt Brothers.

Clockwork mechanism Made of machined brass and steel and used to animate toys for as long as 30 minutes as interlocking gears move to uncoil a spring. Produced as a drive system for toys by clock makers beginning in 1862 and ending about 30 years later in the northeastern United States, most notably in Connecticut.

Composition An inexpensive substance made from a combination of cloth, wood, wood pulp, plaster of Paris, glue, and sawdust, used for making dolls' heads, bodies, and limbs, as well as other toys, notably civilian and military figures.

Crazing A random pattern of fine cracks in the paint of hand-enameled toys—usually a sign that the paint is old, but it can be copied by the finest restorers.

Die-cast The term for a shape formed in a metal mold under pressure. Lead was initially used as the main ingredient of this material, but this was replaced in Britain in 1934 with **mazac** which was safer.

Disc joint A joint made of discs of cardboard held in place by a metal pin; used to articulate soft toys and teddy bears.

D.R.G.M. (Deutsches Reichs-Muster-Rolle) The German term for the official government roll of registered patents.

Embossed Describes pressed decoration on tinplate, done by a hand- or steam-powered press from the inside (rather than the outside) of the item.

Excelsior A soft mixture of long, thin wood shavings used for stuffing teddy bears and animals. Steiff still uses it today for its limited edition bears.

Floor-runner A carpet train or toy that is propelled along the floor by a hand movement.

Flywheel A mechanism used in some toys before 1914 that operates on the inertia principle, which states that a body at rest will remain at rest or if set in motion will remain in motion unless disturbed by an external force.

Friction wheel A central inertia wheel, also known as a flywheel, activated by springs in the rear wheels to set toys in motion. American toys utilized cast-iron friction wheels; European toys used cast-lead. Friction toys were popular from 1900 to the early 1930s.

Horse-drawn vehicles The early cast-iron toys of the 1880s and 1890s replicated in miniature life-sized, horse-drawn vehicles popular during this time period. The names associated with those vehicles also apply to the toys.

Horse-Drawn Vehicle Types and their Descriptions:

- **Barouche**: An open, four-wheeled rig with the driver's seat elevated in front and two facing seats behind.

- **Brake:** An open, sporting, four-wheeled rig that seats two or three people. The driver sits with the other passengers.

- **Brougham:** An elegant, closed, four-wheeled carriage with an exterior driver's seat. Named after Lord Henry Brougham, the Scottish leader of the House of Commons in Britain between 1830 and 1840.

- **Gig:** An open, sporting, two-wheeled vehicle that is high off the ground and often used to exercise trotting horses.

- **Hansom cab:** A popular, covered two-wheeler used to transport one or two passengers. The driver controls the reins from a platform at the rear of the cab.

- **Landau:** A four-wheeled carriage with a divided top that can be thrown back or let down. It features a raised seat for the driver.

- **Phaeton:** An elegant, open, four-wheeled carriage; also a type of touring car.

- **Tally-ho:** An open, four-wheeled rig that could carry as many as 12 passengers inside and on the top of the vehicle.

Impressed Describes the method whereby a maker's mark is indented into the surface of a toy, as opposed to raised or **embossed.**

Incised Describes the method whereby a maker's mark is scratched into the surface of a toy's head, as opposed to **impressed.**

Kapok An extremely lightweight fiber used for stuffing English and German teddy bears, sometimes in combination with other material.

Lead A main ingredient in some die-cast toys until 1934; most widely used in making toy figures until the 1960s.

Licensing The process whereby manufacturers compete to earn the right to produce toys on behalf of other companies; often associated with film and television productions.

Lithography The process introduced to toys in the 1880s by which sheets of tinplate are printed in color in the flat before being pressed into shapes. The term also applies to paper items.

Mazac A magnesium-and-zinc-based metal alloy regularly used in the die-cast technique from 1934 onward.

Mechanical bank A money box in which the depositing of coins depends on some mechanical action, usually made from cast-iron. These were particularly popular with both children and adults in the United States after the Civil War—from 1869 to the late 19th century.

Marriage The term used to describe a toy constructed using parts that did not originally belong together.

Mohair plush A fabric woven from the silky fleece of an Angora goat and commonly used for making teddy bears and animals.

Nickel-plating A technique for coating cast-iron or steel toys with molten nickel to prevent rusting and to enhance the appearance of the items.

Papier-mâché A combination of molded paper pulp, a whitening agent, and glue used during the 19th century for the construction of dolls' heads and bodies.

Patent The exclusive right for manufacture. The stamp "Pat," "Patd," or "Pat Pending" often appears on American and British toys.

Patent date If the patent number appears on a toy or the box it came in, one can get a good approximation of the year any American toy was manufactured, as each number refers to a specific decade between 1860 and the present day. German toys produced after 1890 usually have patent dates.

Penny toys Inexpensive toys usually made from lithographed tinplate that have a simple push-along action. Production was mainly between 1900 and the 1930s.

Plastic A synthetic material with a polymeric structure, which can easily be molded when soft, and then set. Flexible, safe, and durable plastic increasingly replaced tinplate as the main material with which to make toys from the late 1940s, and today, nearly all toys are made of plastic.

Plywood A type of inexpensive laminate sometimes used to make wooden toys.

Provenance The documented history of any antique item passed on to each new owner. An unusual or notable provenance may enhance the value of a piece.

Reproduction The term used to describe any copy of an antique object, including those toys made in molds taken from an original toy.

Shoe-button eyes Black wooden eyes with metal loops on the back, used on early teddy bears.

Still bank A money box which has no mechanical movement involved in the deposit of coins.

Tabbed Describes the method of joining two pieces of metal by folding a small tab through a slot.

Tinplate Thin sheets of iron or steel which have been coated with a tin-based alloy.

Turned A term used to describe a wooden toy that has been shaped on a lathe.

Vinyl A nonflammable and flexible yet tough form of plastic used for making dolls from the 1940s on; it virtually replaced hard plastic by the 1950s.

Wind-ups A term often used interchangeably for both clockwork and spring-driven toys. Clockwork offers superior quality and length of activation: 30 minutes as opposed to the 2 or 3 minutes for a coil or barrel-spring mechanism.

BIBLIOGRAPHY

Brooks, Jacki. *The Complete Encyclopedia of Teddy Bears*, Cumberland, Maryland: Hobby House Press, Inc., 1990.

Freed, Joe and Sharon. *Collector's Guide to American Transportation Toys,* Raleigh, North Carolina: Freedom Publishing Company, Inc., 1995.

Gardiner, Gordon and Morris, Alistair. *The Illustrated Encyclopedia of Metal Toys*, Avenel, New Jersey: Random House Value Publishing, Inc., 1984.

Goddu, Krystyna Poray. *A Celebration of Steiff, Timeless Toys for Today*, Portfolio Press Corporation, 1997.

Heide, Robert and Gilman, John. *The Mickey Mouse Watch*, Singapore: Disney Enterprises, Inc., 1997.

Korbeck, Sharon. *1998 Toys & Prices*, Iola, Wisconsin: Krause Publications, Inc., 1997.

Leibe, Frankie, Agnew, Daniel and Maniera, Leyla. *Miller's Soft Toys: A Collector's Guide*, London: Octopus Publishing Group, 2000

Luke, Tim. *Toys From American Childhood: 1845–1945*, Cumberland, Maryland: Portfolio Press, 2001

Miller, Judith and Martin. *Miller's Toys and Games Antiques Checklist*, London: Octopus Publishing Group, Limited, 1995.

Murray, John J. and Fox, Bruce R. *Fisher-Price, A Historical, Rarity Value Guide,* Florence, Alabama: Books Americana, Inc., 1991.

O'Brien, Richard. *Collecting Toy Trains Identification and Value Guide*, Iola, Wisconsin: Krause Publications, 1997.

O'Brien, Richard. *Collecting Toys Identification and Value Guide*, Iola, Wisconsin: Krause Publications, 1997.

O'Brien, Richard. *The Story of American Toys*, Cross River Press, Ltd. 1990.

Pearson, Sue. *Miller's Teddy Bears: A Complete Collectors Guide*, London: Octopus Publishing Group, 2001

Whitton, Blair. *The Knopf Collectors' Guide to American Antiques Toys*, New York: Chanticleer Press, Inc., 1984.

Dinky die-cast oil truck with white wheels, 1930s.

INDEX

Page numbers in *italic* refer to images.

accessories, G.I. Joe 193
The Acrobats wooden figures *34*
action figures *190, 191,* 192, *208*
airplanes 119–20, 123, *127,* 128, *132*
alarm clocks *103*
Aldrin, Edwin (Buzz) 145
alloys 167, 170–1, 175
ALPS 184, *199*
aluminum 130–1
American Flyer *98,* 119–20, 181
Antiques Roadshow 208
appraisal fairs 27, 144
Arcade Manufacturing Company 72–3, *110–11*
Armstrong, Neil 145
art deco *182*
auctions
    Internet 22–3, 140
    live 18–19
    record bids 18–19, 44, 135
    tips 18–19
    viewing 91
automobiles
    Arcade 72–3, *72, 110*
    Carette *54*
    Corgi *152–3, 168–9*
    Dinky *150, 170–1*
    Hot Wheels *172, 196–7*
    Hubley 76
    Japanese *204–5*
    Keystone *126–7*
    Kingsbury 80
    Lehmann *94–5*
    Märklin *68*
    Matchbox *174, 195*
    oversized *126–7*

Schuco *157*
Steelcraft *133*
Toledo *134,* 148
Wyandotte *182*

BB gun 179, 180
baby boom 145
Baetz, Walter 165
Bandai 185
Barbie *172–3,* 193
Barclay Manufacturing Company *155,* 166
Barton, William 75
Batmobile 169
battery-operated toys
    ALPS 184, *199*
    Bandai 185
    Cragston *185, 201*
    history 13, 183
    Japanese 188, *202–3*
    Linemar *186, 187, 198*
    Lionel 121
    Metalcraft 129
beach toys *149*
Berryman, Clifford 139
Bettendorf, J.W. 125
Bing, Adolf and Ignaz 42
Bing, Gebrüder 10, 42–3, *42, 43,* 45, *112*
Bixler, Louis S. 78
Bliss, R. Manufacturing Company 33, *52*
Blue Streak trucks 134
board games
    history 8–9, 86
    McLoughlin Brothers *59, 88*
    Milton Bradley *87–8*
    Parker Brothers *53,* 89–90
Bonnet, Victor Company 93
Borgfeldt, George & Company 27, 98, 177

Bowen, James H. 64
boxing toys *116–17*
Bradley, Milton 87–8
brass 107
Britain, William Ltd. *99,* 162–3
Brown, George W. Company 18, 44, *52*
Buddy "L" Manufacturing Company *99,* 124–5
Bull Dog trucks 134
Bunny Tiddledy Winks *53*
buses *72*

Cabbage Patch dolls 13
cards, history 8–9
Carette, Georges & Cie. 45–6, *54*
carved wooden toys 8, 32, 38–9, *38, 39*
cast-iron
    Arcade *110–11*
    Dent Hardware *55,* 74
    Gong Bell *56,* 75
    history 9, 10, 28
    Hubley *57,* 76–7
    Ives *58,* 65
    Kenton Hardware *58,* 78
    Kilgore *79, 104*
    Kingsbury *80*
    Keyser & Rex *59*
    Pratt & Letchworth *62, 81*
    process 71
    reproductions 24–6, *25,* 71
    Shepard Hardware *63, 83*
    Stevens, J. & E. *82–3*
    Watrous *56, 84*
    Wilkins *85*
cast-metal 130–1
Castoys 168
celluloid 10, 28
Character Toy & Novelty Company 136, 154

character toys 176–8, *177, 178*
The Charles hosereel *19,* 44, *52*
Chein, J. & Company *92,* 100
Chitty Chitty Bang Bang *153*
clay marbles *8*
cleaning, collection 17
clockwork toys
   see also wind-up toys
   Bing *112*
   Borgfeldt 98
   Britain 162
   Brown *44*
   Carette *45–6*
   history 9, 91
   Ives *65, 66*
   Lehmann *106*
   Linemar *186, 187, 198, 199*
   Lionel *122*
   Märklin *60, 68*
   Marx *96, 108, 113*
   mechanisms 29
   Schuco *157*
   Strauss *116*
   Tokyo Playthings *200*
   Unique Art *117*
   Wyandotte *160*
Coleman, William 119
collections
   battery-operated toys 183
   cleaning 17
   cross-over 176
   die-cast toys 167
   display 16, 89
   novelty toys 179
   plastic toys 189
   plush toys 135
   psychology 14
   repair/restoration 17
   Star Wars toys 192
   tinplate 41
   toy soldiers 161
   trains 118
   wind-up toys 91

collector's items 13, 193
comic strips 176
company logos
   ALPS *184*
   Bing *43*
   Borgfeldt 177
   Buddy "L" 124, *125*
   Carette *46*
   Chein 92
   EFFanBEE *177*
   Fernand Martin *93*
   Fisher-Price 36
   Gund *138*
   Heyde *164*
   Ideal *140*
   Keystone *126*
   Knickerbocker *142*
   Lehmann *94*
   Linemar 187
   Manoil 165
   Märklin *67, 68*
   Marx *96,* 113
   Ohio Art *69*
   Schuco *115*
   Smith-Miller 130, *131*
   Steiff *144*
   Tokyo Playthings 115
   Wyandotte *182*
company mottoes
   Arcade 72
   Gund 138
   Hubley 76
   Kenton 78
   Kilgore 79
   Lionel 121
   Wyandotte 182
composition
   history 12–13, 28
   Ideal 139
   Knickerbocker 105, 141
   Linemar 198
   toy soldiers 165, 166
condition 15

configurations, trains 118
conservation, board games 86
contracts, Internet auctions 23
copper 107
Corgi *152–3,* 168–9
corrosion problems 183
cottage industries 8, 9
Cowen, Joshua Lionel 121–2
Cragston 185, *201*
Crandall, Charles M. 34
Crandall's *10,* 34, *54*
cross-over collectibles 176

Daisy Manufacturing Co. *100,*
   180
Darrow, Charles 90
dealers, tips 20–1
decoration 44, 47, 48
   see also hand-painting;
     lithography; stencilling
Dent Hardware Co. *55,* 74
Dent, Henry H. 74
desirability 15, 27, 86, 118
die-cast toys
   Barclay *166*
   Castoys 168–9
   Corgi *152–3,* 168–9
   Dinky *150–1, 170–1*
   history 28, 167
   Hot Wheels *172–3, 196–7*
   Hubley 77
   Manoil 165
   Matchbox *174, 195*
   Mettoy 168
   Smith-Miller *148*
   Tootsietoy 175
dimensions
   cast-iron 26, 71
   mechanical banks 30–1
Dinky Toys *150–1,* 167, 170–1
Disney characters
   clockwork *122, 157*
   cloth *105*

licensing 176
plush toys *136, 141, 154*
pull-toys *147*
timepieces *103, 178*
tinplate *157*
display
board games 89
collections 16
train sets 118
distressing techniques 26, 43
dolls
Barbie 172–3, 193
Cabbage Patch 13
EFFanBEE *101,* 177
houses 32–3, *33, 52*
Ideal *103, 139,* 140
Donze, Leon 166
dot-matrix printing 26
Dowst, Samuel 175
durability 15

Eaton, Seymour 140
educational toys, Victorian 10
EFFanBEE *101,* 177
electricity 13, 29, 76, 121–2
electronic games 193
enamel 196
Erector sets *102,* 120, 179,
181
Etch A Sketch 69

fakes, detecting 24–6
Fallows, James & Sons 47, *55*
felt 136, 143–4, 156
fine print, Internet auctions 22
Fisher, Herman 35
Fisher-Price 35–6, *146–7*
flea markets 21
Flying Colors *196*
Francis, Field, and Francis 47
friction motors 29

futuristic toys 145, *198, 199, 201,
202–3*
Gamage, Fred 163
Game of "India" *59*
Gameboy *13*
Garfield, James A. 49
gauges, trains 118, 120
Gebrüder Bing 10, 42–3, *42, 43,
45, 112*
General Mills 191
George W. Brown Co. 44
German marks 29
G.I. Joe *190,* 193
Gibbs, Lewis E. 37
Gibbs Manufacturing Company
37, *101*
Gilbert, A.C. Company *102,* 120,
181
Gilford, Ira 197
Gong Bell Manufacturing Company
56, 75, 82
Goodrich, Chauncey 44
Gund *102,* 137–8
Gund, Adolph 137

Hafner, William 119
hand-painting
cast-iron 71, 77
tinplate 10, 41, 48
wooden toys 32
Handler, Elliot 172
Happy Farm figures 166
Hasbro, Inc. 90, 190, *208*
Hassenfeld, Helal and Henry 190
Heyde 162, 163, 164
Heyde, Georg 164
Hill, N.N. Brass Co. 84
hollow-casting 162–3
Hornby, Frank 170
hosereels, The Charles *19,* 44, *52*
Hot Wheels 169, 172–3, *196–7*
Hough, Louis Cass 180
house brands 132
Hubley, John E. 76

Hubley Manufacturing Company
57, 76–7
Hull & Stafford 48
human hair 177
Ideal Toy & Novelty Company
103, 139–40
Ingersoll Watch Company *103,*
178
insect damage, plush toys 135
Internet 6–7, 22–3, 140
Ives, E.R. & Company *58,* 65
Ives, Harry C. 65
Ives Trains 120

Japanese marks 29, *184, 188,
202–5*
Jolanda luxury yacht *60*
Judd Manufacturing Company 77
Judd, Morton 77

Kahle, Joseph and Marcell 177
Kahn, Adolph 114
Kenner 191–2, *206–7*
Kenton Hardware Company 58, 78
keys, wind-up toys 115
Keyser & Rex *59,* 73
Keystone comedies 97
Keystone Manufacturing Company
104, 126–7
Kilgore Manufacturing Company
79, *104*
Kingsbury, Harry Thayer 80
Kingsbury Manufacturing
Company 80, *105*
kits, Metalcraft 128
Knickerbocker Toy Company *105,*
141–2

lead
Dinky 170
regulations 166
toy soldiers 161, 164, 165–6
Zeppelins 132

Lehmann 10, 94–5, *106*
Lehmann, Ernst 94–5
Lesney Matchbox 174, *194–5*
Letchworth, William P. 81
Levy, Jack 136
Levy, Michael 166
licensed products 13, *136,* 176,
   189, 191–2, *206–7*
lightweight electric mechanism 29
Li'l Abner and his Dog Patch Band
   117, *158*
limited editions 6, 7, 13, 193
Lincoln, Abraham 87–8
Lincoln logs *13,* 39
Linemar 186–7, *198–9*
Lionel Corporation 122, 142
Lionel Manufacturing Company
   107, 121–2
lithography 10
   board games 86–8
   paper *62, 66*
   reproductions *24, 26*
   tinplate 45, 47, 70
   wooden toys *32, 33*
live auctions 18–19
Lively Horseman tinplate toy *10*
locomotives
   American Flyer *119, 120*
   Gilbert *181*
   Lionel *107*
   steam 29
   tinplate *11*
logos *see* company logos
"Lottery of the Pious" 8
"Lotto" *88*
Lovejoy, Bob 197
Luke, Tim *18*
Lundahl, Fred A. 124

McKinley, William 37, 49
McLoughlin Brothers 59, 88
"Made In Japan" 29, *184, 188,*
   202–5

Mangiapani, Caesar 136
Manoil, Jack 165–6
Manoil Manufacturing Company
   Inc. *155,* 165–6
marbles, clay *8*
Märklin 10, *60–1,* 67–8
Märklin, Caroline and Theodor 67
Märklin, Theodor 67
marks 29
Marks, Ben and Isidore 126
Martin, Fernand *51,* 93
Marx, Louis & Co. 96, *108,* 113,
   116, 186
mass production 9, 41, 96, 113,
   135, 161
Matson, Harold 172
Mattel 172–3
mazac 167, 170–1
Meccano 170
mechanical banks *18,* 30–1, 63–4,
   77, *82–3, 104*
mechanical toys 10, *100,* 183–8
Metalcraft Corporation *109,*
   128–9
Mettoy 168
Michtom, Rose and Morris 139
Mignot 162, *163*
mohair
   plush toys 115, 135, 141–2, 156
   teddy bears 50, 143–4
"Monopoly" *53, 90*
motorcycles *76, 95, 155, 160*
motors 29
Mr. Potato Head 190
Muller, Heinrich 114
musical toys
   ALPS *184*
   Fisher-Price *146–7*
   Marx *113*
   Schoenhut *109*
   Schuco *157*
   Wolverine *159*
Mysto Magic Co. 181

nickel 56, 58, 72, 85
nostalgia 14
Novelty Iron and Brass Foundry
   72
novelty toys 179–82

"Occupied Japan" 188
Ohio Art 69, *149*
"Old Woman in the Shoe"
   mechanical bank *18*
oversized toys
   Buddy "L" 124–5
   Keystone *126, 127*
   Steelcraft *133*

packaging
   board games *53*
   Linemar 187
   Star Wars toys 192
   The Acrobats 34
   Tinkertoys 40
Packard Motor Co. 126–7
Pajeau, Charles 40
paper
   history 28
   lithography *62, 66*
papier-mâché toys 9, 39, *39*
Parker Brothers *53,* 89–90
Parker, George S. 89
Parrish, Maxfield 89
pedal cars *134*
penny toys 167
Perkins, F.M. 78
plastic toys
   battery-operated 183
   celluloid 10
   dolls 140
   Fisher-Price 36
   Gund 138
   Hasbro *190*
   history 28, 41, 189
   Hubley 77
   Kenner *191, 206–7*

Kilgore 79
Tonka 123
vinyl 102
Play-doh 191
Playstation 13
plush toys
  ALPS 184
  Character Toy & Novelty 136, *154*
  Gund *137, 138*
  history 135
  Knickerbocker *141, 142*
  Steiff *50*, 143–4, *143, 144*
popular culture toys
  ALPS *199*
  Cragston *201*
  history 193
  Hot Wheels *196–7*
  Japanese *202–3*
  Kenner *206–7*
  Linemar *198–9*
  Ohio Art *149*
  Tokyo Playthings *200*
Pratt & Letchworth *62*, 81
Pratt, Samuel and Pascal 81
pressed-steel
  Buddy "L" *99, 124–5*
  Daisy *100*
  history 27, 123
  Keystone *104*, 126–7
  Kingsbury *105*
  Märklin *68*
  Metalcraft *109, 128–9*
  Smith-Miller *148*
  Steelcraft *132, 133*
  Wyandotte *182*
Price, Irving 35
printing
  see also lithography
  dot-matrix 26
  history 8–9
  impression 32
product numbers 36, 37

product placement
  Buddy "L" *125*
  Corgi *152–3*
  Dinky Toys *150–1*
  Matchbox *195*
  Metalcraft *128–9*
provenance 15, 24–6
psychology of collecting 14
pull-toys
  cast-iron *75, 84*
  Fisher-Price *146–7*
  wooden 35–6, *35, 36, 101*

racing tracks, Hot Wheels *196*
rarity 15
Reed, W.S. *62*
regulations 166, 193
repair, collections 17
reproductions 24–6, *24–5*, 71
restoration, collections 17
Roosevelt, Franklin Delano 97
Roosevelt, Theodore 49, 139
rubber
  Gund 138
  history 13, 28
  tires 72–3, 127, 133, 134

sailing ships 60, *62*
sand casting 9, 26
Sandy-Andy Automatic toys 70
Sax, Stan 18
Schoenhut, A. Co. 38–9, *109*
Schreyer, Heinrich 114
Schuco 114–15, *156–7*
secondary markets 6, 189
Sennett, Mack 97
Shepard Hardware *63, 83*
"Siege of Havana," The *89*
slush casting 165, 167
Smith, Leslie and Rodney 174
Smith-Miller 130–1, *148*
Smitty Toys 130–1
soldiers *see* toy soldiers

Southard, Frank E. 134
space age toys 145, *198, 199, 201, 202–3*
spinning tops *149*
"Spiritual Treasure Casket," The 8
Star Wars toys 7, *191*, 192, *206–7*
steam 13, 29, 120
Steelcraft 132–3
steering mechanisms *131*
Steiff *50*, 143–4
stencilling *110*
Stevens and Brown Manufacturing Company 44
Stevens, Elisha 44
Stevens, J. & E. Company *64*, 75, 82–3
stick toys, Victorian *9*
storage
  die-cast toys 167, 171
  plush toys 135
  toy soldiers 161
  wind-up toys 117
Strauss, Ferdinand 96, 113, 116
Strauss Manufacturing Corporation *51*, 116
Superfast range, Matchbox 174
"Susceptibles," The *59*
Swedlin, Jacob 137

Tariff Act 1891 29, 49
teddy bears
  Gund *137*
  history 49
  Ideal 139, *140*
  Knickerbocker *142*
  Steiff *50, 143, 144*
"Teddy Girl" 135
Tinkertoys 40
tinplate
  ALPS *199*
  American Flyer *98*
  auctions 18, *19*
  Bing 42–3, *42, 43, 112*

Borgfeldt *27, 98,* 177
Britain 162
Brown *19, 44, 52*
Carette 45–6, *45, 46, 54*
Chein *92, 100*
Cragston *201*
Dent Hardware *55*
Fallows 47, *47, 55*
history 9, 28, 41
Hull & Stafford 48, *48*
Ives 65–6, *65, 66*
Japanese 188, *202–5*
Keyser & Rex 73
Lehmann *94–5, 106*
Linemar *186–7, 198, 199*
locomotives *11*
Märklin *60–1, 67–8*
Marx *108*
Meccano 170
Ohio Art 69, *149*
penny toys 167
reproductions 24–6, *24*
Schuco *156–7*
Strauss *116*
Tokyo Playthings 115, *200*
Unique Art *117, 158*
Wolverine 70, *159*
Wyandotte *160*
Tokyo Playthings Ltd. (TPS) 115, *200*
Toledo Metal Wheel Company 134, *148*
Tonka toys 123
Tootsietoy *12, 112,* 167, 175
toy soldiers
    Barclay 155, 166, *166*
    Cape Town Highlanders *162*
    Heyde *164*
    history 161, 162, *164*
    Japanese cavalry *162*
    Manoil *165, 166*
TPS *see* Tokyo Playthings Ltd.
tractors 72, *110–11*

trade shows 21
trademarks 29, 47, *184*
    see also company logos
trains
    see also locomotives
    battery-operated 121
    configurations 118
    electric 13, 121–2
    gauges 118, 120
    Hornby 170
    Ives 120
    Lionel *107, 121*
    steam 13
    tinplate *60–1, 98*
trucks
    Arcade 72, *110–11*
    Blue Streak 134
    Buddy "L" *99*
    Bull Dog 134
    Dinky *150–1*
    Hot Wheels *173*
    Japanese *204–5*
    Keystone *104, 126*
    Märklin *68*
    Matchbox *194–5*
    Metalcraft *109, 128–9*
    Smith-Miller *130–1, 148*
    Wyandotte *182*
Tutankhamen 86

Ullman, Philip 168
Union Manufacturing Company 48
Unique Art Manufacturing Company 117, *158*

value 15, 27
vehicles *see* automobiles;
    motorcycles; tractors; trucks
vinyl *102,* 142

Watrous *56,* 84
Watrous, D. W. 84

Whisstock, F. 162
Wilkins, James S. 85
Wilkins Toy Company 54, 85
wind-up toys
    see also clockwork toys
    Chein *92*
    history 91
    Japanese 188
    keys 115
    Lehmann *94–5*
    Linemar 187, *199*
    Marx *96, 113*
    Schuco *114–15, 156–7*
    storage 117
    Tokyo Playthings *200*
    Wolverine *159*
window displays 40
Winzeler, H.S. 69
Wizzwheels 169
Wolverine Supply & Manufacturing 70, *159*
wooden toys
    Bliss *33, 52*
    carved 8, 32, 38–9, *38, 39*
    Crandall's 34, *34, 54*
    decoration 32
    doll houses 32–3, *33*
    Fisher-Price 35–6, *35, 36, 146–7*
    Gibbs 37, *37, 101*
    Knickerbocker 141
    qualities 28
    Schoenhut *109*
    Tinkertoys 40
Wright, John Lloyd 13, 39
wrist watches *103, 178*
Wyandotte Toys *160,* 182

Yellow Cab Co. 72–3
yo-yos 113

Zeotrope 88
Zeppelins 132

ACKNOWLEDGMENTS

This book is dedicated to all collectors of playthings and the author would like to thank the following individuals who supplied photographs and support in the preparation of this book:

Greg Strahm, Bonnie and Scott Luke, Bill and Jeanne Bertoia, Ray Haradin, Elizabeth Schwartz, Judy Buel, Elyse Luray-Marx, Dave and Brian Weinthal.

PICTURE CREDITS

All pictures supplied by the author, except the following:

Bertoia Auctions: pages 18 *right*, 27–33, 37–39 *middle* and *left*, 41–47, 49, 51, 52, 54–66 *bottom*, 67–68, 70–83, 84 *bottom*, 85–88 *bottom*, 89, 91–92, 94–96, 98, 99, 100 *top left*, 100 *top right*, 101–103, *middle*, 104 *middle* and *top*, 105 *top*, 106–111, *middle*, 112 *middle* and *top*, 113, 114 *left*, 115–129, 132–134, 139, 148, 156 *top*, 158–160, 162, 163, 167, 175–178 *right*, 179, 181–188, 198, 199, and 203.

Christie's Images, London: pages 51 *bottom left* and *bottom right*, 104 *bottom*, 145, 150 *all*, 151 *all*, 152 *bottom*, 153 *top*, 159 *top*, 168, 169 *bottom*, 170, 171, 174, 194 *bottom*, 199 *bottom*, 208 *bottom*, and 217.

Collectors Old Toy Shop, Halifax, Yorkshire HX1 1XF, UK: pages 153 *middle*, 169 *top*, 194 *top*, and 196 *top left* and *top right*.

eBay website: page 22 *right*.

Mr. Ray Haradin (private collection): pages 161, 164, and 165 *all*.

OPG/P. Anderson/Chuck Steffes: page 50 *all*.

Sotheby's website: page 22 *left*.

Peter Lowry for Craig Stevens: pages 7, 191, 193, 206 *all*, and 207.

Mr. Brian Weinthal (private collection): pages 172, 173 *all*, 196 *bottom*, and 197 *all*.